JOURNAL OF HAWAI'I LITERATURE AND ARTS

bamboo ridge

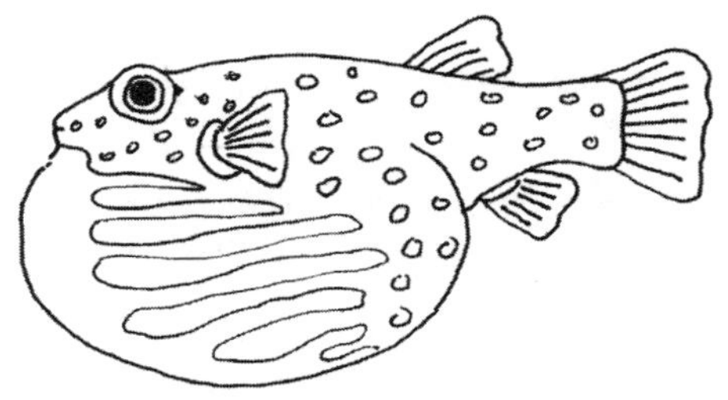

NUMBER ONE HUNDRED

ISBN 978-0-910043-86-1

This is Issue #100 (Fall 2011) of *Bamboo Ridge, Journal of Hawai'i Literature and Arts* (ISSN 0733-0308).

Published by Bamboo Ridge Press

Indexed in the *American Humanities Index*

Bamboo Ridge Press is a member of the Council of Literary Magazines and Presses (CLMP)

Artwork courtesy Cane Haul Road by Grant Kagimoto and Arthur Kodani

Back cover image from *Bamboo Ridge* Issue #2 by Darrell H. Y. Lum, concept by Guy Agena

Editors: Eric Chock and Darrell H. Y. Lum
Managing Editor: Joy Kobayashi-Cintrón
Copyeditor: Milton Kimura
Business Manager: Wing Tek Lum
Typesetting and design: Wayne Kawamoto

"dual citizenship" by Ahimsa Timoteo Bodhrán originally appeared in *Platte Valley Review.*

An earlier version of "Apo Baket" by Amalia B. Bueno was first published in the "Babaylan Series," curated by Eileen R. Tabios through Meritage Press (www.meritagepress.com).

"His 53rd Autumn in Michigan" by David James was originally published in the winter 2010 issue of *Oyez Review.*

Bamboo Ridge Press is a nonprofit, tax-exempt corporation formed in 1978 to foster the appreciation, understanding, and creation of literary, visual, or performing arts by, for, or about Hawai'i's people.

This project is supported by funding through the Hawai'i State Foundation on Culture and the Arts, and through appropriations from the Hawai'i State Legislature (and by the National Endowment for the Arts).

Bamboo Ridge is published twice a year. For subscription information, back issues, or a catalog, please contact:

Bamboo Ridge Press
P.O. Box 61781
Honolulu, HI 96839-1781
(808) 626-1481
brinfo@bambooridge.com
www.bambooridge.com

Bamboo Ridge Press gratefully acknowledges the generous donations of the following individuals and organizations in 2011:

Carol Abe
Guy Agena
Alex Alba
Nancy Aleck
Haunani Alm
Steve Alm
Pam Amii
Anonymous (11)
Jane Aquino
Larry Araki
Geoffrey Bannister
Brad Bate
Buzz Belknap
Jodi Belknap
Mary Bell
Henry Bennett
Perle Besserman
Teresa Bill
David F. Bird
Betsy Brandt
Dominique Brown
Frank Brown
Amalia B. Bueno
Judith Buffington
The Cades Foundation
Donald & Danielle Carreira Ching
Dennis Carroll
Casey Charitable Matching Programs
Karleen Chinen
Eric Chock
Ghislaine D. Chock
Sue Lin Chong
Byron S.C. Choy
Sammie Choy
Hingson Chun
Kaliko Chun
Sheila Chun
Xander Cintron-Chai
Barbara Clemens
Cooke Foundation
Roger Couture
Doodie Cruz
Linda Cunningham
Leanne Day
Porscha Dela Fuente
Lisa DeLong
Charlotte Dias
Kathy Doering
Marie Shirlyn Dom
Arnie Drill
Bev Drill
Carol Egan
George Engebretson
Deanna Espinas
Regina Ewing
Valerie Falle
Victor Falle
Sabra Feldstein
Virgilio Menor Felipe
John Fleckles
Eric Fombonne
Foodland Super Market, Limited
Aurora A. Fruehling
Royal Fruehling
Marie Fujii
Curt Fukumoto
Alvin Fuse
Karen Fuse
Grace Gonser
James Gonser
Norma W. Gorst
Karen Yamamoto Hackler
Arlene Hagen
Lynne Halevi
John Hara
Marie M. Hara
Mavis Hara
Mayumi Hara
John Hara Associates
Kasumi Hara-Mau
Gail Harada
Ermile Hargrove
Cheryl Harstad
Jim Harstad
Hawai'i Council for the Humanities
Hawai'i Literary Arts Council
Hawai'i State Foundation on Culture and the Arts
Linda Hee
Leonore Higa
Melvin Higa
Christina Higgins
Karen Hironaga
Blossom Lam Hoffman
Charlene Hosokawa
Craig Howes
Dennis Ida
Sherri Ida
Dennis Ihara
Ginger Ikenberry
Ann Inoshita
John Ishihara
Leslie Ishimi
Roger Jellinek
Akemi Johnson
Eric Johnson
Megan Johnson

Lisa Linn Kanae
Steven Katz
Barbara F. Kawakami
Evon Kawamoto
John Kawamoto
Wayne Kawamoto
Melvin Kawashima
Nora Okja Keller
Patrick Kennedy
Carol Jean Kimura
Milton Kimura
Tomi Knaeffler
Vernon Knight
Gloria Kobayashi
Joy Kobayashi-Cintrón
Martin Kogan
Juliet Kono Lee
Andrew Konopka
Brenda Kwon
Joan C. Lancom
Melanie Lau
Terry Lau
Laurie Leach
David Lee
Gail Ann Lee
Lanning Lee
Lucretia Leong
Michael Little
Phyllis Look
Eulalia Luckett
Jack Luckett
Darrell Lum
Lisa Lum
Mae Lum
Russell Lum
Tan Tek Lum
Wing Tek Lum
Marion Lyman-Mersereau
Sheryl Lynch
Suzanne Marinelli
Diane Mark
Lesli Marumoto
Jean Matsuo
Greg Mau
Val Mau-Vetter
Mayor's Office of Culture & the Arts
Arthur Mersereau
Tamara Moan
Nancy A. Mower
Mary Lombard Mulder
Eden-Lee Murray
Birte Myklebust
Charlotte Nagoshi
Terri Nakamura
Eric Nemoto
Amy Nishimura
Ethel Aiko Oda
Janine Oshiro
William T. Ota
John Palomino
Christy Passion
Bill Potter
J. Arthur Rath III
Stacy Ray
Karen Richards
Regina Roberts
Colleen Rost-Banik
Donald Rost-Banik
Warren Sakamoto
Kent Sakoda
Milton Sakuoka
Electa Sam
Misty-Lynn Sanico
Kenneth K. Sato
Nealson Sato
Suzanne Sato
Calvin K.Y. Say
Kaimana Seymour
June Shimoda
Stanley S. Shimoda
Sally Sorenson
Muriel Stitt
Oded Stitt
Mitsue Stout
Matthew Stuckey
Monica Sullivan
Richard Sullivan
Raynette Takizawa
Hazel H. Takumi Foundation
Happy Tamanaha
Noe Tanigawa
Andrew Tanji
Ginny Tanji
Malia Tanji
Moriso Teraoka
Delaina Thomas
Bob Torrey
Joyce Torrey
Dennis Toyama
Jean Toyama
Joe Tsujimoto
Lan Tu
Bette Uyeda
Anna Viggiano
Darlene Weingand
Western Union
Curtis White
Lindsay White
Frederick B. Wichman
Christie Wilson
Wai Chee Chun Yee
Ann Yoklavich
Lisa Yoshihara
Beryl Allene Young
Adrian Zecha

Contents

ARTIST PROFILE AND PORTFOLIO

WAITING FO DA BIG FISH: 100-WORD/100-LINE ONLINE CONTEST SELECTIONS

Tribute to Albert Saijo

Contributors

From the Editors

No literary journal of any kind makes it to issue 100 without support from unexpected places. And in many ways the support mirrors the writing we have published: surprising, shocking, generous, challenging, and gratifying.

We were young literary radicals in 1978 when we walked into Pioneer Printers with the dream of printing up a couple of hundred copies of the first issue. Owner Dennis Watanuki quoted us a price about twice as much as the $200 we had in our pockets. We must've looked so forlorn that he just sighed and said he'd do it for whatever we had.

We had already spent maybe 50 bucks to have the issue typeset by Alice Matsumoto, who used an IBM Composer, a glorified typewriter that she had used to typeset the *Hawaii Observer*. And because printing a photograph of Bamboo Ridge, the fishing spot, meant additional expense, Darrell learned how to do a line drawing by tracing from the photo instead. We priced that first issue at the handsome sum of $1.25. Little did we know that it would cost us more to mail than what we were charging!

Somewhere along the line, after a few years of saddle-stitched (stapled) issues still without photos, another unexpected angel: Jim Uyeda—who at the time ran a small computer/software company called Software Library—challenged us to look like a real journal. He suggested a color cover and perfect binding (glued, not stapled). Yeah, right, we said. You gonna pay for it? Okay, he said and wrote the check.

And, of course, Grant Kagimoto, our first (and pretty much our only) advertiser, bought ads starting in issue #4 in 1979 and gave us a space at all the Cane Haul Road events and he kept doing so throughout the years, never asking for our circulation figures or charging a table fee. The first distribution system was Eric driving his '63 Valiant with the Bamboo Ridge logo stenciled on the doors, delivering a handful of copies to places like Mānoa Longs and long-forgotten bookstores from Fort Street Mall to Hale'iwa.

We knew we had something when printer Watanuki complained that our jobs took longer than usual because the issues were hand collated (the old walk-around-the-table method) and the boys were stopping to read. So take a look at the list of donors. Help us thank them. We also hope you will join them. And we hope you will stop "walking-around-the-table" and sit down to enjoy reading.

* * *

The cover of this issue is not only a tribute to the many "characters" who have contributed to our success but also alludes to an essay, "Waiting for the Big Fish: Recent Research in the Asian American Literature of Hawaii," by Stephen Sumida in *The Best of Bamboo Ridge*, published in 1981. In it, Sumida traces a literary history that, in the minds of some, did not even exist. For many of us, growing up in the Islands, attending local schools, and studying English at the University of Hawai'i, we never encountered local literature. Sumida points out that this was confirmed by the lack of work by Asian American writers (to say nothing of Native Hawaiian writers and others) in popular anthologies of Hawai'i literature. Were there really no Asian American writers of sufficient quality to include? Sumida and fellow researcher Arnold Hiura set out in 1978 to find out. They searched the public libraries and the University of Hawai'i libraries for work written in English by people of Chinese, Japanese, Filipino, and Korean descent in Hawai'i. Not expecting to find much, they were surprised to discover nearly 750 works—ranging from individual poems to novels and plays dating back to the 1920s—and published their findings in *Asian American Literature of Hawaii: An Annotated Bibliography.* These findings were liberating for many local writers because no longer did we feel that we were pioneers (in some ways "inventing" local literature) but simply following many writers who had come before us, a part of a tradition. We've taken the title of Sumida's essay and placed it on our cover to represent the Big Fish in this volume and the many more to come.

This issue celebrates work selected from the traditional mailed in manuscripts with a 100-line limit as well as from the entries from the 100-word and 100-line online submissions. The limits were an attempt to squeeze in 100 authors but instead we chose 100 selections from 70 authors, so that we could include a posthumous tribute to Albert Saijo, a pioneering Beat Generation Asian American poet.

Although we are still committed to the printed version of *Bamboo Ridge* (we're so old school) we're tiptoeing into the digital age with e-books and online writing. The unexpected: several familiar names took up the challenge to write something online based on themes selected from the early issues of *Bamboo Ridge*. We'd like to think that reading good writing on the website inspired others to give it a try. And while all this was happening, the four renshi poets, Ann Inoshita, Juliet Kono, Christy Passion, and Jean Toyama, continued their linked poetry experiment for another year, this time focusing on the Massie Affair. Their inspiring example of the intersection of history and creativity, the public and the personal, also contributes to the vitality of our community.

With over twice as many authors and selections in this special anthology, we couldn't limit our Editors' Choice Awards to just one in each category. Of course, all the pieces in this issue are editors' choices, but these are our favorites:

Best Prose –
Donald Carreira Ching, "Traditions"
Christine Kirk-Kuwaye, "Humor Me"
Best Poetry –
Elmer Omar Pizo, "Warning!"
Joe Tsujimoto, "Night Blooming Cereus (La Pietra, 1988)"
Best New to *Bamboo Ridge* –
Christina Low, "Where You From?"
Mayumi Shimose Poe, excerpt from "Constellation of Bodies—Emiko"

The Editors' Choice Awards are made possible through a bequest from the Majorie Edel Foundation. Professor Edel was a writer, teacher, and a mentor to many of the authors in these pages.

—Eric Chock and Darrell H. Y. Lum, Editors

PS: If all this inspires you, check out BAMBOO SHOOTS online and our continuing monthly contest that features "writing starters" based on selections from past issues of *Bamboo Ridge*.

PPS: Want to take a trip down memory lane? Check out the issues #1 and #2 that are out-of-print but viewable online. Go to www.bambooridge.com, scroll down to DOCUMENTS to find them. Keep checking back to find more as we archive our out-of-print issues.

KAKAĀKO BLUES
©1998 Grant Kagimoto
beware the Kona winds...
CANE HAUL ROAD, HAWAI'I

Ahimsa Timoteo Bodhrán

DUAL CITIZENSHIP

I was born not to this village but that one.

i was born to the tribe of men, not women.
but i was taken by them at a young age.
and turned against them.
or rather, they were turned against me.
we are still healing this rift.
i am still waiting, as are we all
from the camp of women, for a warrior,
messenger, to welcome me on home.
and home, i'll come. without relinquishing
my dual
citizenship.

I was born to the tribe of men, taken in by that of women, raised by the elders and sisters of that community. A different fire. Still it burns in me, and I wait at the edge of the village, peering out over the fields, for a messenger, on foot, a warrior walking by night through the woods, listening for the crackle of our fire. I am not the first to rise, as our warrior women stand, armed, to see who is coming. I sit by the elders, the grandmothers, watching through smoke, through ember and flame, to see if he will know my name, the one I was called at birth, the one I have carried all these years in this pueblo. He emerges from brush, from flame, surveys the gathering, nods, shows he is of peace, warrior-strong true, but his battle for me, by me, is another day. Seen and seeing, he walks toward the fire to kneel on one foot and make offering, whisper prayers to the fire. I lick my lips, not for him, maybe, but because I realize there is a dryness in me I cannot name. It is he who shall name it. I wait for the whisper of his words against the drum of my ear, a clear flute singing in my throat. Elders watch, say nothing. Offer a few other things to the fire. They have barely raised their eyes to greet. He begins to talk, low, over the flames, to see if they will be heard, his words, his offering. He marks the birch as he walks by, a way to find his way back, if needed. If needed for him ever to return. He talks to the fire, to us, to those Ancestors gathered, to those still coming. He works, talks through the flames, them rising to snap with his words. He offers the names of his people, his life, the gods he worships, his path. He has come for me. I have been called home, from home, to home. I am of age now, thirties, learned my skills of fight and war, love and healing, hunt and gather. He has come to ask for me, not only for him, but his people, once mine. To resurrect a bloodline, heal the rifts between our tribes. I look at my elders. They do not look at me, speak towards the fire. They say it has been long time since he came to their people, that he is one of us now, that he cannot leave his obligations to the people, his tribe, the one he was adopted into, the fields, this fire, he cannot leave this fire. He cannot leave the braiding of the young girls' hair, cannot leave the songs he must teach them, the braiding of voices he must do, the braiding of twine and reed into the baskets that carry our people through his days. He is no longer of that people, they say. One of us, now. One of us, always. Born to us before, born to the wrong village, now his claimed. He was a gift to us from the Creator. It is here he shall remain. He was born here, reborn here, given a name, purpose, path, people. Clan and totem, tribe. What could this other people, across the way, offer him? Memories of a childhood that was not his? A family that did not want him? A brotherhood that did not know what to do with him? Some warriors, they say, discarding their most proud, most noble and strong, most wise. A wasteful people, they say. Raised him we have, they say. Ours, they say. I look towards fire, flame. Eyes misting wet. The truth of their words, my longing. To stay, to come be with him and learn their ways. I do not want to leave my women, I say. I do not want to leave this fire, I say. Your people, my people, did not want me, I say. He cries, tears. He has been many years in waiting. He remembers the day I was taken away and cried.

I am to go with him. We are to live in the middle between both camps, visiting both. We are to start, create a new village. And call it wholme.

We will take embers from both fires.

Sally-Jo Keala-o-Ānuenue Bowman

KA'ELEMAKULE

My wife. Ho. Long time she stay *make.* Dead. You know. Stay inside Homelani Graveyard. Can still find the grave, but all inside the cane grass, get mongoose inside. I no like take care the grave. Get ghosts inside the cemetery. Ghosts no scared mongoose.

My wife, she stay so young for *make.* I think, when was it? So much time ago, so much time. I think, hard, hard. When? Back I have to think.

Hilo one small village then. Small kine. Now come big. Steamer come every time from Honolulu. Before time, before my wife come sick, get sailing ships inside the harbor. Was before I come one ship's carpenter. Before I went on top one ship.

I think back. Who the King then? Even to Hilo, sometime the King, he come. One time I see him. I stay young, more young than the King. I go down the wharf for see the King. Alex, they call him. Alex one *haole* kine name, the whole t'ing stay Alexander Liholiho, Kamehameha Four.

I go down see Alex the King. And over there plenny people like see the King too. I see one girl. One beautiful girl. So big, the eyes. But plenny people there, you know. I see her only from far, inside the crowds. I look and look, watch her moving to the side. She stay with her mother, I think. Can see her good, she wearing one white kine *haole* dress. How come? What kine Hawaiian this, wear one *haole* dress? Not even one *mu'umu'u.* One dress. I like know how come, but I no like be pushy, you know, *maha'oi.* Cannot go to her and just say, Eh, how you? Must have introduction.

I look her mother. Who that? I ask one old man, who that? He never know, tell me ask one 'nodda old man. Hoo, the next old man say, Why you like know?

The girl, she so pretty, I say.

Pretty going make you come crazy, he say. *Pupule.* You watch out, boy. You see the mother? The mother look like the girl, yeah?

Nah, I say. The girl look like the mother.

More worse, he say. More worse. That mother, she no live Hilo. The girl, she no live here. Bad, bad, they come see the King. The King, he going *make.* You watch. *Make* before he come thirty.

You sound like one *kahuna,* I say. How you know this kine stuffs? I know, the old man say. I know. Just you believe, keep away from *kapu.*

But I like meet the girl, I say.

You go meet the girl, maybe you *make* like the King. Maybe you die sooner, *pau* before you twenny-five. Then you say in your coffin, Hoo, one *kahuna* told you.

The old man, he try go. The King, he leaving too. But I shake the old man's shoulder. His bones, they rattle inside his skin.

Tell me where she live, I say. Plenny people crowding around. I lose hold on him and he walk feet fast. Sideways he so skinny I no can see him good.

I call out, loud: Where she live? Tell me! Where she live?

He turn around. The crowd making plenny noise, but I can hear him good.

Kīlauea, he say. The small pit, Halema'uma'u. Deep inside.

Amalia B. Bueno

Apo Baket

Apo Baket makes her own cigars, smoothing
The dry leaves like leather, rolling the sweet
Pungent sheet into a not-too-tight spiral
Then knotting its thickness with black thread.

She trims, twists and snips the ends clean.
She tucks the secret stash in a wooden drawer
Of her ancient Singer sewing machine. These hidden
Treasure sticks she'll share with friends and neighbors.

Apo Baket smells like the homemade coconut oil
She awakens from its solid white sleep. She scoops
A dollop onto her warm palms, then massages the glow
Into her thick hair falling on shoulders, down to hips.

Oiled and coiled, round and round, she forms
The classic Filipino grandma hairdo, a gray bun
Against the nape of her neck, held hostage
By her arched tortoise shell comb, its translucent golds
And deep browns passing for sunshine, earth.

In the narrow halls of Apo Baket's home she walks
Hunched and soundless on black velvet slippers,
Their gem-splashed embroidery shiny with beads.
Like a snake turning her head side to side
She slinks up on us with mean, squinting eyes
Ready to pounce, never missing a single detail
Of proof we were up to no good.

She takes her whiskey straight, swigging Seagram's
From a bottle kept safe in the gunmetal gray dresser
Keeping company with other medicines—the overused

Tiger Balm, White Flower, Salonpas for her aching bones.

Dr. Ramos asks if she's been taking the pills
He prescribes. He also tells her she smokes too much,
Drinks too much, and to please, for her gout's sake,
Please, stop eating tomatoes, patani, dinuguan and shellfish.

She hisses at the kind doctor, asking what kind of Filipina
Can live without tomatoes, mongo beans and blood,
Then spits out a stream of phrases—lateg mo,
I am too old, leche, I cannot change now, puneta—
Her cussing worse than a longshoreman.

It was at Cousin Bino's house when I first saw her pluck out
A good-sized bisukul, a freshwater black snail
Floating in a soup of tomatoes and onions.
She held the snail up between her thumb and pointer,

Tapped its back end with a spoon quickly, just once,
Crushing the shell at its most fragile point
Then sucked out the meat from the front with such gusto
I felt sorry for the snail, all of its body gone so suddenly.

Apo Baket outlives her only son, wearing black
For 365 days, becoming harder, more bitter
Striking out and recoiling at loved ones.
She outlives her husband and decides
Not to leave her house for one year.

She outlives her friends, then her neighbors
And relatives, one by one. I remember her sadness,
Her open palm revealing shriveled fingers pressed
Against her forehead, her eyes scanning the street for visitors.

I watch from inside the screen door, her profile puffing
That familiar Ilokano toscani, her cheeks sucking air,
The tabako's fiery end inside her mouth, a habit of survival
To withhold any glowing red light from wartime Japanese.

She nods to passersby at dusk, her quiet exhale
A solemn recognition. Resigned, she spits
Now and then into a plastic wastebasket
Lined with shredded newspaper by her feet.

Her calm breath relaxes her face, shadowed
In the twilight beneath the bittersweet street lamps.
The cigar smoke curls and twists above her
Disappearing with the memories of loved ones,

Bending and sliding like the wisps
Of her long past, unwinding away from her
The white smoke trailing slow, moving up
Toward the rafters of the darkened porch.

Amalia B. Bueno

From a Native Hawaiian Woman Shipped Out to Oklahoma Because of Prison Overcrowding in Hawai'i *

1. I left three years ago.
2. If you want to know about my crime, ask Prosecutor Peter Carlisle.
3. If you want to know how much cash and drugs I had on me, ask my husband.
4. If you want to know where my husband is, ask his attorney, the guy who plea bargained so the State could get bigger fish.
5. If you want to know why the dealers don't get caught, ask my cousin at W triple C who's also a mule like me.
6. If you want to know why my cousin is a drug runner, ask her boyfriend who threatened to kill her if she didn't do it.
7. If you want to know where my daughters Liana 6, Shawneen 10, and Cody 14 are, ask Human Services Director Lillian Koller.
8. If you want to know why I was moved from Women's in Kailua to O triple C in Kalihi, ask the suicide watch supervisor who gives out the meds.
9. If you want to know why I got shipped thousands of miles away from home, ask the case worker who recommended me because she said I wouldn't be a management problem.
10. If you want to know what the first Oklahoma winter was like, I have never been so cold in my life I thought I was going to die.
11. If you want to know why me, a kanaka maoli, is among so many Native Hawaiians in prison, ask the Office of Hawaiian Affairs.
12. If you want to know why I had to leave the place where I was born, ask Governors Waihee, Cayetano and Lingle.
13. If you want to know if I still get family visits like before, the answer is no.
14. If you want to know if I'm allowed weekly phone calls to my daughters like before, the answer is no.
15. If you want to know if I'm off the waiting list and got my required substance abuse treatment class, the answer is no.

16. Sometimes I think no one cares about me, or remembers mothers and daughters who've gone away, or notices Hawaiians, or thinks prisoners matter because we're out of sight, out of mind.
17. I don't want to think about it any more.
18. I couldn't wait anymore. So I left.

* After Bino A. Realuyo's "From a Filipino Death March Survivor Whose World War II Benefits Were Rescinded by the U.S. Congress in 1946."

Amalia B. Bueno

Lovely

You go to your first concert at fifteen
and you're going to sit in the lah-jez
until your sister says its called low-jess, dummy.

You're up high, and worth it because
the Jacksons are at the Blaisdell
even though there's no Michael anymore.

You are wearing a new wrap-around dress
in lavender, sleeveless, because you forgot
to tell your mother that the concert was this Saturday

so she just turned the armhole facings under.
Everyone thinks you bought it at Liberty House
and you smile and your sister doesn't say anything.

It's the first time you see so many drunk people
in one place, advertising beer in plastic cups
and such long, long, long lines for the bathroom.

A fight breaks out between an angry Samoan
who has given the stink eye to a wild Tongan.
Their bruddahs from Wai'anae and cousins from Lā'ie

jump in to break it up. You are secretly thrilled
to witness the violent stupidity and think the adults
could have planned better for more bathrooms.

Your sister gets your cousin to buy beer
for both of you and the joints get passed around.
The giddy sensation of standing on your seat

and dancing to music that you know
all the words to, even without the main man Michael,
makes you feel so lovely.

Donald Carreira Ching

What Was

When I was a kid, there was a woman going door-to-door asking all the kids in my neighborhood to take a survey. Fifty bucks if you can believe it, and all you had to do was fill out a form. She asked me how old I was, where I was born, what my parents did for a living; all things I was then. The topic changed quickly, and soon she started to ask what I knew about Special K, Oxy, pakalōlō. The valley had just begun rallying to rid itself of something we were finding out had claimed more than anyone knew, more than anyone *could* know. I was probably twelve then, what did I care about this shit anyway, just give me the fifty dollars and move along. Five minutes later, she did.

Even in high school, it was more about weed than anything else. A neighbor up the road gave me rides to school in his hamajang red Integra, the W2 making the trunk rattle as we swerved in and out of traffic on days we were late, trying to make it in five minutes flat only to cut out of class anyway. He would smoke occasionally, never heavy, while I shot Southern Comfort in the back roads near Kapunahala. Weed was weed, you could get high and still laugh at chronics like our friend Mike, telling us about seeing the world in a different color while he loaded himself with painkillers from his mother's medicine cabinet right outside the gas station where he worked.

A few years later, I started to hear things. The breeze that sweeps through the Ko'olau mountains carries with it whispers that no one dares discuss, and that I finally began to put together. It still wasn't your son, your daughter, it was theirs. It was the neighbor who paces back and forth in his house, yelling at the birds he keeps locked away in cages so filthy the smell spills out onto the street.

Was da guy from high sku, y'know da one, good guy, played football, real akamai. *Fo' real? You sure? No can be.* And when you saw him that first time, even if he looked the same, you saw him in the light of a thousand stories, countless news breaks and special editions. His picture in the same paper that lined the cages, shitted on daily, and suddenly no one wants to knock on his door and ask him even once, where he's from or what his parents did for a living. When the news van pulls up, they don't ask if everything is all right, how he got this way, who he was before.

I-C-E in capital letters, pictures of termite-ridden homes and carports overgrown with weeds, a toothless male in the background now like a mongoose afraid of the rats behind the lens. The same rats that took the valley so many years ago and that have now come with their cameras to record what development has done. He says nothing to the reporter, looks as if in mourning, afraid to speak about this thing that has taken not just sons and daughters, mothers and fathers, children still-born—their blood a clear mix of generations, of culture—but himself.

Growing up in Kahaluʻu for me was about the windward rains that ran through her valleys and fed the rivers I'd catch crayfish in as a child. It was about walking with my friends down to the bus stop and catching the 65 to Temple Valley, and then down to the pier where my father would be pulling in with whatever he did or didn't catch.

But the same rains that find their way to the ocean, bring with them a deeper sense of something that has long since been polluted by tar and concrete. The chronics in the paper are not nameless; they have just forgotten their names, unable to remember on shores now eroded with time. Nowadays, these same shores, once viable, once vital, like the ahupuaʻa of which they are a part, are documented with single-word captions, and images of mongoose scurrying for the shade.

I was too young then to understand, or maybe I was just too ignorant to see that what Mike was doing was waiting to die beside those pumps. The Integra that I rode in smelled sticky sweet, and even though I hadn't taken a single hit, I might as well have taken the lighter and lit it for him. Others too shame to admit what once was, now pray for what is, and what is yet to be. Growing up in Kahaluʻu for me, for many, was never about ice so when the woman with her degree and her fifty dollars asked me what I knew about meth, what was I supposed to say? Five minutes later, she too would be gone.

Ghislaine D. Chock

The Path

Wandering alone in Kyoto
I am pulled again toward a shrine.
The stone floor changes under my feet
From large stones to smaller ones.
"Slow down, feel the ground."
Running source water from a well
Asks to leave my worries behind.
"Wash your hands,
Wash your mouth."
After sweeping my face with incense,
I approach the giant aged rope
That attaches to heaven.
It has held so many strong and weak hands.
Bong! Bong!
Greeted by golden statues in a dark background
Surrounded by old scrolls—
Special ageless treasures.
I ask for protection
For myself and my loved ones,
And to be a better person, always,
On my path.

A joyful elderly priest-like lady
Sits behind a desk in the corner.
She asks her younger assistant
Where I come from.
I tell her Hawai'i, and before that, Canada.
She is so puzzled!
She laughs and tells other bystanders.
Then reaches for my hand.
I do not hesitate to reach for hers as well.
Her handshake is feminine,

But strong, without hurting.
Usually, I dislike handshakes;
I prefer hugs.
Those never hurt.

I pull my little traveling book
For the assistant to calligraphy
The shrine's logo.
Different widths with each stroke of dark ink
Done swiftly without hesitation.
It occupies the whole page!

Her eyes gaze at my kimono jacket.
She reaches for it.
I tell her that I wove it.
I sway my hands from side to side with an imaginary shuttle—
this motion is part of the universal weaving language.
She understands.
And laughs some more with appreciation.

The lady agrees to a picture,
But unfortunately,
Removes her smile for it.
Then, she returns to her beautiful smile again.
When I attempt to photograph her ageless treasures,
She teaches me "iie"—
Her arms form an X across her chest.
Her way to tell me "kapu"
I understand.
Then, she teaches me "hai"—
Arms bent at the elbows,
Up on each side of her head.

When leaving,
I follow a path of single stones.
"Pay attention,
It is said that
To stay on the path

You must slow down,
Be in the moment,
And feel the space."

Enjoy your path.
I bow deeply.

Ghislaine D. Chock

The Talk

In front of a large rock garden,
An ageless monk sits with us,
Dressed in a black robe.
He talks firmly with his eyes closed
But always smiling softly:
"Stand erect, hunchbacks!
It will open your hearts!
You wore your parents' faces
For the first 20 years.
But now, it is your true face that I see.
Put a smile on it.
Be thankful
For the air you breathe.
You need each other."
Then he walks away.

Myles De Coito

Go Sleep Already, Irene

The reflection staring back at Daryl reminded him of Jerry Rice's three-touchdown performance in Super Bowl XXIX. Joe Robbie Stadium, Miami, Florida, 1995. The last hurrah of the 49er dynasty. The wide receiver wearing number 80 had all the facial accoutrements of an NFL player: sweat, mouthpiece, eye-black. Visible even to the casual observer, however, was one more piece of equipment being worn by the all-pro. It was a strip of plastic adhering to the bridge of his nose. Not quite a Band-Aid, it was something else. Daryl, like others, would later learn this face gear was a novel performance-enhancing tool. It dilated an elite athlete's nasal passage, allowing for optimum intake of oxygen.

For Daryl, however, the Breathe Right strip was an attempt to enhance his wife's ability to sleep. He grinned—open-mouthed—at the irony, revealing his nighttime dental guard. The two items, snore strip and anti-tooth-grinding mouthpiece, were cumbersome—anathema to a good night's rest. No, he was not Jerry Rice, and he definitely wasn't about to score any touchdowns.

Sandra had scooted over to her side of the bed. Eyeshades drawn, cotton candy-blue HEAROS ear plugs inserted, the blind and deaf woman had pulled her share of sheet, blanket, and comforter over and around herself. "Fricken mummy," Daryl mumbled.

"What you said?"

Return of the Living Dead, Daryl thought. "Notting," he said. "Goodnight, Mommy."

"Ha? Talk mo' loud next time."

He couldn't believe it. Why couldn't she just leave the earplugs out if she wanted to hear him? He kept this to himself as he slumped into his familiar indentation. Grasping the near edge of linen with one hand, he turned off his lamp with the other. Here, in the dark, the familiar ritual began. He would try to wait for Sandra to fall asleep first, allowing her to slumber free of his barely checked, incessant snoring. He bit down on the piece of plastic in his mouth, testing the air through his wide-open nostrils. *Down, set, ready, hut-hut-hut . . .* And just like that, he was off and dreaming.

The first whack hardly stirred him. He merely brushed an imaginary mosquito from his ear. Then came the shove, which only caused him to reposition. The third blow stung, a flick on the arm that drew a flinch. Daryl's eyes opened, or so it seemed. He could see himself, lying on a twin-sized bed, its mattress swathed in hospital-white flat sheets. Pulled up over his chest, but under his arms, was a gray flannel blanket. An assortment of colored cables crawled out from beneath the blanket, toward his head. The mess of lines reminded him of his job as a telecom wire splicer: a baffling snarl of Crayola strands, which wove into end points upon his torso and crown.

The woman in this dream was definitely not Sandra. Even under her starched, sterile lab coat, he could trace the silhouette of petite curves, which ran down to two-inch pumps that looked more playful than professional. She fed through her hands a stream of paper being inscribed with wave patterns. The machine doing the work made steady sounds, as some cartridge-housed stylus droned back and forth, emitting the mosquito-like noise he'd heard before waking.

The louder, more apparent noise in the room, however, was his snoring. Like his Craftsman weed whacker that grunted to life only after many cranks, his throat rasped raggedly, reverberating as if a flap of bulldog skin were stuck within it. He thought of his neighbor Ronnie's Shindaiwa, a little power-stroking piece of Japanese engineering. That thing always started on the first try. He felt slobbish beside the pretty, young monitor who was witnessing—as Ronnie had done so many times—his impotence.

"Oh my God, shut up already," she razored in a whisper. "Pity your wife." A tendril of polished black hair fell out of its neatly tucked position behind an ear. She puffed it back, mouth skewed to one side of her face, hard enough to blow out candles on a five-year-old's birthday cake.

Hhhwwhuh! The blast of air from Daryl's mouth shot his head back. His eyes opened skyward as his hard hat slid off. He grabbed at the protective shell with both hands, losing his grip on the top railing of the lift bucket, which was suspended thirty feet in the air. Feeling the vertigo overcome his knees, he instinctively dropped to the metal mesh floor in a squat.

"What Daryl, fall asleep again?" his spotter yelled. "Brah, nuff already. You fall down *make*, as my ass!"

Daryl was shaking, but he confidently retorted, "You know what, try move da bucket smooth next time! Nevah mind blaming me, ah." The narrow, yellow brim hanging over the slumped man's eyes prevented him from seeing the fingered riposte of the ground crewman. Intuitively, though, he felt the mouthed cussing and gesture burning a hole in his back. Daryl pushed against the rusted metal grating beneath him. He rose: head bent forward, mouth aimed dead center of a space amid the ferrous floor. His tongue sucked to the roof of his mouth, creating a vacuum. The action drew forth a cavern full of saliva that he let drop in a stretched-out sling of viscous elastic that snapped the ground three feet from his co-worker.

"Oh, *no*, he nevah!" came the sassy reaction between clenched teeth. Daryl watched as she hopped to her left, and then checked her foot nearest his bed for evidence of splatter. "Not my fricken new Taharis," she hissed, looking over her right shoulder as she bent the same side lower leg for a good look. "Ugh!"

Daryl tried to apologize, but his words merely fell to the floor, lying in the pool of spit his body had just issued. He reached for a towel near the bed, intending to place it over the wet spot, when—*clang*—a catapulted combination wrench ricocheted off the bottom of his bucket. The impact loosed a rain of rust flakes. Daryl launched his hardhat, a fastball of retaliation, "Wait till I come down, you son of a bitch!"

"Daryl, shut *up*!" Sandra stood at his nightstand, feet spread apart to avoid the lake of dribble bedside. Oscillating toothbrush buzzing away in one hand, she smacked the top of her husband's alarm clock with the other. "What, sleep good—*all-star*?"

He looked down, searching for black, patent leather heels, but found only faded, pink fuzzy slippers. Dejected, he elongated: toes pointing and fingers stretching up from parallel, reaching arms. It was an empty salute, as no ball had crossed the goal line. He closed his eyes and saw pressed, white poly-cotton, and anticipated the morning's warm shower spray, its engulfing steam. His back arched, glutes tightened—pelvis thrust forward, upward. "Aah," he groaned a waking yawn. "I jess was about fo' score touchdown."

Jesse S. Fourmy

The Breakwall

I've paddled days when the sun itself
disguises the distance you cover from the shore
to the breakwall and back, playing its tricks upon you
with the colors of the water of the bay.
Sometimes green and bright
or deep blue. Sometimes black (if a cloud covers the sun).
You become confused by keeping track
of its colors and its depth. You fatigue.
The sun does not relent with its game
until you concede, weary from the constancy,
that barrage of rays and heat which lap at your temples
like a dog in the backyard of a relative
who still lives in the place you were born.
The heat just lingers there, lathers in your face
and without the hat you wore you'd wish yourself
back in the shade of the regatta
watching the outriggers file across the bay
in that perpetual motion of paddlers.
Steersman's cadence ringing them on.

Those hot, windless days when the water itself's slick
and inviting—a mirage luring you to the breakwall
in its infinite distance until you're upon it
and the black crabs clinging to its mass shift
from your sight to the cracks between the stones
and the water on the other side of that rock wall
that you can't see but know is there
because you've paddled across the bay
to the breakwall before and have seen it
a million times in photographs or from the air
and wondered what exactly was out there behind it.
And there you are, having paddled across the bay

which at times seemed peaceful and bright and green
and smooth, or deep blue then black—as if clouds crossed the sun.
The whole time the shore near the regattas shrank
smaller and smaller with each monotonous stroke.
I went there. I went there to see hammerheads
and the breakwall which was much larger than I imagined
or could see across the bay or from the air.

It's not the breakwall or the ocean divided against itself
that creeps inside you, feeds the monster of anxiety
chained to your reason that you and others have vouched for
time and time again. It's what's on the other side
of the breakwall if you paddle, stroke by monotonous
stroke to its end, where the openness of the ocean swells,
lifts your craft as tall as the breakwall itself
where the wind and sun shift instantly like the crabs
you witnessed on the black rocks of the breakwall
moments ago when you arrived. Tired and amazed
at how big the breakwall is, how large the bay,
how far the shore, how small the regattas with their tin roofs,
and, no longer visible, the canoes with their steersman,
wearing a wide-brimmed hat and calling
for his paddlers to dig, dig, switch, dig, dig,
switch. The water, gray and wind-damaged
beyond the breakwall where no sun seeks itself
on its surface, and buoys clang in unison warning
freighters and cruise liners, with neon green and red
strobe, of the breakwall splitting the gut of the bay.
This is what you wanted—to cover a great difference
alone, to paddle where *hammerheads* are believed
to haunt the deepest section of a bay.
The *breakwall*, undeterred and uncaring,
lies about its size, its magnificence—
what it keeps from you, keeps you paddling back.

J. Freen

A Halloween I Remember

"You too old for Halloween," my maddah tell me, the morning before I go school, on the Halloween I going tell you about.

"I know," I tell her. "You tink I nevah know dat?"

Still yet, lunchtime, I stay eating with Edgar, Donut, and Chuckie, like always, and Chuckie says even though Halloween for kids, and we sure as hell not kids anymore, maybe we could, you know, charge em one moah time, dress up and everyting, like back in da day. You mean like lass year, Donut says.

Later on I tell my maddah I pau with my homework, now I stay heading foah da park. She gives me the look, but she nevah say nothing, so I jet outta deah, go meet da guys. Almost dark already. On the way I wen put on my pirate costume.

Da guys stay waiting for me on da corner. If you nevah know was them, you would tink, one pumpkin head standing next to Barack Obama—but jus Donut and Edgar. But, next to dem, get one girl!

And not jus any girl. For like one second, I tink, ho, cannot be, naw—and then I see, no, not *her,* jus Chuckie, the jokah, dress up like her, with hair like hers, and where he got dat skirt? Radical. People walking by, mostly girls from school but some guys too, they sure recognize who Chuckie supposed to be. Pointing, laughing—specially da girls.

Da girl Chuckie impersonate, dass Carlita Wong, da mos beautiful girl that evah was, da whole history of girls. Carlita Wong walk by, you almost pass out. Girls hate her cause they know maybe they live long time, but they no going look dat good, not evah.

But, Carlita Wong strange. She pale like anyting. Her hair beautiful, but all big, fluffy kine. Edgar's oldah bruddah says, "She tink she Farrah Fawcett already. Stay in one time wop."

Her clothes strange too—all wild-kine colors and stockings look like get spider webs all ovah. One time I stand close to her, she smell like mothballs.

One more ting. She live in da most had-it house on our street. Old, two story, lean sideways, no paint, mango tree cover da whole place, gate stuck half open. And Carlita she nevah talk to nobody. She jus go to school, come back home. Somebody say her faddah wen leave long time ago, now only get da maddah—but nobody see her, years and years already.

So, we walk around, us guys. We trick-or-treat little bit. Rain coming down the valley now. We stay on da sidewalk in front da Wong house. Even more spooky and sideways, in the mist and dark. No reason, but we push open da gate and go inside da yard.

Nobody like knock. The wind stay making noise in da tree, you cannot hear traffic or people on the street, nothing.

After long time da door open. One old lady standing there, her white hair like one da kine, halo over her head.

"Oh," she say, "is it that night again? Come in, children. I must have something for you."

Da parlor smell like mothballs. Dark, except one small lamp. After while, da lady wen come back with milk and cookies.

Nobody going touch da cookies—we jus like leave, cause creeping us out already. The old lady sit with us, and, first time, we can see her face. Now we creeped out for real. Cause, you know she old, and supposed to get one old face? But no moah lines, smooth her face. In fact she beautiful, like da old Chinese vase stay on da mantel, Edgar's house. And she look exactly like Carlita. By the way, I tinking, where Carlita stay?

Pretty soon, da other guys, they notice all dis stuffs too, and also notice the old lady only looking at Chuckie, in his Carlita costume.

"So, little boy," she tell Chuckie, staring like one laser beam, "who are *you* pretending to be?"

We look at Chuckie. Chuckie shaking, sweating, nevah say nothing. He stay in one trance—cannot move his eyes from da old lady's eyes.

Den, my heart skip. I see something, white, pass by, jus outside the lamp light. I notice Edgar wen see um too. Den, I see it again—one white shape, like one pale shadow, float past, behind Chuckie's head.

Dass it for me. I look da oddah guys. Then me, Edgar and Donut we jump outta our chairs and charge out dat front door so fast da old lady nevah even notice we stay gone. And Chuckie? He nevah move. Paralyze, I guess. We stay rats, but we wen leave him there.

Aftah dat, we run home fast, lock our doors.

Next day one school day. Lunchtime I go foah sit with da guys, except no more Chuckie. I look at dem, dey nod deah head, raise eyebrow, I look two tables over, deah Chuckie. Only he look different. And, he stay sitting with Carlita Wong!

Da oddah guys say dey gotta go study now—ha, ha—but me I go ovah, cause I feel bad bout last night.

So now they both looking up at me. One ting everybody always notice about Carlita is she get blue, blue eyes, but almos no moah pupil in da center, so she stare out at you, her eyes more like two blue TV screens. And weird dis, but when he look up at me, all of a sudden I see Chuckie's eyes stay different now—used to be brown, but now they changing, right in front of me, coming blue, da pupils smaller and smaller, like he and Carlita on da same TV channel already!

After Halloween, da gang only us tree guys now—Chuckie spend all his time with Carlita. We see him every now and den, and every time he little bit more different. His hair grow long, his pants come tight, his shoes get checker pattern, he wears little jackets, too short da sleeves.

"Dat kid tink he Michael Jackson," says Edgar's oldah bruddah.

Time pass, bombye we nevah see Chuckie around at all. Chuckie's mom tell my maddah Chuckie run away. Da cops look, posters all ovah, but till today nobody evah see Chuckie again.

Carlita, she still walk to school, and back again. Same, same, except now she get one small kine smile all da time on her face.

One time I stay walking fast around da cornah and almos crash into her—her face, her eyes, up close to mine.

And I swear I not crazy now, but inside her blue eyes I see something in the middle, where da pupil supposed to be, some damn ting, one dark dot. I look closah.

I'm telling you, I see my friend Chuckie's face inside deah, da kine, da original Chuckie, and seem like he stay reaching out to me, trying foah say something, but den Carlita blinks and walks around me. I turn and watch her go. And tink naw, couldent be, couldent be. Could it?

Norma W. Gorst

Going Under

Once the sea closes overhead,
the world turns gray, dense water
presses the body, molds veins
into flat tracks running wild

under skin, till the blood chills
to stillness. The soul moves on,
at these depths no longer connected
with time, with the need to be

in time, floating, cradled in
the water's arms. How beautiful
to rest so, to watch the dolphins
slip by, curious, their darts

coming as if across the retina,
effortless as sunlight probing
the body that's left, stirring
the halted cells of memory—

what it was like to be. Something
wants to laugh at their antics, their
smooth waltz, the spinning, caroming
bodies—down, under, over—in a dance

impossible to resist. Arms and legs
would join in, but the water holds
them. Now only spirit leaps to meet
the dolphins' grace and time-bound reel.

Marie M. Hara

Sugar (Territory of Hawai'i, 1948)

I went outside of our house by myself to see the sugar cane up close. Another bright day of dazzling sunshine in a quiet patch of houses far from anything you might call city life greeted me. Kapa'au on the Big Isle was next to Hawi town in Kohala with the sugar mill, far away from Kona where they had a few cars, markets, and the government-paved streets. Already bored by the quiet life at five years old, I longed to play with somebody besides the older boys who threw guavas at me in the lane. Nobody stirred out of the other rickety plantation houses. So many of the adults had left for Hilo where there was hope of work for the military. The younger men had already left the camps to fight as Americans in the war. Only old people stayed behind.

My obaban and ojiji moved so slowly watering plants or fixing our rice and poi and sometimes fish that they made me impatient to hop around or run whenever I could. When they looked in my direction, they sometimes frowned. What I saw was their fine attention to the front yard where she raised a batch of chickens in a wooden shed, and he clipped at bonsai plants. My mama had left me with her parents so that she could find a job as a nurse in a real hospital, not a plantation office.

I wrote her letters covered with drawings of airplanes and my name spelled in block letters next to a small girl waiting on the ground, looking up at the sky. Auntie from the house with the peeling paint in the other dirt lane near the Lucky Strike store would write the address on the fold-up envelope then let me lick a three-cent stamp to send the message to Mama in Honolulu.

I sat on the weathered back steps staring out at the fields of cane that grew closer and closer to our clothesline. From where I surveyed the back of the property everything was deeply green in the flat afternoon sunlight. The night rain had left some drops that glittered on the windblown rows of the sugar crop now waving gently. The cane had grown taller even by my quick measure. *Abunai.* Dangerous. In Japanese the grandparents often warned me, "Don't you go out there. You'll be sorry if you do. Your feet will get all cut up." I looked upon the big field ahead and noted the far neighbors' mango tree. No fruit yet.

Well, I had slippers on. I loved to dance like a tree in the breeze while imagining that almost transparent fairies could appear out of the shrubbery that grew wild around the Kapa'au Library. I had read stories about them, studied illustrated storybooks and wanted to see for myself. Carefully, silently, I made my way down into the rows of cane, remembering every so often to look backwards to locate the house. I left no bread crumbs or little stones from my pocket to mark the way back. No fairies, elves or *menehune* emerged anywhere.

I knew better than to go farther than the mango tree, but I still got lost. The big field of cane was far taller than I thought—or I was much shorter. Turning around, I began to head back, but lost my way again. I couldn't make out the darker top of the mango tree anymore. Then I remembered my obaban's voice telling me how when she was young she joined the other lady workers with weeding hoes. As they cut away the stray cane seedlings or dug out weeds from the straight furrows, they laughed and sang. They could find each other that way. I sang out the words of "The Easter Parade." Loud. No one heard me yell about "My Easter bonnet with all the frills upon it . . ." I meandered through row after row. No one, anywhere. I wanted to get back home where the back door was always left open, where the old ones were waiting for me.

Ojiji once told a neighbor, while I was in earshot, about the pitiful "be-be mama" who lost her little child when a cane fire flared out of control and whipped into her field. She was at work not too far away but couldn't get to the baby sleeping under a little blanket canopy. She had worried about crawling centipedes but not fire spreading wildly over the area. The baby cried in screams, and the mother screamed, but she and the other hoe-hana ladies couldn't get through the curtain of flames in time. The mother was scarred with burns then lost her mind. Ojiji touched his head and used the word "lo-lo" to say that she was still crazy, whenever her name was mentioned. We walked silently past her place where the empty front porch had rags of curtains, windows that were never open.

I spotted a stalk of cane half broken off from a shorter plant, the one miniature plant in a tall row. I thought about how the boys used their pocketknives to cut and peel nice stalks of cane then chewed on them to suck out every bit of the sweet sugar juice from the fibers inside. They liked to eat in front of me, but they never let me taste any of it. I grabbed to yank the cane off the main stalk then froze.

The shiny green stalk sprouted fine, almost invisible prickly hairs that poked my hands immediately. I sure felt the hot rush of irritating pain jabbing across my palms. It made me pull up my fingers in a clench of agony. I moved my right hand up to reach a big leaf hanging from the stalk. I could hold onto that instead. The leaf, ridged with its own thorns, ripped through the flesh on the backside of my fingers. Auwee, the sting of pulling the jagged leaf away.

Yelping in pain, feeling under attack, I dropped the hateful green thing and swooped away, running down the row, racing back to where I hoped was home. Like a fluttering hankie blown away by a strong wind might fall back to its clothesline, I jerked myself into motion. In a few minutes I flopped on the back steps, frantic to turn on the nearby faucet. I washed water over my itchy, stinging hands and dusty feet. I turned the remnant of spume hose over my hot head as I tried to shake the bits of nasty stuck stuff off of me.

Even then, for days my pudgy skin carried tiny hurt places from the sticky hairs and jagged leaf of sugar cane. It had promised something sweet that I couldn't get, no matter how much I wanted it. Most of all I felt hurt to know that way inside I was truly stupid. I didn't like to look out at the fields of green any more. I stared at the Bull Durham bag tied onto the mouth of the kitchen water spigot, gazed toward the scary outhouse with too-large seat holes hanging over a swampy stream bed.

In Japanese Obaban said, "What have you learned?"

I was sad. I shook my head, shrugged and stayed silent.

She smiled at me.

Gail N. Harada

Sky Watching

It was many years ago that a father took his two children up Tantalus to witness Ikeya-Seki's huge comet tail sweep the eastern sky. They were impressed by this astronomical phenomenon, and did not comprehend its impact on them. Later, occasional shooting stars flashed through their lives—fleeting, unarticulated wishes waiting to be fulfilled nevertheless. When Halley's comet re-entered Earth's orbit, something about the angle of its path to that of Earth's diminished its tail to human eyes, so it seemed small compared to the clouds of galaxies and rivers of stars stretched across the black dome of sky above the obsidian expanse of Kīlauea crater. The configuration of Venus, Mars, and Jupiter clustered beside a sliver of crescent moon one June night in 1991 inspired curiosity and anticipation, but the *Honolulu Star-Bulletin* declared the grouping had "little scientific significance." In July of the same year, solar eclipse devotees from around the world descended on the Big Island, only to be foiled by cloud cover that parted for just a few moments during the four minutes of totality. At the same time in a parking lot near Diamond Head, a community gathered, straining to see the moon's penumbra on the sun through special optical grade solar filters. The birds grew quiet, a dusk that never deepened into night settled and lifted, and life went on. In the spring of 1993, the Perseid meteor shower raised spectacular expectations—visions of hundreds of falling stars streaking the night sky. The predictions were not fulfilled, though the faithful who kept watch claimed they were not entirely disappointed. Then, late one November evening as the moon emerged from its eclipse encircled by a faint lunar rainbow, like the princess of clouds and mist on the seventh day of the seventh month in the old Japanese folk tale, a woman began crossing over the Milky Way toward a mystery that could not be denied, a memory that could not be forgotten, and an unexpected path.

Ann Inoshita

Finding an Exit

She is the only one here,
and the doors are locked.

There are books on shelves
that have no order or titles.
Everything she finds
disappears in her hands.

She looks for a window,
a table, a chair to break out.
Every object she runs to
moves farther away.

She's breathing hard,
her skin is hot,
and her voice turns
to steam.

She cannot speak, but she hears music
outside the room.

She feels a tap on her shoulder,
and she is outside in the courtyard
with her classmate.

Her classmate pauses,
then asks if she should continue talking.

She nods and hears music in every syllable.

Ann Inoshita

Public School: 1983

When the last bell rang,
she ran home.

She opened her backpack
and threw away
her report card with A's
homework
reports
books
journals.

She opened the refrigerator
and threw away
sashimi
tsukemono
sushi
manapua
Spam
Portuguese sausage.

She opened her closet
and threw away
an old kimono
jeans.

She hit the garbage bag.
Ripped the plastic.
Kicked the cans.

Thought of
cutting
burning
herself.

Thought of
electric sockets
water
pills.

She left everything
on the floor
and walked
to the cabinet.

She emptied
a bottle
feeling
every
pill
in her hand.

Everything
would be
gone.

She looked
around
the room
for the last
time.

She notices
a picture
of her family
and pauses.

She slips
every pill
slowly
back
into the bottle

and puts
her backpack
and clothes
in her room.

David James

His 53rd Autumn in Michigan

Early November and it comes down to this again: the man sheds, losing his hair, ears, face, a leg dropping in the driveway, his arms torn loose, blown across the yard like fleshy Styrofoam. He dissolves into an autumn day, his soul turning that pale shade of sky gray. It happens every year as the evening temps flirt with 30, as trees strip down to scarred bark, as certain birds become memories.

He resigns himself to this fact of living, which is like a fire, bright and consuming at the same time. Thick, cut logs are tossed into the flames; within hours they're glowing piles of ash, sparking up in the stiff wind.

The man waits for spring when he hopes to reassemble for another year, to piece himself together with what's left from the bitter winter months. This ear is not working well; that arm carries a peculiar ache; his left eye trembles now. As with every blessing, there's a price to pay.

David James

You Can't Always Be What You Want

I moved
to get away from myself,
figuring with a brand new start
I could set things right:
a clean slate, a blank sheet,
a cloudless sky, all blue
and noisy with birds.
I left everything behind—
books, tools, cars, golf clubs—
lessening the chance that I would
be able to track me down.
No forwarding number, no change
of address on my license.
One early morning, I kissed my wife goodbye
on the forehead as she slept; my kids
were absorbed in their own lives
so there was no need to tell them—
they wouldn't realize I'd gone
until they reached their 30s.
I shaved my head bald, grew a beard,
bought all new clothes. I flipped a coin
at the train station to find my new home.
Rented a small apartment there, took a job,
paid under the table, at a fruit market.
At least I'd have something to eat.
But mostly, I stayed out of sight, hiding,
Stowing away below the main deck.
To pass time, I memorized the stars,
counted every hair on my body, watched the leaves
turn red and yellow, predicting which one
would fall next.

I moved to lose my old self and live the way I wanted.
And it worked
for about a week.
Six days into my new life, I felt like someone
was watching me, that obese lady at the plum display,
fingering every piece of fruit; that blonde girl staring
at me like I had blood on my face.
As I walked home, two pigeons, obvious spies,
charted my path using electronic sensors
(I later found out this was untrue).

But it was 10:00 when the knock on the door
broke my meditation of ankles. Standing on the porch
with five suitcases, smirking like a raving idiot,
my old self greeted me.
"Yo, dude, why'd ya leave?"
"You know why," I said.
"Not really," he said, "but here's most of your stuff,"
pointing at the suitcases. "I only took what
I thought you'd need."
We stood there for two or three minutes, staring,
me glancing down at his feet,
him peering behind me into the apartment,
until I let him back in,
my first and last
mistake.

Darlene M. Javar

For Robin, Unclaimed

Thin as hibiscus petals—
sick for a month, unable to breathe,
you finally went to the emergency room,
but no one accompanied you
when you were transported
to the next hospital sixty miles away.
Not wanting you to be alone
I drove to Hilo Medical Center
and claimed we were related.
You talked through your oxygen mask
until the doctor came in and reported—
disease had claimed your body.
I used the phone at the nurse's counter
to call your home,
to tell your lover to hurry, to get here.

Unable to breathe,
again you were transported
to another hospital an island away,
again unaccompanied,
again unclaimed.

I called your mother after searching the directory,
explained I was a new friend,
acknowledged your absence of seven years;
the mother who once saved you,
adopted you, sheltered and loved you
when you were her little boy.
She told me you were already
damaged beyond repair
by the time she got you,
that she had lost you twice—

she calling you by her chosen male name,
me calling you by your chosen female name,
both of us not claiming your birth name;
and then the daughter she could not accept
disappeared for seven years.
"*Terminal, Saint Francis Hospital,*" I reported
then she contemplated
flying across the Pacific
to see you, to help you, to love you.

Your mother and I talked each week
and she shared
that she would sing to you over the phone,
love you, pray with you,
and she would come.

I called your friend in Alaska and shared with her
that you were dying. She said she would come,
to see you, to help you, to love you.
Each week we talked and she was still coming.

I called the transgender support group.
I called the nurse to complete your forms.
I called the doctor when you wanted to lessen the pain.

Flown to O'ahu, an island away,
your lover said he would come,
to see you, to help you, to love you.
When the doctor called me
to say that you might not
make it through the night,
I bought the airline ticket for your lover,
so you wouldn't be alone and unclaimed anymore.
After a week, you sent him home.

When the doctor called me and said you had died,
I called your friend, your lover, your mother.
Alaska wanted your body, Arizona wanted your body,
but O'ahu had your body.

A month after you pulled
off your oxygen mask,
two months after
you were admitted with AIDS,
a voice over the phone explained,
"Unclaimed bodies are incinerated."
Like you changed your name,
I changed my number.

Darlene M. Javar

Pyrex and Pipe

Arranged your pipes
in the 13 X 9 Pyrex dish, glass on glass.
Pipe from the top shelf of your wood shop—
measure, saw, assemble;
pipe under the dash board of your truck—
weld, rivet, paint;
the bathroom you remodeled—
floor, sink, shower— pipe behind porcelain décor;
inside your hunting boots, under your Budweiser hat,
in your jeans pocket.

Pinched the piece of glass,
jagged remnant of pipe bowl—
glass dropped, overlooked on the kitchen floor;
a day spent cooking for a nephew's birthday.

Rearranged your pipes in the Pyrex dish.
Glass with meth residue, glass of charcoal film,
glass rinsed clean, broken neck glass,
oval bowl glass, round bowl glass,
I-might-even-try-this glass.

Placed my forearm over the 13 X 9 Pyrex dish,
examined the keloids. Lateral lines of self-infliction;
glass taken to flesh, the jagged neck of your pipe,
the bowl crushed on cement. I slashed at your insanity.

Selected a piece of glass from the Pyrex dish.
Careful incisions carved out keloids,
a hunt for pipe under the dashboard of my forearm;
glass on glass, glass in flesh, red on glass.
Blood welding, Pyrex painting keloids
arranged on the top shelf of your woodshop.

Frances H. Kakugawa

Post Notes to Pearl Harbor and Hiroshima

Pearl Harbor, 1941

Under the rising sun
The enemy came
Wearing my face.

Immediately, a new word was added to my childhood vocabulary.

Eh Jap
It claws my spine
Tearing skin.
It enters my body
To devour who I am.

What do you do
With Eh Jap
On your face?
I spit it out. Bull's eye!

Hiroshima, 1945

In a brilliant flash, my ancestors were vaporized and my history came to an abrupt halt.

We sliced the chrysanthemum
Off its stalk and left it
Naked in the sun.

Over the ashes of Hiroshima,
Our victory was hailed.
Beneath that, my ancestors lay buried.

Years after Japan surrendered, my grandmother hurried up to our house. In Japanese, she called to my mother. "I heard from the emperor, I heard from the emperor! He called and said Japan won the war! Isn't that wonderful?" Her eyes, her smile, such ecstatic joy.

"Obaban, Obaban," I told her in English, "Japan surrendered thirty-five years ago."

My name is either Hideko Frances Kakugawa or Frances Hideko Kakugawa, depending on what document I am holding. My birth certificate carries the name my parents gave me and tells one story. My Social Security card bears my American name first and tells another.

Rust
"Leave," I beg you.
"Japan surrendered,
My ancestors were fried.
The *Arizona* is rusting
At the bottom of the bay."
My mirror whispers in sorrow,
"I can't let them go.
We are prisoners of our face."

Either way, the history of the young girl I would have become is gone. The only face left for me to wear was my own.

Portrait
A crayoned flag: red, white and blue
Waves from a chopstick
Clutched in my hand.

In the other: a chrysanthemum
On a rice paper fan
Covering half my face.

Frances H. Kakugawa

Sounds of Old Plantation Days

I miss the sound of the cane trucks tonight
Hauling cane through old sugar towns.
Not the bounce and rattles of the empties,
As they head back to the fields
Over the twists of narrowing country roads.
It's the dull muffled thump of trucks
Laden with tons of fresh cut sticky cane
That pass my silent, sleepless nights.
I'm not alone on these nights,
In company of faces sitting high
In darkened cabs, the glow of half-burnt cigarettes
Hanging from their lips like summer lanterns.

Lisa Linn Kanae

Bobby Pin

All us girls at the Lewers Street McDonald's get one small Tupperware container full with bobby pins. You cannot have enough bobby pins. This McDonald's is probably the busiest one in Hawai'i, so once you punch in and hit the floor, you cannot be fixing your hair. You no more even time for stop and check out what you look like. Not like get planny mirrors behind the counter anyway. The only mirror get is the one inside the French fry warmer, so maybe, if you get couple seconds, you can check out your face when you scooping fries into the cartons. Remember now. I said couple seconds. I don't know why they call that thing a French fry warmer because the thing is not warm. It is frickin' hot. Get those orange heating lights too, da kine that make your face look like one jack-o'-lantern. And you can forget about seeing your reflection in the stainless steel equipment. Basically, you better do all that make pretty-pretty shit before you grab your time card. Remember, this is Waikīkī; we suppose to be pretty.

This is my routine. I pull back my hair into one ponytail and then with my fingers, pick at my bangs so they drape naturally over my forehead. I get what Tūtū call one "high forehead." She get one too, but she no can cut her hair because she one hula dancer. She almost had one heart attack when I cut my bangs, but I told her times are different. I liberated, I said. I free for do what I like—like spray Aqua Net on my bangs. I gotta shut my eyes and hold my breath because Aqua Net is stink and can sting. I slick back any loose strands and then slide in some bobby pins for keep everything all neat. All together. Your hair cannot be hanging in front your face. Health regulations. My mother's boyfriend tell me that rule is stupid because I come home smelling like cooking oil and burnt salt. He said I might as well sell chemotherapy on the side. One time he told me, "Every day your mother carry huge trays of dinner plates at the Sheraton, all you do is push hamburgers." Whatever. I no listen to him. When I bring home leftovers, he the first one for grab one Quarter Pounder. He's nothing but a broke-ass, bum. At least I get one job.

Every couple weeks, I go Woolworth's for buy my hairnets. Buy the black, nylon kine. No buy Honeycomb. The color look like peach fuzz on your head. This is how you put on one hairnet. You grab the elastic rim with both hands and spread your fingers for hold the rim open like that string game you play when you one kid, and then slide the net over your head like one shower cap. Underneath the hairnet, my ponytail look like one fish inside one fishnet. Us girls have to wear one flat, orange aloha print bow on our heads too. The bow match my aloha shirt uniform, which by the way, is so big for me, I look like I stay six years old, not sixteen. Couple more bobby pins for hold the bow in place, and my head look like one Christmas present.

Get one bag of orchids on top the time clock, so before I grab my time card, I have to pick one orchid—the assistant manager said take only one—and pin it to my bow so the flower look like it's behind my ear. Poor thing those orchids. I'm night shift, so by the time I get to work, those orchids looking pretty tired already. Not their fault they wasn't born for be decoration at one wedding or in one of those fancy offices downtown.

One time had this customer. Could tell she was all into being in Waikīkī. She had one flower behind her ear and one hot pink batik pareo with too much fringe—da kine made in Thailand. She take one look at my orchid and she tell me, "I love it that everyone wears flowers in their hair. It must be so cool to pick a flower from your yard everyday on your way to work." I tell her, "I no more one yard." She look at me like I from Mars or something. "Excuse me?" she said. "No more . . .?" That's when I realize she no understand me. Happens all the time. "Sorry. I don't have a yard, ma'am," I said. Could tell she was little bit embarrassed, but she no need be shame. I no more one yard. I live in one apartment. Nobody I know get one yard. It is what it is.

"So I was wondering," she said. "What side do I wear the flower if I'm single?"

I look behind her at the long line of customers getting all antsy. "Well, it's like your wedding ring, yeah?" I tell her. "You wear the flower on your left ear if you married, just like you wear your wedding ring on your left hand."

"Oh my goodness!" she said. She take the flower out from behind her right ear and shove um behind her left ear. "Wouldn't want anyone to think I was single, now do I?"

She make like she all worried that every single guy in Waikīkī going mack on her in the next five minutes. I wanted for tell her get real; this is McDonald's, not one disco. I wasn't trying for be mean or anything, but the truth is I pulled that right ear, left ear answer straight out of my ass. My mom always says you gotta think on your feet if you like be in food services. My mom should know. She been on her feet for the past fifteen years.

Then the lady had hard time keeping that flower behind her left ear. The thing kept slipping out.

"Here," I told her. I take the orchid out of my bow and give her my bobby pin, but she just look at me and then at the bobby pin.

"Oh, I appreciate it and all, but that thing was, um, in your hair," she said.

I know you can use one bobby pin for do all kine stuffs. Clean da wax out of your ear, separate your eyelashes when they all clumpy with mascara, pick one lock. I wen offer this lady something for help her keep her act together, but she couldn't see that. All she saw was one bobby pin that was stuck to my flat, orange bow. The thing neva even touch my hair.

"Can I take your order?" I ask her real robot kine.

"How about a strawberry shake," she said.

"How about it," I say real sassy kine. And das how I know you cannot see your reflection in the stainless steel equipment. I turned my face towards the side panel of the shake machine, and all I saw was blurry brown and orange.

Milton Kimura

Thank You, Miss Halstead

It was Miss Halstead, my high school biology teacher, who started it all. During second period on a Friday of my freshman year, she ended her description of the difference between meiosis and mitosis with "If any of you are interested in music, there'll be a performance of Mozart's *Don Giovanni* tomorrow on channel 2, and the tenor is Charles K. L. Davis, who's from Hawai'i."

For me, this wasn't a seed sown on completely unprepared ground. While Waipahu in the 1950s was decidedly not operatic bedrock, I had heard snippets of this exotic form on TV, "The Ed Sullivan Show," to be specific: Robert Merrill and Richard Tucker in Verdi duets and Roberta Peters soaring into the stratosphere in bits from *Lucia di Lammermoor.* For some reason I liked these segments and begged my parents not to change the channel when they were on Sullivan's "tonight on our show" list. Now was my chance to see a whole opera and with someone from Hawai'i singing.

I knew I'd have to battle my father for viewing time with Saturday afternoon reserved for sports telecasts, but I got him to let me watch the opera by saying that it was a class assignment, which it kind of was, I rationalized.

It's been a half century since that Saturday, and I don't remember many details of the performance. But one impression stands out, loud and clear. It wasn't Charles K. L. Davis in the demanding lyric tenor role of Don Ottavio. It wasn't Cesare Siepi, the Metropolitan Opera's leading Don Giovanni in the '50s and '60s, or Judith Raskin, an esteemed Met lyric soprano, in the role of Zerlina. No, what I remember is the woman who sang Donna Anna: Leontyne Price.

Through the puny speaker of our 21-inch, black-and-white Zenith came a sound that wasn't like any other voice I'd heard up until then. The middle part of Price's voice was full and rich, almost as though more than one voice were singing at the same time. It had a pulsing vibrato that seemed to embody the ancients' "harmony of the spheres"; I had a hard time imagining how one could create that vibration without grabbing hold of the throat and oscillating it manually. Her lower notes were easily produced, that is, she didn't have to push her voice down into that range. And then the high notes. All the voices I had heard until Price narrowed as they moved up the scale. And with the narrowing came a hardening of the sound, the highest notes sometimes verging on screams. But there was no such ceiling to Price's voice. It moved up with no indication that more effort was required. Rather than taking on a hard opacity, it retained the rich vibrato, urgent and life-like. Each time she executed a phrase, I wondered how she created that sound.

On Monday Miss Halstead asked if anyone had watched the opera on Saturday. I didn't raise my hand because no one else did. But I stayed after class to tell her that I had. She asked what I thought and I told her that what I remembered best was Leontyne Price's voice. She smiled and said that I had good ears. I asked her if Price sang at the Metropolitan Opera; she said no but predicted that it was only a matter of time. Then I made a 14-year-old's promise to hear her in person someday, if nothing else, to see if she could really make that sound.

It took another 11 years before I saw her live as Giorgetta in Puccini's *Il Tabarro* at the San Francisco Opera. She did not disappoint. It was all there: the glorious middle voice, the ample lower range, and the amazing top, at once pure and seductive. She had a habitual way of moving when she held high notes: she would slowly turn her head and upper body from one side to the other, as though to encompass the audience and give everyone a share of the magic. In subsequent years I saw her in *Manon Lescaut* and *Ariadne auf Naxos* and at an autograph session at Tower Records. While she was signing my albums, I asked if she would ever again sing her signature roles, Leonora and Aida. "Oh, can't give those up," she reassured me.

She was true to her word. The last time I heard her was as Aida on June 16, 1984, again in San Francisco. It was her last role there, to be followed by her final performances at the Metropolitan, again as Aida, a few months later. All her San Francisco performances were sold out, so standing room was my only option. When I got to the opera house at 5:30, the line for standing room tickets doubled back on itself in the lobby and then snaked down Van Ness Avenue. But there were 200 tickets for sale and each person in line could purchase only one, so I was in luck. When the doors opened, I raced up the flights of stairs but found the Dress Circle slots full, so I continued up to the Balcony and claimed a spot. During the first intermission, someone offered me a seat, saying that the woman in the seat next to his had left to attend a fundraiser. I took it and enjoyed the rest of the performance seated.

The voice had changed: the divisions between registers more pronounced, the low notes huskier, the movement up the scale a bit stiffer though the downward portamento was still an aural luxury. But the top was untouched. Perhaps the biggest challenge of the role comes in Act III, the Nile Scene, when Aida holds the stage alone and sings "O Patria Mia," a mournful reminiscence of her Ethiopian homeland. It is capped by a high C that Verdi marked *dolce* (sweetly) and *senza affrettando* (without hurrying), but the note, as delivered by other sopranos, is too often a desperate, squeezed-out effort that is quickly—mercifully, for the audience—abandoned. Price approached it with confidence, climbing slowly to the summit and floating a C of sublime sweetness and lingering there—she was obviously in no hurry—before descending to the last phrase of the aria. The audience roared its approval. Not only applause and shouts but also foot stomping. They went on. And on. A professional, she did not move except for slightly lowering her head in acknowledgement. In the excitement of that moment, I didn't remember to think a thank you to Miss Halstead, so I'll do it now.

Christine Kirk-Kuwaye

Humor Me

Plotless, my short fiction offered tight character studies, usually with a unity of time and place. I employed epiphanic elements and usually relied on a few images that I relentlessly mined. And the simpler they were, the better. Frequently, I would write a story and then be unable to find an acceptable title. Just as frequently, I'd come up with a title and not be able to write a story under it—"Pearl's Before Swine" is one title still waiting for a story.

Occasionally, I would feel that I was exploiting my family, portraying them in ways that not only were not quite accurate but also not kind or fair. But I suppressed this feeling by telling myself that I wasn't writing nonfiction or biography, just drawing a bucket or two from the well. Besides, family members continued to follow their own trajectories regardless of what I wrote or even whether I wrote. Except for my second husband, I never asked any other family members to read my work. In fact, I hoped they wouldn't since I believed that they would approach each one with the zeal of fact checkers. I also feared that they would believe that what I wrote was what I felt about them. And it was, although in a condensed version.

One of the last pieces of fiction I wrote was an outburst about a bad boss. Because I thought it had legs, I shared it with a friend whose opinion I respected. All she said was: "This is really angry." Meant as homage to my dead colleague who had suffered under the bad boss's supervision and had recently died from leukemia, I hadn't considered that the emotion behind it might trump characterization and overwhelm the series of carefully chosen episodes meant to honor my friend.

So, I stopped. No more spinning episodic 20-pagers based on small real personal events, selecting just the right opening descriptive scenes, experimenting with point of view (and always struggling to break my addiction to the first person unreliable narrator and her parenthetical asides), and then seeking ways to include meaningful, well placed, revealing dialogue.

What I wanted, I decided, was Charles Memminger's job as a humor columnist for the *Honolulu Star-Bulletin*. I don't find him funny or funny all the way through each column. "But he's won awards," husband Jack said to me when I told him I wanted Memminger's job.

"I don't care. He's not funny," I said.

"Well, some people must think he's funny since he's won awards and he doesn't look in danger of being fired."

And here I am straying back to fictional elements. Whereas Jack really did say, "But he's won awards," the rest wasn't his retort. Nor would he have said it, had he retorted, in just that way. *I* would say that and in fact, I just *did*, right here. Curtain pulled back; fiction revealed!

Exhausted is an excellent word to describe what I feel about Memminger and to describe what I experienced with my fiction. Of course, being tired is the most obvious meaning but others are salient as well: to be used up; to be emptied by drawing out the contents; to deprive wholly of useful or essential properties, possessions, resources, etc.; to destroy the fertility of by intensive cultivation, like continuing to sow only cotton season after season. Then there is the image of ejected gases. It must be hard coming up with a weekly column that is at least as good as your best to date but hopefully better than that. The focus has to be on the everyday and familiar but with a kick that makes a connection to the larger. Memminger begins with the everyday and connects it to another everyday. I figured I could do better.

With an Internet connection, nothing is stopping me from blogging. I just jumped on the Internet a minute ago to look up "bane of my existence" then "boon of my existence" and stumbled into a blog about the importance of walking 45 minutes a day with a neighbor, the obvious reasons: good for body, weight control, blahblah. Her larger point, or like Memminger's everyday point, was that she and her friend and neighbor Donna talk about EVERYTHING when they walk—politics, history, religion ("on all levels"—?). Sometimes they cry, sometimes they laugh, this blogger tells us, and often they wave at the neighbors as they stroll past. And here's the punch line: because she's healthier, she's better able to serve her Savior. Ah.

My daughter I have written of previously in poorly concealed fictionalized versions of my life. I can only hope should she read them that I have been transformed into ashes and scattered somewhere. She was the bane of my existence. She was a social child who pushed against boundaries and wore me down with her need for company. I was a harsh young mother in a floundering marriage in economic straits, a story being enacted all over the country at this moment. But things got better as we got older, as I hope they will for my doppelgangers out there. I finally stopped writing about her.

My husbands were cast in supporting roles in my fiction. Sometimes they actually were supportive, but mostly they were foils, really, and generally poor dumb fucks who never stood a chance. All my stories felt compressed as if the world they portrayed did not have quite enough oxygen.

Character (daughter) Pearl's last appearance was as a teenager working at McDonald's. This story appeared in a collection that is still in print, sometimes assigned in local literature classes, and, just a few weeks ago, read on the radio. My son never made an appearance in my writings, but not because of any scruples I had. By the time he became interesting enough, I had stopped writing fiction and so couldn't exploit him.

Hold it, right here. I wrote the above paragraphs a few months ago and then, as is so often the case, did exactly what I said I was done doing: wrote a story that has a version of my son. The story references things I shouldn't really be talking about—unpleasant facts about a student I worked with last summer, my husband's family, a civic duty I'm performing that should be performed without mention.

Jack asked me what makes something fiction when so much of it is true? "The way it's put together?" I said with a lilt that let him and me know immediately I didn't know what I was talking about.

But after listening to my story read by the gifted actress, maybe what I do is make quilts. There's Dad's suit, Mom's wedding dress, a piece of the baby's blanket, my bloodstained blouse cut into squares and then pieced together to make something new. And even as I write this and admire the analogy, I know that this misses the point. I take stuff that "really" happened to people I love and write it down for people to read. I make judgments about my loved ones; I move them around like chess pieces or make them dance like marionettes. There is always an element of ridicule in what I write since I value getting a laugh at anyone's expense. When Jack had finished reading this most recent story, he had much to say. But my first question was: "Was it funny, at least some of the time?"

Juliet S. Kono

Chant Master

To pass him in the hallways
when away from chanting class—
and apart from the soft dunes
of his eyes, nose, and mouth—
is to see his face as a desert
swept by the fine dust of boredom.
He barely looks at us.
Śrāvakas of the Seer of Truth,
we disciples dash through our days,
one class to the next,
in a swirl around him with our
hundred head bows like simple
requests he can't possibly return,
so, ignores.
He wants only, for us
to stay out of his way.

But, at the first sharp slap
of his memory fan
across the palm of his hand
to keep time, his is a face riven,
its mask broken
into sandy pieces on the floor.
Upon the sudden and driven
first intake of his breath,
as in a newborn's
first fierce full note,
his voice sweeps fire
through us and we are greeted
by all Mahāsattvas and urged
to leave the world of Saha,
of birth and death,

and go to one held
by enlightenment,
as upon the dais
of the white lotus.

Breathe, elide. Raise
your voices to suchness
and go as you are.
Let us chant together.

Without much thought
we follow
to where he takes us—
ride the flow of his voice,
the seat of the Larger Vehicle.
We chant away our birth cries,
the years, the centuries,
the times we walked in mud,
rose to a cloud bar,
or crossed the river of fire.
We join the flow of his
voice that promises an oasis,
an awakening,
a samadhi of cooling waters,
like a mother's lullaby.
Soothe and salve
our parched understanding.

Brenda Kwon

Flight

She once caught an avocado between her hands.
Poised on a rock beneath the tree in our backyard,
she leapt, seizing the alligator-green
then landed tender in the grass,
no signs of sore leg or blue veins
in the way she clutched her prize to her chest
then held it out to me when she saw me watch.

I took that prize
because I know the language of a mother's care
and how she feeds to say *I love you*
but her real gift was flight,
those few seconds she lifted up,
left behind the weight of stone,
her seventy-two-year-old body slicing the air the way it did
in the decades-ago pirouettes and grand jetés
that pulsed her blood in the days before my grandmother threatened,
If you become a dancer, I will break your legs.

I have never seen her dance,
her only recital shaped by the ballerina who pas de bourrées
in my head with a choreography composed of fragments:
the lift of her arms pinning sheets to the line,
the point of her toe when she steps on the gas,
the tilt of her chin as she tucks the phone between shoulder and ear,
her stage the story of our lives,
whirling through piano lessons, band practice, basketball, and hula,
three meals per day and reminders to sleep,
her music the waltzes I hear her hum when she is dreaming of the girl
she never stopped being.

Maybe that's why she led me into pink leather slippers,
stitching elastic to hold my girl-feet in,
combed my hair back so it wouldn't fall as I spun,
my child's body reflecting in studio mirrors
the artist she was never allowed to become.
Insisting I learn how to walk above ground,
she watched me graduate from the balls of my feet
to the tips of my toes
'til the only things holding me down to the earth
were wood and a millimeter's thickness of satin
because she believed if I only kept going,
chassé, arabesque, sauté, elevé
I would lift off the ground and learn how to fly.

And so I danced in satin, ribbons, and wool,
but flew in sound, letters, and words,
and the day I untied those ribbons forever
was the day she let go of dreams
that puppeted me across the floor,
me,
the girl whose movement in her womb
must've felt like the dance she carried inside,
stirring
long after ribbons fell unbound,
the cord that tied us clipped and cut.

And she packed away my winged feet
but refused to break my fingers' flight
over the lined platform of clean white pages.
And she followed me through my many stages,
her steps *en avant* and syncopated
by swollen leg and hips tilting, unjustly weighted
while my pen would *glissade* loops, crosses, and points,
each piece a story of what a body does when allowed to dance.

But beneath the lyrics I learned to hear
her earthbound rhythm, her supporting beat,
the way the pause would lengthen between her steps

in what I imagined was flight but knew was time,
silvering her hair, curving her back, measuring her sleep,
and slowing her breath.
And in the silence I remember the way she leaped,
her body supported by the knowledge of flight—
and when she leaps from this rock
to claim her prize,
there will be no stones to break her fall.

Lanning C. Lee

A New Lease

The ad was posted on the Manoa Marketplace community bulletin board. Rent Negotiable. Those words caught my eye. I had to move. Soon. I called immediately.

The phone rang for eons. Finally a strong, soft voice answered. Very polite. No questions. Interviews were in person only.

An hour later I entered Mānoa Starbucks. He said he'd be easy to spot: an elderly Japanese gentleman wearing a Sakamoto for Lt. Governor T-shirt. I scanned the crowded room and spotted the back of a head of steel-gray hair neatly cut. Approaching from behind, I leaned over his right shoulder. In a small notebook, he was sketching a hand, sketching a hand, sketching a sheep.

Astounded, I slid around into his peripheral vision. Without a word, he looked up at me and gestured to the seat across from him.

"You would like to rent?" he questioned softly, closing the book.

"Ah, yes, I do. I would. Definitely."

He carefully replaced the cap on his black Flair pen. "It is just you?"

I said yes, that I'd recently lost my wife.

He examined me with a contemplative nod, picked up his book, stood, and led me outside. "You have a car?"

I pointed to my vintage, multicolored Corolla.

"This is me." He indicated a newer white Camry. "You will please follow me."

I rolled out right behind him, sticking close. Cars came between us. I decided better to drop back to keep an eye on him. Concentrating on his tail, I locked in like a laser as we wound our way to one of those lines of large homes on the valley's west slope. A high-rent district.

The room, on the first floor of this two-story monster, was enormous. It was littered with clothing racks. Fixed, rolling, cascading—but not one article of clothing. I had to ask.

"My wife," he said. "This would have been her closet. She loved dresses."

I nodded. "Would there be a bathroom?"

He strode vigorously to the mauka wall. I saw he wore only his socks; I'd forgotten to leave my shoes at the door.

"My shoes," I said. "Sorry."

"That is not a problem." He slid a large wall panel aside.

The bathroom was cavernous.

"And, ah, is there a kitchen?" I asked, huge dollar signs pounding my brain.

He slid the bathroom door shut. "You may use the main kitchen. It is in back on this floor, just past the living room. I hardly use it. You will be able to cook whenever you wish."

The financial moment of truth had arrived, but I hesitated and walked into the hallway. The walls were lined with photographs. My question about cost waited. "What great photos. Did you take all of these?"

He joined me in the hall. "Actually, I drew them."

"Drew them?" I stepped up to the closest one. Even though it looked like a photo, it actually was a meticulous drawing of a middle-aged looking man, a trombone resting in his lap.

He asked before I could. "What rent could you afford?"

I ran my panicked calculation. If I could sell the condo soon—if—I could afford a little more. Somewhere in the neighborhood of $1500? Maybe? What could I afford for sure?

"Might, ah, $1250 be anywhere near what you were looking for?"

"How about $900," he said, "with no deposit, and I will handle all utilities. I need simply to have this room rented now."

He surely saw the surprise on my face, but I couldn't tell by any expression on his.

He examined the trombone player. "Do you like jazz?" he asked.

In a stunned haze, I nodded slowly, my jaw still floating near the floor.

"Good." He smiled for the first time. "At night I play jazz. I hope this is not a problem."

I shook my head slowly. Even if he were the worst musician on earth, I'd deal with it.

"When can you move in?"

"Uh, do you need me to fill out an application? Need any references or anything?"

He smiled again. "No, you are the one. I know people. Paperwork is later."

Everything was bad. My life was in the toilet. My wife. I wanted change now. "Could I move in now? I just have to go back to my place, grab my clothes. I'm selling my place and everything in it. If the next owner wants to toss it all, fine."

"I understand," he said. "I have a new twin bed, never used. You can help me move it downstairs when you come back."

The drive to my building was over before I realized I was there. I threw all of my clothes and toilet articles into some Longs plastic bags. I'd go to Kmart to buy sheets and towels.

The sun was sinking. I took one last look around what had been a good home for nearly eight years. How long can someone go on missing someone? I stepped out on the lanai and sat to watch the sun set one last time. This place, I would not miss.

In a place far away from anyone or anywhere, my wife's voice whispered to me; I couldn't understand her. Moving closer, she whispered again, some strange language.

"Huh?" I awoke in darkness. "What the . . ." The clock read 8:30. "Cripes!"

I stumbled through the dark to the front door, grabbed my stuff, and walked hurriedly to the elevator. Go to Kmart now? No. Better call him.

The phone rang on until the cows had come home and were deep in REM stage sleep.

"Freakin-A!" I jumped in my car and jammed it as fast as I could and still be safe.

I flew into the valley and turned up ʻAwapuhi to Puʻuhonua. Now which one was it? Puʻuhonua dead-ended. All the houses could be his. I drove slowly back. Nothing. There. No. That white Camry was too old, and that one, too. "Does everyone in this neighborhood own a white Camry?" This house was three stories. That one set too far back from the road.

At Five Corners . . . we'd turned left, right? Hold up. I drove all the way back to Starbucks. Do it again. Out the back on Kahawai, left onto Lowrey. The Five Corners. Left, right? Left onto Mānoa. This time up Kōmaiʻa. Nothing. I tried Puʻu Nanea. The street was bumper to bumper white Camrys. Every house could be his. None looked right.

Did we go right at Five Corners? Rainbow Drive? Fartle-doots! A herd of heart attacks was thundering my way. "Don't panic, brah," I breathed to myself.

Back to Safeway, dammit. Racing to the community bulletin board, I tried dialing the number again. It rang until a day and a half beyond doomsday.

I reached the board and looked at the ad. But it wasn't the ad. It was a card for Tai's Yard Service. Really? He'd already come back, already removed the card?

My heart was beating the climax of the "In-a-Gadda-da-Vida" drum solo. Double-time. I rang again. Redialed. Again. Aga—

Finally! "Hello."

"Hello!" I tried not to scream. The phone was still ringing. "What the fu—?"

"Hello," the voice said again. Then I felt a tap on my shoulder.

I wheeled around. Air roared into my lungs. He was standing there.

"Mr. Murakami!" I blurted out. "I'm so sorry. I fell asleep. I tried to call you. I couldn't find your hou—"

For the first time, he laughed out loud. I could see he could see that I was in full panic mode. "But everything is okay now," he said, his eyes twinkling. "I had to have rocky road ice cream." He held up his Safeway bag. "My favorite." He pointed. "Your car is there?"

I pointed to where he was pointing, nodding, my breathing slowing but still ragged.

"Everything is good now," he said softly. "Again, then, you will please follow me."

Jeffrey Thomas Leong

Five Star Baby Palace

for the Nanjing Grand Hotel

Not her regular duty as deluxe headquarters for the Party elite
nor even as five star spa for China's new entrepreneurs,
bringing Wal-Mart to city center.
But on a mid-winter Monday, hostel for the China Adoption Bureau,
whisked up twin round towers to the 10th floor,
we pop into a sleek rosewood nurture.
In a parallel near, down a tube of new Taizhou-Nanjing highway
an egg of a daughter, burst from the ovary of orphanage.
Pulsed through traffic tie-ups, cuddled by Auntie nannies,
who speed press *xiao xin*, "little new,"
directly to our attach.

A call down to "Conf. Roam 703," and we first see
writ upon whiteboard, her temporary given: *Maile*.
In a womb lit fluorescent, to our shock, a Her!
bundled under red sweater, turtleneck lime green,
and blue puppy booties, dazed as any cellular
drifting dangled before amniotic rest.
Flash! a snapshot, the blind of instant union,
Congrats! and back to our womb-like private nursery,
where, when stripped of wrap, she revels,
joking, kicking.

Then a gestation, for next five days,
of something altogether new. Parents learn to baby care,
intuition splitting and replicating, acquire *how-to*'s with speed:
each gesture, shitting or not shitting,
the constituencies of it,
to initiate a bottle, chopstick-stir local formula,
her tepid bath's first swirl.

In *jook* and hash browns Western-style,
we clique hungrily for clues,
comforted in familiar cues of Kenny G's sonorous "White Christmas."

When, at week's full term, something emerges,
sleepy-eyed, like the slime-impaired sight of primeval sludgers,
coming into light, a new to be spanked south
to the U.S. Consulate Guangzhou, then further across borders.
Tzai jian! plush, superior stork hotel, a new family wails,
breached from its harried rooms,
and, as usual, handed off
to dwell in a house more foreign.

R. Zamora Linmark

Vigil

11:57 a.m. A bus terminal outside Madrid's Méndez Alvaro metro station, he waits with a one-way ticket to Mojácar, home to Spaghetti Westerns, like *Marcha o Muere* and *Treasure Island* with Orson Welles as Long John Silver.

Mojácar: home for the next month, with cacti, lemon and orange groves for neighbors.

Blood, like sakura petals, blossoms on a crumpled napkin.

Biting one's lip is no accident. Filipinos believe it means someone is remembering you as though you were already dead.

The deeper the gash, the more vivid the memory.

Over beer and platitas of tortillas on toothpicks, Filipinos conversing in Spanish-Tagalog.

Espangalog? Tagañol?

In Spanish there are two ways of being: *ser,* permanent, for poets, and *estar,* temporary, for when one is ill or waiting. In Tagalog, there is no verb *to be.*

Keep digressions out of the conversation, and you ostracize 99% of Filipinos.

12:28 p.m. A seventeen-year-old memory of Madrid:

"I told you to stay in London."—his Brit bf.

"I got bored waiting."

"You can't stay here. Alison's parents—"

"Fuck London, fuck your homophobic friends."

Fortunately for him, Filipinos, who make up the largest Asian group in Spain—90% of them are women working as maids—believe in the "mi casa es tu casa" code.

He ran into Lani at Plaza de Chueca, 3 a.m., managed to vent without disclosing his sexual preferences or talking about how love had gone through more break-up/make-up cycles than one of Edward Albee's couples.

"What a dump!"—Martha.

Lani offered him the studio apartment she and her boyfriend rented; it was their weekend love nest.

Ring on her finger told another story.

Next day, Lani's boyfriend, accompanied by another woman, and mistaking him for a vagabond in boxer shorts, nearly killed him.

Lani's boyfriend gestured at him to put his money away; a tight lip insured him free lodging. Over chocolate con churros, the only meaning he could squeeze out from his year-old relationship with Joseph:

"Who's afraid of Virginia Woolf?"—George.

"I am, George, I am."—Martha.

First major symptom of doom: a phone call from an American Express agent.

"Yes, sir, cut the card in half. Yes, sir, now."

2:55 p.m. Window seat #5, next to an old woman with a gummy smile.

3:50 p.m. Miles of dry earth like
skin of dying lions
Next exit: Ikea.

Nineteen hours ago, he was in Newark with Robyn and Allan, chain-eating Swedish meatballs.

"I sleep on IKEA, I eat on IKEA, I think on IKEA."—Robyn.

"When do they find time to furnish the world, they only have the sun for three months?"—Allan.

He misses Allan, Robyn, Swedish meatballs, massage, ABBA.

Honey, if you change
Your mind I'll be first in line
Take a chance on me
—ABBA haiku.

5:00 p.m. "Death laid eggs in the wound"—Garcia Lorca.

5:45 p.m. A hilly, whitewashed pueblo and an overdeveloped playa make up the centerfold of Mojácar's tourist brochure.

Every four years, Río de Agua, the pueblo's river, touches water.

8:29 p.m. The route to Lorca's death, as described by his biographer Ian Gibson in *The Assassination of Federico García Lorca*, was a five-mile march that began in front of the Archbishop Moscoso's palace and ended under an olive tree, on the edge of Alfacar, Viznar.

Lorca's comrades that August night: Dióscoro Galindo González, a one-legged schoolteacher, and two bullfighters, Joaquín Arcollas Cabezas and Francisco Galadí Mergal.

Ainadamar: Arabic for "Fountain of Tears."

"Here all I want is wide-open eyes
to see that body that can never rest"—Lorca.

"Wait a while / Till a little moonbeam comes peeping through"—
Billie Holiday crooning despite the iPod battery icon glowing red.

12:45 a.m. Ivan Morris, in his introduction to *The Pillow Book of Sei Shōnagon*: "I have however, preferred to retain the confused time-sequence of the traditional texts"

"I have however, preferred to retain the confused time-sequence of the traditional texts"

"not because this was necessarily the order"

"necessarily the order in which she arranged her book, but because"

"in which . . . because any systematic reorganization"

"arranged her book, but because any systematic reorganization"

"reorganization would be arbitrary"

"arbitrary and possibly"

"arbitrary and possibly"

"any systematic reorganization"

"confused time she arranged her book because systematic organization would be arbitrary and possibly misleading"

3:04 a.m. Sleep interrupted. Bergman's *Hour of the Wolf,* when nightmares play in slow motion.

"The soul, without the body, plays"—Petronius.

Hour of unforgiveness.

3:33 a.m. The memory of Ireneo Funes shines upon him. A Borges creation, Funes was paralyzed after getting thrown by a wild horse. The accident reduced him to days and insomniac nights in a room with unlit candles, staring out at a fig tree, examining cobwebs, contemplating the sunset, remembering in English, French, Portuguese, and Latin.

"My memory, sir, is like a garbage disposal"—Funes.

How many faces does a dead man wear throughout his wake?

In lieu of sleep, he busied himself instead with memories—his and not his—like being hounded in a dream with one eye opened.

with azuki beans
and ice cream

Michael Little

Walter Gets Romantic

On February 12, with Valentine's Day fast approaching, Walter Yamada decided to do something special this year for Janice. Something more than flowers and a Hallmark card. Something extra romantic. Something to rekindle the embers of their love. Something so romantic she would fall in love with him all over again, just like years ago in 11th grade, when he couldn't afford a dozen roses but did take her on a dozen inexpensive dates, including several high school basketball games and a couple of shave ice dates.

This was the one time of the year that Walter gave much thought to romance. Christmas was all about the kids. New Year's Eve was for watching fireworks and opening a bottle of domestic champagne from Foodland after dinner. Valentine's Day was just about Walter and Janice. If only Walter thought about romance more often, at other times of the year, he might not be so clueless about this "extra romantic" business. Maybe he should set aside 30 minutes on the first of each month, or at least on major holidays, to contemplate romance. He watched Valentine's commercials on TV, but they only increased his anxiety.

On the morning of February 14, Walter began to panic. He didn't think that a trip to Waiola Shave Ice on Valentine's Day would rekindle anything. In desperation he asked Shirley, the secretary at his accounting office, for help. For an idea. For *any* idea. Shirley smiled, thought for a second, then curled her finger for Walter to move closer. When Walter leaned in, Shirley whispered slowly, "Write her a poem."

"Oh," Walter said. "A poem? Are you sure?"

"Of course I'm sure," Shirley said. "Write her a poem. She'll love it."

"Hmmm," Walter said. The idea seemed to make him look even more worried.

"You've never written her a poem?"

"No," Walter said, as if it were the craziest question anyone had ever asked him. "I wouldn't know where to start. I've never written a poem. You mean like 'Roses are red, violets are—'"

"No!" Shirley said. She exhaled and leaned back in her chair. "Something better than that. Something new. Something fresh. Something . . . from your heart." Shirley raised her index finger, then moved it straight at the middle of Walter's chest, touching the spot where she imagined his heart must be.

Walter stepped back from the contact. Beads of sweat began to form on his brow. He regretted having asked Shirley for help. Even if she was right. A poem? Really? Walter started to say something but finally just threw up his hands in despair. He turned and began walking away.

"Wait," Shirley said. "Maybe I can help." Walter watched as she reached into a bottom drawer of her desk and pulled out a small object. She handed it to Walter.

Walter read the writing on the object. "Numi, Monkey King, Jasmine Green Tea, Certified Organic." He looked at Shirley. "So?"

"Read the rest, up in the corner."

Walter held the tea bag wrapper closer. "I shall be a cloud, you the moon, and this our tea." He stared at Shirley.

"Hello," she said. "It's a poem."

"Oh," Walter said. "Can I use it?"

"Why not? I think it's quite romantic." Shirley took the tea bag wrapper from Walter and read the lines aloud, her voice deep and emotional. "I shall be . . . a cloud . . . you . . . the moon . . . and this . . . our tea."

Walter felt that he might be blushing, so he quickly took the tea bag wrapper back from Shirley, thanked her politely, and went back to his desk.

That afternoon, on the way home, Walter stopped at Longs and bought an expensive Valentine's card, one with lots of blank space on the inside for the poem. Back in his car he began to write the words of the poem on the card. "I shall be a cloud," he wrote in his best hand. Then below that, "you the moon."

Then he paused. "And this our tea?" Wouldn't that give away the fact that he had stolen the poem from a tea bag wrapper? But the poem looked so short without it. Only two lines. What would Janice think? He decided that he would pick up roses on the way home as well. He looked at the two-line poem again. Should he add another line? Something personal? Did it need to rhyme? Moon? June? Spoon? Cartoon?

What if he just changed the one word at the end? Walter read aloud, "I shall be a cloud, you the moon, and this our . . ." Walter was stuck. He decided to leave it at two lines and hope for the best. Then another thought attacked him. What if Janice didn't want to be the moon? What if she was insulted because the moon is big and round? And made of cheese? What if Janice wanted to be a cloud instead? He could imagine her voice. "Walter, why do you get to be a cloud?" Or worse yet, "Walter, what kind of poem is this? It doesn't even rhyme. You wrote this?"

Walter grabbed his cell phone and quickly called the office, hoping that Shirley would still be there. When Shirley answered, Walter poured out his worries to her.

"Calm down, Walter," Shirley said. "It's gonna be all right. Janice will be surprised and excited that you wrote her a poem. Just think romantic. Think romantic. Pretend you're one movie star and Janice is your biggest fan. And let me know tomorrow how it worked out."

As Walter drove home, he had a new problem. Which movie star should he pretend to be? Who was the one that Janice liked? Think, think. Sean Connery? Brad Pitt? No way he could pretend to be Brad Pitt. Then he imagined himself as James Bond. All those old Bond movies he and Janice had watched together.

When he finally arrived at home and carried the roses and card into the house, Walter decided to announce his entrance. He could hear kitchen sounds. Probably Janice cleaning up before they went out to dinner.

"Is that you, Walter?" Janice called out as she walked out of the kitchen.

"Bond," Walter said. "James Bond."

"Oh, Walter," Janice said. Then she saw the roses. The poem she would read later. Walter sighed. Valentine's was so exhausting. Then he felt Janice's arms around him and decided that this Valentine's Day would be extra romantic, no matter who was a cloud and who was the moon.

Mary Lombard

Building Blocks

The cartons arrive after his stroke. After he came home from the hospital and before the smell of the place has begun to fade. The coughing down the hall. The crack in the ceiling. Like a mouth up there, yawning wide over his head, every night, leering. He's looking up now, as if to . . . to . . . but he doesn't see it. All is fog, all . . .

"Oh, what have you done?" she cries. "Gone and ordered a library?"

Library? His eyes water at the clear space opening before him. Cartons all over the place. Books. Sure, uh, oh, a long time ago . . . he bought . . . Of course. His books. His *library*! What he's wanted all his life. Why he built the shelves, for God's sake. Years ago. Not out of pine, either, none of that flimsy ply board. Nope, only sweet koa, warm and hard at once—only the best wood for the Classics. She'll have to move her knickknacks, of course. His library will now occupy the koa shelves, along with his other books, of course, his favorite ones. He has a lot of local books. History. Missionaries. Whalers. He likes history. He has, uh, he has *Shoal of . . . Shoal . . .* He has *To Raise a . . . To Raise a Nation*. Maybe . . .

That paper she's waving—he won't look, no, no, no, no.

"Paid in full. *In full*!" Spitting. "I don't believe this, I don't *believe* it! What do I do with all these books? These bills stealing my life? What do I *do*?"

He watches her stacking them on the floor. His books, by God, filling the room. All Classics. Leatherbound, the complete set, every solemn one the same height, every title stamped in gold, every single one new. Plato, Cicero, Milton, Chaucer, Herodotus. Saint Augustine said . . . he's always wanted to read Saint Augustine. She tips a carton and more slide out. Volumes. One after another. His heart shivers: Melville. Oh, take care!—don't drop Melville.

She plunks one in his lap. He hefts it, chuckling. He'll put this in his head and gain weight. It's ink that feeds his hunger and ink he'll gorge on till he walks loaded—no, runs, takes off—lit up and lumbering and word besotted and minus brakes. Nope, no brakes. Nothing to stop him ever anymore.

She sits back on her heels crying. His mother cried. His mother crying because he was crying. He crying because, when he finally got sick enough to take to bed, he couldn't hold *The Three Musketeers*, it was too heavy, the words danced all over the page. Wouldn't stay put. Not any more, though. Nope, no more coughing up and down the hall. No more tears, no more chores, no more work. He's surrounded by his own books! All classics. A whole library. And all the time in the world for feasting.

Shakespeare, it says, The Tragedies. Shakespeare. He's read some of the poems, he's sure of it. And stories. No—plays. Yes, plays! A long time ago, though. He presses his nose into the smell of new paper, of print and glue. Runs his hand along the sleek spine. He riffles the gilt-edged pages, and the book falls open, as if by itself, magically, at the ribbon marker. He stares at the page. Touches it, gingerly, aware of the glassy smoothness under his rough hand. Turns it, slowly. Smells it. Strokes it. Look at that—the words flow under his hand. Streams, rivers, oceans, the stir of continents—in his fingertips. Every word a promise, a universe.

"Well, maybe now, at least, you'll quit wandering off for a change."

He's worked hard all his life. He quit college to work. There may have been other reasons, but he can't recall them. What he remembers is work. The house he built on weekends and vacations, the nights he put in at the office. As the only executive in the company without a degree, he was obliged to do the extra time, to compensate. For the kids. Then off they went. He lost them. One son to Vietnam, another to drugs, his daughter to a foolish marriage. While he watched in helpless rage. He managed some Dickens and Mark Twain and Gavan Daws, though, and now and then a bestseller. He might've borrowed more from the library, but parting was too hard. He liked to dip back into a beloved book now and then, respond in the margins, make it his own. Money was tight, that's all. And time a persistent echo in his ear repeating, Get off your duff and finish that report to the stockholders; pay on your loan, fix the toilet, the whatchamacallit, the floor damage from the leak in the water heater. Shell out for a new heater. Get ready for church.

These cartons are building blocks, by God. He'll build his own church.

Slowly, he rearranges the ribbon. Gapes at the rows of black on white. Runs his fingers along a line. "Never, never, never . . ." He bends over the book, cradles it in his arms, hears the words, feels them sinking into his flesh. "Never, never . . ." His eyes keep leaking. He rubs them. "Never . . ." He caresses the page. His gaze wanders. There's no hurry, is there?

Daylight darkens at the window. The lamp throws a flicker of gold across the page. Clatter in the kitchen. The steamy smell of simmering meat. And all around him, building blocks. Books to unpack. Worlds to uncover.

She clumps in with his tray. "What are your glasses doing on the floor?"

He blinks, but not at her. At the glow of words. And beyond, to the passing banks of the Mississippi. The muddy water churning up ahead. She says something, but . . . He's listening to Huck. Or Lear, perhaps, or Ishmael or um, even good old Natty Bumppo. And, closer to home, his old books, the ones . . . Waiakane, oh and *Ka'a'awa,* and, uh . . . and yes indeed, the king! Kam, Kam, uh, Kamehameha something . . . the third? He couldn't forget that. And Hiram . . . Hiram Nihoa . . . that feast with Princess uh, Ka'ahu . . . uh Ruth, uh . . . practically in his backyard . . . and all the while he's bedazzled, caught in a wave, churning, lost in the current. At last.

Christina Low

Where You From?

I'm not from here, really. Yes, I was born at Kaiser Hospital on Ala Moana Boulevard—the place where the two-tower Prince Hotel now boasts the same view of the Ala Wai and Magic Island my mother must have enjoyed just after giving birth to me.

Yes, I was raised here, reared in Kāne'ohe, and sent to Saint Ann's. I watched the undeveloped field of weeds—that, Velcro-like, stuck to my tube socks when I ran through—become monolithic Windward Mall.

And yes, when people ask me, "What school you went?" I answer "Maryknoll," beginning the routine of naming people who went to my school until we stumble upon a person in common, however far removed. "You know Trudy Vierra? She wen grad '90? Her aunty is Violet Vierra? Her cousin went Farrington, grad same year as me." Because that's how locals appropriate the strangers we meet, force-fitting them into our collective pasts by association so that the "other" becomes almost familial.

But I maintain: I'm not from here. I never belonged—my parents weren't Issei or Nisei, and my friends were mostly one thing. How I rued not being full Asian! My community may have been mixed like me, but at least they *looked* Japanese or Korean, Filipino or Chinese. I was a quagmire of ethnicity and I still am.

My people are from two other islands but go back a few generations, and they're not from *there* at all. My mother was born and raised in New Zealand, about a half-hour's drive outside Christchurch on the South Island. There in the now destroyed city square, a plaque once named her great-great-great-grandmother, Sarah Stokes, one of the immigrants on the first colonizing ships from England into Lyttelton Harbour.

I imagine her, black-haired and mousy, long strips pulled out of her up-do by the rushing wind, on the deck of New Zealand's equivalent of the *Niña*, the *Pinta*, or the *Santa Maria*. Of course, she and her husband were in steerage with their five sons and three daughters, so the likelihood of this wind-blown fantasy could have only happened during the very un-sexy daily mattress-airing, when she and twenty-one other families with their sixty-five children did the same, peeling their bedding from the wall-to-wall bunks built into 875 square feet of shared living space.

Let's say she's got a minute during the one hundred and three days she spent on the *Randolph* (did I mention she was pregnant with child number nine, and gave birth en route?). She's there on deck trying not to puke, thinking about the life she'll have on that other shore; the England of her birth so close behind her heels she can still feel the cobbles beneath her feet. She knows she'll never return to that home again, or does she? Could she ever imagine her great-great-great-granddaughter (my mother) one day sailing across another expanse of sea, even farther East?

My grandmother was the only grandparent I ever met. She was kind to me and gave me great bosomy hugs, but she lived in New Zealand, which was much too far away for me to know anything about her. We wrote letters on aquamarine stationary I bought for her during the trip I made there before she died. I was eight, I think. Whenever one of those envelopes came in the mail, I felt important and loved. My grandma didn't have an address. Instead, she lived at "the Knoll," where prize-winning roses were grown and a babbling brook was spanned by two hand-carved bridges, married to my grandfather—who had kind eyes, blond hair, and wore bow ties.

I'm not sure either of my grandparents ever left New Zealand. They may have tooled around Akaroa Bay or caught the ferry to the North Island, but they mostly stayed close to the street where my grandfather owned a liquor distribution company. Four of their six children also remained relatively close to King Street. One moved as far away as Perth, Australia, but my mother, the eldest, hitched herself on two other boats, first to Fiji, then to Hawai'i.

Fiji sucked. It was hot and she had to live with her in-laws, who weren't kind. To them, she was a white devil who stole their perfect number one son. For a year, she endured living upstairs from her mother-in-law, who had nothing good to say about the way her daughter-in-law cooked, cleaned, or breathed. Then, Mom became pregnant. Nine months later, she gave birth to a son she named Paul, who died about 24 hours after he took his first breath. This loss wasn't easy for my parents, who probably left Fiji to start fresh. But forty-plus years after she reached Hawai'i's shores, my reticent mother still speaks with a slight accent, still drinks cups of tea, and eats toast with Vegemite.

My deceased father did the same.

And likewise, a boat carried his father's father from China to New York, where he worked for years, perhaps on the railroads in NY. He died there, but his body would make the trip back and be buried somewhere in Hong Kong. His two sons (one of them my grandfather) made sure their father was interred in Chinese earth. I hear he missed his wife, but I don't actually know anything about his life or what he looked like—all I have is a photo of his gravestone; the characters of my name: a waterfall of tears carved into stone. I don't know whether he loved opium or whiskey, what kind of white men spat at him as he walked the unpaved streets in NY. Was his queue amputated with his chi, or did he learn enough English to protect himself? Chances are he was illiterate, or he might have sent for his wife and two boys, gone West, opened a laundry, and I would be cut into eighths.

I know more about his son—my father's father, who rode another boat from China to Fiji, and would not return, ever. Born January 27, 1893, my granddad looks the stud. In his twenties, he posed for a shot with legs crossed and white patent leather lace-ups, the cuffs of his pants crisp and the creases of his blazer so very F. Scott Fitzgerald. In one hand, a book. His other elbow rests on a potted plant, the hand open and relaxed. With a slight frown he penetrates the sepia page, gazes hard at me. Later pictures of the curly-headed man with glasses prove he never went gray. I think he loved whiskey, gambling, and not opium. He smoked cigarettes and owned lots of sharp suits.

A long time passed before granddad sent for his four-foot-nothing Chinese wife. As a young woman, my grandmother shaved a couple of inches from her widow's peak and tied her hair in a bun that covered her ears but not her gold earrings. Fierce, her dark brows frame eyes that aren't really sure whether the camera will steal her soul, but her lips are soft and stifle a smile. Aging, she became a tight scowling woman with wiry hair cut at her chin. She must have sewed because all her dresses look the same, all with round collars, all cut from stiff material like old curtains that don't seem to touch her skin.

A long time after they reunited, when they were both past forty, and had established themselves on the island of Gau (pronounced *n-gaow*) with a coconut farm and a bakery, my father was born. When Dad sailed to Suva for boarding school at age five, then to New Zealand for university where he'd befriend my mother's brother, I know he wasn't just a little afraid.

But when the time came to pick up his new wife and move her from her hometown, he was already well acquainted with diaspora. My mother, on the other hand, was not. I can see my mother, like her predecessor, on that other sunny deck staring into her future, her past trailing so close behind she can still hear her mother's voice in her ear, feel her father's warm hand on her shoulder. Does she know the son she buried would not be her only child? That she would bear three more children, returning each time to that same Waikīkī maternity ward next to the movie theater?

Probably not. And it likely wouldn't have mattered so much to me *not* being from here had things been different growing up. If my friends did not go to their grandmother's house after school or garden and fish with their grandfathers, if they didn't tell stories about their cousin's cousin's cousin who was now their aunt or share star fruit and lychee from their great-great-uncle's farm at lunchtime, perhaps I wouldn't have felt so disconnected.

When I was five or six, my father's brother immigrated with his four children to O'ahu and ended up buying a house not more than half a mile from where we lived. My cousins went to the same school as us, and though they weren't much quantity-wise in comparison, at least they were *something.* But having all been born in Fiji, they were even less from here than me.

I'm Polish, English, Irish, German, and Chinese, but my parents are essentially Pacific Islanders. Where's the box I'm supposed to check that encapsulates all of that? There is no "home place" with people exactly like me, and there never will be. To make matters even more confusing, perhaps I should move to Russia and marry an African-American Latino who was born and raised in Bangladesh.

But maybe that's what everyone here *is* from—a great long line of crossed wires and discombobulated connections. And here's the thing: coming from a place, coming from a people only means you have roots, and no matter how convoluted and twisted up, no matter how skinny mine are from stretching, they do exist.

Wing Tek Lum

The Murder

> "This was different from the death of people in war, with weapons in their hands, the deaths of people who had left behind their houses, families, fields, songs, traditions and stories. This was the murder of a great and ancient professional experience, passed from one generation to another in thousands of families of craftsmen and members of the intelligentsia."—Vasily Grossman, *A Writer at War*

The barrel maker is dead
    caught in a mortar barrage
    unable to know which way to run.
The gaunt herbalist is dead
    wounded by a stray bullet
    his life then slowly bleeding away.
The ladies' tailor is dead
    his shop set on fire
    bolts of fabric ablaze all around him.
The bald nun is dead
    drowned trying to escape upstream
    when her overcrowded boat capsized.
The cobbler is dead
    killed while at work on the sidewalk
    shrapnel splattering flesh onto his shoes.
The photographer is dead
    shot in the face when he tried to stop
    the looting in his studio.
The stout policeman is dead
    slain by a machine gun burst
    when his barracks launched a counterattack.
Two spinster sisters are dead
    bayoneted on the floor of their home
    after being gang raped.

The stonemason and his apprentices are dead
    buried alive in a large trench
    they and others had to dig.
The tall amah is dead
    poisoned by stolen opium she swallowed whole
    her choice of suicide over humiliation.
The waitresses are dead
    ripped apart by a grenade
    thrown through the door of their tea house.
The lantern maker's baby is dead
    her head bashed against a wall
    her parents speechless, unable to cry.
The newspaperman is dead
    tortured before being strangled
    for printing broadsheets urging resistance.
The burly fishmonger is dead
    his head split open by a sword
    to test how sharp the blade was.
The pregnant teacher is dead
    blown up by a land mine
    as she scoured alleyways for food.
The sign painter is dead
    pummeled into a coma,
    then lingering for days, defiant to the end.
The rice merchant is dead
    hit by a truck
    begrudging his hard life, his last thought.
The noodle shop owner is dead
    struck mute, unable to work,
    then refusing to eat.
The itinerant mender of pots is dead
    stabbed with his own pliers
    in front of his son who swore revenge.
The blind singer is dead
    chased down by dogs
    after she had been given a head start.
The tai chi master is dead
    starved in his cellar

too shell-shocked to come out.
The young stevedore is dead
beheaded on a wharf
red-faced, full of tears, begging for mercy.
The street barber is dead
thrown into the river
along with his washstand, razors and mirror.
The petite mother and son are dead
fallen from a second story window
from which they had jumped or were pushed.
The fortune teller is dead
his heart stopped when he heard
that all of his children were dead.

Christina Minami

Last Minute Changes

My ex-wife finds me in the produce section. "You're buying a vegetable, Justin?"

I nod. Since we were married for thirty years, there's no real need for a greeting. I've begun to think about my health lately and say as much. "Sometimes I think about the future, you know."

She flicks the fennel stalk, leaving a wet impression of her nail. "Fancy way to start with health food. I gave up when you refused the peas. Even babies eat peas."

I'm sorry about that incident. Even at forty years of age, I could be a bit of a heel. Her parents had been over, and they were good local folk who remembered the Depression and the war, so my staunch refusal to touch anything colored by chlorophyll was met with disappointment. They split my portion and complimented Theresa more than once on the meal, a very out-of-the-ordinary indulgence. "I always liked your meats."

There's a slight pinking to her cheeks. I think it's a high point on which to leave the conversation but she follows me to the cereal aisle. To convince her I've changed, I choose a high-fiber one. My new concern with the flaccid aging of my heart has nothing to do with my doctor's lectures. It was the shirtless muscled jogger in Kapi'olani Park who passed me as I dawdled around the asphalt perimeter and the subsequent realization that such physicality has also passed me by. Calisthenics and fiber and vegetables may not recapture my youth but it's a gesture in the right direction. "So what are you up to these days?" she asks.

I want to say, "What do you care," but it's so rude that I cringe even though I haven't said a thing. She mistakes it for pain and rubs my sleeve between her fingers as she used to when we were in the midst of Rachel's difficult teenage years. "Same old," I say. "Except for the vegetables. I saw Ted the other day in Chinatown. He looked good." Ted might have been the beginning of the end for us but we both know if it hadn't been Ted, it would've been a Fred or Tom or Dan.

She says, "Well, we just got back from Greece and as it turns out, he's not such a fan of Mediterranean food. He thought he'd love it when we bought the tickets."

"Funny how that can happen, right? You just keep finding out new things about yourself until the day you die."

She shrugs and adjusts her glasses to look at me. Really look at me, as if I'm a bug lanced by a pin. "Some of us, I suppose. But really, how are you, Justin?"

"Fine. Great, in fact. You wouldn't recognize me." We're walking away from the cereal and turning towards the dairy, when Nancy Lee wanders out of the frozen section. She was in my class at McKinley and always had something in her nose and corners of her eyes and was always the first to volunteer to do something for the teacher. She and Theresa were friends back then. She even came to our wedding. I can't bear to see her, not when Theresa is so obviously not with me (we have separate carts and I'm in a T-shirt and khaki shorts and slippers while she's in her trim brunch attire), so I swerve to the checkout line. The fennel and Fiber One are the only things in my cart but surely there are other people who come to the market for more incongruent items. Cheetos and bouillon. Diapers and frozen corn. Lemonade powder and sour cream. "This is me."

"Drive safe, Justin." Theresa's brows knit up towards her hairline in theatrical concern but that's just her. She's a tiny woman and big facial expressions are her way of standing taller. What it really means is a more banal "It really wasn't so bad seeing you."

I watch her go even as I hear the checkout boy ask, "Rewards card? Rewards card?" because I've been thinking lately that there's not much of a difference between thirty years and the rest of your life. Really, we missed fulfilling our vows by so little. But like so many other things, it's passed and since Theresa was never the type to linger on wrongdoings, neither will I. The fennel is more expensive than I'd anticipated and as I poke through my wallet for a bigger bill, it occurs to me that in addition to the vegetable thing, I'd really like to become the kind to volunteer in the hospital and return library books on time and call Rachel on a weekly basis, just to check in as a father should. Maybe I'll even buy a boat and invite Theresa and Ted and Rachel aboard for an afternoon. It'll be a glassy day with only the slightest spit of breeze. We'll all be dressed as our better selves, in white shirts and shady hats and boat shoes, and the accumulation of bitterness and poorly-timed miscommunications will spool away in easy chatter. Rachel and Theresa will agree that I've improved and, instead of taking it as a slight, I'll beam, give a little bow, and say, "Thank you, my darlings, I was hoping you'd say that."

Angela Nishimoto

After Goodwill

Sharon finally selected a pair of jeans and four shirts: two three-quarter-sleeved, one short-sleeved, the last a tank. She went to try them on, the sign at the dressing room entrance warning that the store was monitored by closed circuit TV.

She hung the clothes on a hook, kicked off her Birkenstocks, and then pulled off her sweater and peeled off her tee shirt. She took her shorts off and tried on the jeans, which were too tight, then the tops, one after the other. She set aside the tank for last; it was a style that had flattered her, a peachy-pink cotton/lycra blend, just what she'd been hoping to find. Taking off the last of the sleeved tops, she caught sight of her near-naked mirrored self.

Under the terrible light, her shoulders slumped, breasts sagging. She half turned and saw that her behind hung low and her thighs dimpled. She slipped on her own clothing and didn't look into the mirror again. She put on her dark glasses to protect herself, *From the sun,* she told herself.

After hanging the tank and jeans onto the rack, she got into line. The cashier with long, black hair rang up one shirt at $6.99. Sharon checked the tag; she had thought the tops were $3.99 each. But she was mollified when the other two were rung up at $1.99 each. She wrote a check.

Happier now, she walked past the achingly empty Audi dealership, heading for McDonald's. She inhaled the French fry fat smell and decided to eliminate soda from her diet, starting Monday. She ordered a medium Coke, and then regretted that she hadn't gotten the small size. Free refills.

She sat, crossing her legs. She faced a poster of a handsome man with a good-looking young boy on his back, their hands on a football. They looked a little strained, as if they'd been smiling too long. *Their faces are going to be frozen that way forever.* 'Wilson' and 'Pop Warner' were on the football. Other words squirmed on the ball but she couldn't read them. *They're too small,* she thought, squinting.

In front of the photomural sat a woman with inky black hair, picking her yellow teeth with a black plastic fork. The woman's brown tray held the rumpled wrapping of a cheeseburger, an empty French fry package, crumpled napkins, a small-sized cup with a straw, and a colorful box. *A Happy Meal,* Sharon thought, telling herself not to stare.

A silver-haired man seated himself opposite the woman. Suddenly animated, the woman spoke rapidly, rolling the Rs and clucking, her black eyes sparkling behind thick-lensed glasses, magnified. She grinned at the man, her teeth big and square, and then sucked on the straw in the cup.

At the table next to the couple lounged four boys in baseball uniforms, black with white numbers. The boys were about thirteen years old. Each of the boys had a cup of water and leftovers of Extra Value Meals before them. They seemed weary but relaxed.

The boys got up, picked up their trays. All four looked at Sharon as they walked past. Her breasts, her legs. She sat up straight, moved her foot up, then down, and curled her toes as she sucked on her straw, the sweet, acid taste of Coke flooding her mouth.

Carrie M. O'Connor

Plagued

A year after I left the cult, I decided I would go back for you.

"Go down, Moses, Way down in Egypt's Land," I hummed softly.

I boarded the No. 1 Lunalilo Home Road bus at Fort Street Mall.

We planned to meet at the Kaimukī dim sum restaurant alone, near the place where you pawned your Hawaiian heirloom bracelet for a special mission contribution a couple years back.

My fuchsia dress was clinging to me in the day's heat. There was no air conditioning. Flies buzzed and danced in a huge mass above the bagged carp in a woman's lap. The girl in front of me smelled of cheap pikake perfume. The tourist behind me had slathered on coconut oil and was poring over maps of Hanauma Bay with his wife.

Near King Kamehameha's statue, a UH student wearing a black-velvet yarmulke got on and sat down next to me. He eyed my art history textbook and we began to discuss Judaism and Marc Chagall.

"How do you know so much about Judaism?" he asked.

"I was once trained to convert people to a Bible church. From any background," I told him matter-of-factly.

"Well, I'm a pretty tough nut to crack," he said with a laugh.

"Good to hear."

"So, were you good at selling faith?"

"A regular whore for God," I told him.

At the Straub Hospital stop, I fingered your last letter to me—the one that accused me of being a coward for leaving once the newspaper did an article about the church and mentioned "aggressive recruitment tactics" and "brainwashing." I was now all the words True Church liked to call people who left: a marked woman, a fall away, a dog that returns to her vomit.

Once we got to Blaisdell Arena a blind man got on with his dog. As the bus continued on, I began to scratch my itchy legs already covered with bites from the fleas that attacked me.

By Mōʻiliʻili I was gulping for air. My asthma was kicking in. I pulled the cord and stumbled off. The Jewish student was behind me.

"Are you OK?" he asked.

"Bad asthma attack."

He led me to a bench where I yanked my inhaler out of my backpack. In a few minutes, I was breathing normally again. I pulled out my cell phone and dialed your number. When you picked up, I could hear them talking in the background. Leaders.

"I'm late. Who's with you?"

"Melinda and Shelly. They wanted to see you so badly," you said.

"The last time they saw me they told me that I was prideful, selfish, and going to hell. You promised to come alone. I don't want to see them."

"That's because you're afraid of the truth."

"Listen to me. I love you. Please. I'll call you again and we can meet alone."

A click. Then, silence. You were gone.

It had started to rain, and after saying good-bye to the samaritan, I walked to the cracked seed store where I bought li hing cherries. I sat at the bus stop and sucked them. One by one I spat the pits out on the sidewalk. I began calling out the plagues in Hebrew. *Dam*, blood, *dam.*

Tell old Pharaoh, Let my people go.

Then, I knew.

I am not your Moses.

I'm just a haole girl in a plus-size Hilo Hattie muʻumuʻu running to catch the No. 22 Sea Life Park bus.

And I will always love you.

Shelley Ayame Nishimura Ota

excerpt from HAWAIIAN KALEIDOSCOPE

Mrs. Martha was different from the other church ladies who talked of charity but practiced little charity. Mrs. Martha didn't scold or preach. She just looked a little sad when the Hawaiians got drunk. This disappointed look stopped many a Hawaiian who had been drinking too much.

"Jubilee!" Once more the loud voice shattered the Sunday peace.

"Boss wants you," Jubilee's wife said. "That awful man. Yell, yell, and yell some more." She wished someone would put a curse on him and let him die an unnatural death. He wouldn't be missed. Mrs. Martha and her three girls would be better off without that devil around.

Bepen's temper had reached an explosive point by the time Jubilee appeared.

"Good afternoon, Mr. Bepen."

"Damn! Get on your horse and come along," Bepen ordered.

"On Sunday? A day of rest and prayer?" Jubilee threw up his hands in mock horror.

"Don't give me that Sunday talk!" Bepen yelled. "I know better!"

Bepen knew the missionaries had hardly influenced the Hawaiians. True, the Hawaiians enjoyed the hymns and the majestic phrases of the Bible. Outside of this, they clung to the old ways, believed in many gods, and even practiced witchcraft. Blast 'em!

"Get on your horse!" Bepen ordered, swinging his riding crop viciously.

"Sure, sure, Mr. Bepen." He thought it best to humor the Boss. Without enthusiasm he unhitched his horse from the *'ōhia* tree, mounted, and rode behind a silent, brooding manager.

If he wished, Jubilee could accommodate himself to situations as readily and as smoothly as the peel of a banana. But today, cheerful accommodation was not part of his heart and soul.

Far in front of him, he suddenly heard Bepen shouting, "Damn. Look at this!"

Jubilee stirred his horse and came upon a group of newly arrived Japanese workers squatting in the shade of a breadfruit tree, playing cards. He slowly whistled.

"This bad! Playing cards on Sunday. On day of rest and Bible reading. This Devil's work."

The workers bowed and smiled. One of them held up his cards and said in Japanese, *"Hanafuda."*

"Playing cards on Sunday!" Bepen's eyes flashed with displeasure.

The workers went on playing, unaware of the manager's mounting indignation.

"Jubilee!" Bepen's voice lashed the air. "Take their names. Tomorrow morning, ride over to the magistrate and tell him to hold court. Tell him I've got Sabbath Day violators."

"Yes, sir," said Jubilee, unable to look at the workers who were looking at the angry manager and wondering what was happening.

As Jubilee reluctantly took out his pencil, Akimoto the interpreter and Takeo Miyake appeared.

"Good afternoon, sir," said Akimoto. He appraised the situation and turned to Bepen inquiringly.

"Sabbath Day violators!" Bepen snarled.

"Sabbath Day violators?" Akimoto's thick eyebrows went up. "Surely you are not serious. These men are new arrivals. Besides, they are not Christians."

Akimoto was not inclined to take the manager seriously, until he looked around. Jubilee's stricken face, the pale faces of the workers, the belligerent set of the manager's mouth. The scene was incredible.

"Please explain, Mr. Bepen," said Akimoto.

"Playing cards on Sunday!" Bepen snapped.

Akimoto glanced around and saw the flower cards in one of the worker's hands. Quickly, Akimoto assumed control.

"You are aware, Mr. Bepen, that the contract states that these men are to be free of persecution of any kind while they are on the plantation."

"I don't need your damn advice," said Bepen. His nose quivered with disdain. "Now, get off my plantation. You're trespassing."

He ordered Jubilee to make sure the interpreter was off the plantation by sundown. Whipping his horse, Bepen thundered away.

After the manager's departure, Jubilee explained the situation as best as he could.

"These men are ignorant of Sabbath Day violations," said Akimoto, very much concerned.

"Big Boss make rules. Same everywhere."

"Yes, Jubilee-san. Tyrants are like that." Then he turned to the workers and explained the situation.

The explanation fell ominously upon the workers. Furtive glances were filled with anxiety and dismay. This was not a propitious beginning. It was a curse blighting their future.

"We should quit this land," shouted one of the workers. "Yesterday the filth, today this!"

"What will come next?" asked another.

The workers avoided one another's eyes. If one of them went back to Japan, it would make it harder, lonelier, and more distressing for the others. They all sensed this.

Akimoto spoke gently to counteract the increasingly dark mood of the men.

"We must not lose hope. Men of power often use a flimsy excuse to further their ends. But such conniving and scheming will ultimately come to a bad end for them." The interpreter turned to the *luna*.

"Please take their names."

"Take their names?" asked a surprised Jubilee. "What for? You say, contract say, no persecution."

"Yes, Jubilee-san," Akimoto gently explained. "The contract is clear on this point. It states that the laborers are to be free of any persecution while residing on the plantation."

"Then why should I take names?"

"You were told to take their names," said Akimoto. "It is your job. I cannot ask you to do otherwise."

"I won't!" Jubilee stood firm. He had been slippery about many things, but now he was determined to make right. In the past he had laughed with Boss, flattered him. Acted the fool. No more!

"I will take up this matter with the proper authorities," Akimoto declared. "You must obey your superior's command as long as you are in his employ." Then Akimoto explained the situation to the workers, emphasizing Jubilee-san's stand.

The men bowed to Jubilee. Once more they were indebted to him, for his generous show of support.

Jubilee bowed. If only he could tell these men that he hated to see honest men abused by bosses like Bepen. He stared at his heavy boots and asked himself how long he would allow the Boss to kick him around. On a sudden impulse, he asked the interpreter a question.

"You think I'm too old to learn?"

Startled by the question, Akimoto replied, "No one is ever too old to learn."

"Me, 18," said Jubilee. This was a guess, for he had no record of his birth.

"Go see Mr. Tail," said Akimoto. "He will help you."

"Mr. Tail. Fine man. Kind man. I go see him."

"Now take their names."

"I can't."

Once more the interpreter explained the situation to the workers. One by one, bowing and smiling, they came forward to Jubilee and gave their names and registration numbers.

With great reluctance Jubilee took down the information. He had never met men like these Japanese, who willingly sacrificed themselves so that Jubilee could keep his job.

When the last name was taken, Jubilee went down the line of men and gave them his hand. He couldn't resist laughing. Soon, the workers joined in the laughter, for they too felt they had risen above an ugly situation and saw something comical and pathetic in Bepen. A small man, asserting his will, over a small incident.

Bowing once more to the Japanese contract workers, Jubilee mounted his horse and rode away.

Christy Passion

Lineage

You were only a black and white photo—
a woman with short curly hair, flowered housedress,
tired averted eyes.

From my father's lips
a saint that made perfect pasteles
and watched over my aunt's virtue until
it was safely delivered to a nice Chinese boy.

I kept you at a distance.

Much later I discovered you
through more insidious scraps discarded
in dark corners of family functions—
a scarred lung, the older daughter who overdosed,
things done to pay the rent when your husband ran off.

I kept each shred and built a nest of you
one I could safely curl into, grandmother,
and as each groove was filled
saint or sinner, fabled charm, clotted blood
you breathed me alive.

Now there is so much to ask:

Was your heart filled with a thousand sparrows
thundering against your cage screeching to get out? *Mine is*

Or did they burst out; tear flesh from faulty valve
leaving hunger and bitter true stories
that eventually did you in? *Oh grandmother*

I am here now
Warrior, bone bridge, raucous clang
making a wreath of past and present.
Unflinching you formed the words that would be me,
I will not leave your story in famine.

Christy Passion

The Compromise

I do not have the same things with him
that I had with you, but I have different
things, good things, quiet things

a terracotta tiled roof and mock orange hedges
sheets of lined paper and unbrushed hair
old patchwork quilt, blue seashells,
a bowl of Portuguese bean soup.

I also have a tiger in the basement.
He sniffs at the door constantly
pacing between old age and remembering.
He never blinks
and waits for my shadow
to cross the floor.

Christy Passion

The Walls of Jericho, 1973

And the city and all that is in it shall be devoted to the Lord for destruction.

Joshua 6:17

There is nothing left to offer
except a linoleum floor, thin rug
and 40-watt light bulb.
You flutter and smile, little bug,
as if this is enough

Look at your wellspring
my cracked palms, my swollen feet
my unnoticeable short hair,
as necessary as the air
and as easily dismissed.

The night shift is tiring, little bug
but you want, your father is gone
but you need. With your curls
and stuffed bear you point and say please
but the rent is due, and the rent is due.

Each child's cry is a trumpet blast
tearing down these walls
a new city built on the back of this
broken one. In the rubble are
thrift store clothes, a small warm light
and dust.

So tell me of being a ballerina,
a cat doctor, a chef who makes purple berried
tarts. I live there now as I carry you
in the wrinkle of my eye.
With each breath I will level mountains
for you, so you can fly to places
I will never see.

Christy Passion

Poor in the Pacific: a Remembrance

I put on the skirt Chris gave me late for my birthday—a nice soft skirt with pinks and corals and browns. I look like the Micronesian women I see in the thrift store wearing long colorful skirts, same as their daughters, who run to the back of the store looking for toys while the mothers rummage through tables of spatulas and spoons looking for a perfect fit. So joyful these running girls, their laughter sparking a glint of pride from mother to mother, bright skirt to bright skirt. They never speak to me. Though I have never attempted to speak to them either, and I will never have a child. I think.

I clean my house after breakfast and feel that this must be also what the women do with their mornings. Put away the clothes; ignore the dishes in the sink for a little while more. Feel the skirt against my knees, feel the bright colors clash at the paunch of my belly. I carry on as if this is always what I do, always what I wear. I turn off the morning show, annoyed by the host telling me the seven steps to living. I know there are many more. Poor people move in millimeters at a time, imperceptible steps. Clean the clothes. Wash the children. Scold them. Make the food. There is no food to make. Make something anyway and be thankful.

You can forget the sting of poor but not the shame.

I live in this house and know it will never be mine no matter what the papers say. Things get taken away. You win writing awards then your father gets diagnosed with cancer. Perhaps you believed you deserved some recognition. But with all recognition, come all recognition, and there are jealous gods out there too. Gods who listen out for the boastful and quickly take away what you worked so hard for. Prayed so hard for. Maybe that's why the women do not talk, at least not to me. Maybe that is why they brag about little triumphs but keep quiet about the big ones. *Hear this, God, You gave me my daily dose of hardship, no more for now, no more.*

Like the old, they do not pray for gain, they pray just to hold on.

They smile with their toothy grins capped in silver and offer me a yellow T-shirt from the three-for-a dollar table. Is it me? The girls look up at me from behind mama's knees and I smile: afraid. They smile back in wonder, show me the one-armed Barbie being sold for just a nickel. Just a nickel for all this joy.

In the parking lot the women share their catch: gently used shoes, almost complete set of forks, and soap. They pack them away into plastic bags as they gather themselves for the bus. They travel in communities, more than one woman always. I travel alone in a large SUV just in case there may be a time when I need this much space. Even my home, with its excess of room, is filled with things I only thought I needed. Things I'll eventually bring to the thrift store. So I make my donation and wander through the store looking for treasures among the discarded. The Micronesian women and I. See their dark teeth and even darker eyes. See their curves covered by opposing colors, colors fighting it out for the landscape. See their untoned bodies, bodies that give birth and sweep floors and catch buses to thrift stores open only on Wednesdays and sometimes Saturdays. See them laugh, but quiet when others pass by, move slightly to the side because they are in the way. See them live their life trying to hold on, yet losing ground. Never asking for too much. Hoping they paid the toll for at least one child to pass through free. This child will wear matching clothes and drive a big car with no one in it but herself. She will never consult others or the rantings of traditions that no longer make sense. She will buy her mother gifts: brand new crock-pots and T-shirts bought from Sears. And those would not have been on clearance. The mother will wear matching outfits to church and the colorful-skirt-thrift-store-T-shirt-wearing women will cluck at how beautiful it looks. Whisper that it must have cost a lot of money. They will rub the hem of the sleeve or pull the skirt away to admire the stitching and the softness of the material. It will smell new, it will be crisp and free of wrinkles. The woman in the new clothes will deny the clothes' worth as anything good. Say that it would have been better to get four skirts for this price at the thrift store but she wears it to make her child happy.

But that is years from now.

Any prideful boast from the mother about the child is about the mother. Any years given up with fathers that go out to bars to see other women is made up for in that small moment of glory. All the dented cans of corned beef, all the forms from smiling social workers, all the calluses and salty tears are worth it. To wear a matching outfit not bought at a thrift store makes up for it. To not look down when others pass by but to look them in the eyes and say, "See, I am like you, I have a leather purse too. I have a nice outfit. I shop at the same shops; I am worthy just like you. My child has made me worthy. All my sacrifices paid in full."

Elmer Omar Pizo

Warning!

Reading these poems
with your bare eyes,
you feel at once
a nasty, stinging sensation
in them.

Rubbing them makes
matters more worse.

I recommend welder's
goggles. You are best
protected using them.

As much as possible,
read these poems only
in areas with adequate
ventilation.
And shield the words
from sources of heat
to prevent them from
igniting.

Vapor coming off
from the words,
if inhaled,
wears out
the outer linings
of your lungs
forcing them to work
harder.

Those vapor residues
may settle in
the pores
of your exposed skin.
Take a shower
as soon as you are done
reading them.
Half an hour or longer
will do.
But of course!
It must be accompanied
by a vigorous up and down,
side to side,
even circular scrubbing.

If by accident
or by some other reasons
you swallow the words,
do not thrust
your middle finger
inside your throat
to induce yourself
to puke.
A glass of water
doesn't do any good
at all.

Hurry up!
Do not delay!
Call Bamboo Ridge Press immediately!

Nutrition Facts

Average Serving Size: A *150-word poem
published by the Bamboo Ridge Press

Calories: 75
Calories from fat: 0g

Total Fat: 0g
Saturated Fat: 0g
Trans Fat: 0g
Cholesterol: 0g
Sodium: 0g
Carbohydrates: 0g
Protein: 0g
Sugar: 5g

*Not artery-clogging or a significant source of sugar but it improves and boosts the thinking power of the brain.

Elmer Omar Pizo

Rodent Control

Pier 2/Honolulu Harbor
January 27, 2006

Just before noon was when
I lifted up the lid
of the black bait station I set
3 days ago under an abandoned stairway
at the back of the aging 2-story building
bordering the right side of
Aloha Tower Marketplace
identified by the foot-sized,
Calibri-type lettering:
DOT/Harbors Division.

The *Star-Bulletin* wasn't there.
Or *The Honolulu Advertiser.*
The competing KITV, KGMB, KHNL

and KHON TV stations didn't come as well.
Yes, nobody was there to cover
the breaking news this late morning.

Inside the box I found
the corpse of an anonymous rat,
stiff in its fetal position
as if it were shielding itself from
an imminent, unknown threat.

Shifting my head to a different angle
to grab a better look—
a little smudge of coagulated blood
was barely visible at the base
of clumped whiskers on the left side
of its still face.

On its face,
there was no hint whatsoever
even of the slightest pain except its
extremely sharp front teeth were protruding
as if they're resting after gnawing at something
solid,
hard
and indestructible.
Its nose, blunt;
fur, brownish;
tail, flaking, balding and shorter when
measured against its body that was
a little bigger than a mouse's;
and the 2 small,
round,
shiny objects
below the base of its tail disclosed
what it really was—
a juvenile male belonging
to the Norway species.

Whether it was a safe
or a wild one,
if I were to make an assumption—
his parents couldn't have failed to deliver
to him some oft-repeated warnings
to be wary and not to get into that kind
of box sitting harmless and innocent
along the edge and corners
of commercial
and private establishments.

But I had to admit I was wrong
thinking it was only the good Lord who knew
of the reason and purpose
of the solitary house fly
hovering low and high,
circling tight and wide
over the corpse.

The smell of decaying flesh
could have been picked up
and carried by the wind when
it sneaked into the neglected
backdoor and dropped it
at the fly's doorsteps,
either on purpose
or by mistake,
minutes before I could get into
the building.

Barely I opened the mouth
of an improvised body bag
(a Sack N Save plastic grocery bag at that)
when the fly began rolling
a number of times before executing
an imperfect loop
a few feet away from
the corpse.

Acting on impulse, the fly darted back.
This time, it hovered directly over the corpse
for quite a while before it shifted its move
into a straight nosedive
to plant a quick light kiss
on the corpse's furry forehead.

When it directed its glance toward me,
I bowed then looked back at it,
careful not to break even into a slight
smile.

To Madame Kerima Polotan Tuvera
Distinguished Filipina Essayist/Novelist/Short-story Writer
December 16, 1925 - August 19, 2011

I regret so much that I never had the chance to meet you
to express my deepest appreciation of your fine short stories
that I was fortunate to read during my high-school years.
Aloha and mahalo nui loa, Madame

Elmer Omar Pizo

Kailua Goat December 2010

What holds knife to your throat and eats billy goat?
You are right it's the Manong! Buk-buk. Buk-buk.
— Frank De Lima, "Filipino Purple Danube"

Before the caretaker caught him
by his horns
and dragged him bleating
to the makeshift table,
he was jumping,
running back and forth,

at times even kicking dust
over the dried-up dirt,
together with the other goats.

One hundred
and seventy-five bucks
including tax (I'm not sure
if there's any hidden fee involved),
that's all it had cost me to own
the sole rights to do anything I want
with his 10-month-old body.

With his fore and hind legs bound
together by a nylon rope,
his body is forced to curl like a fetus
inside a mother's womb.

Just as my friend is about
to push the pointed tip
of the stubby ice pick
to punch a hole in his jugular
vein, I place my left hand over
the right side of his chest
heaving with fear
not to assure him everything will turn
all right, but to let him know
I do sympathize with his sealed,
inevitable fate.

As I am about to take a swipe at
the fly crawling on my sweat-soaked
forehead, I chance upon his eyes staring at
the tip of the ice pick: *Although somewhat
distorted, the reflected image is clear
enough—the executioner is wearing
no hood, mask or any sense of shame
and guilt.*

Flame from the hissing blowtorch
melts thick strands of black hair
around the neck,
around the belly,
around the udder;
on the sides of the ears,
the whole of the tail,
above the hooves
giving off a kind of sulfuric smell
some stomping,
finger-pointing,
holier-than-fly evangelicals describe
when it comes to their most-favored
topic: *that sulfuric and flaming kind*
of punishment reserved only for
souls that prefer to hold onto whatever
are their wicked ways.

The shrinking jaws,
misaligned teeth
heavily stained green by months
of chewing grass and weed appear
as the sole bearer of
twisted truth:
It seems the goat is
smiling,
enjoying
the burning.

To the memory of a gifted and very kind literary mentor, Edith L. Tiempo
National Artist for Literature, Republic of the Philippines
April 22, 1919 – August 21, 2011
A hui hou, until we meet again, Madame . . .

Mayumi Shimose Poe

excerpt from ***Constellation of Bodies—Emiko***

Ann cries out "Daddy," and that's when we see him. Yama has materialized as if from deep cover, still wearing camouflage, and is moving swiftly. His eyes are intent on Ann, and she is toddling toward him. I am on my feet and have her in my arms before I know it. I can't explain why I have done this or how I got to her so fast. I have no words, I'm just standing there like an idiot, staring, while Ann whines and reaches for her father. I tuck my nose deep into the honeysuckle of her hair, and my heartbeat thrums against her. There's something about his eyes—they're hard and empty, like staring into the barrels of twin guns. He doesn't push the issue, stays so still it's like he's received an order to do so.

The family closes around us, exclaiming his name, embracing him, and covering him with leis. "What a surprise," Yama manages. But his voice is choked, like we're a noose at his neck. "Now here's the kind of homecoming a soldier dreams of," he says. The lack of affect in his voice is chilling. Maila hovers at his back, picking lint off his uniform. I understand the gesture—any excuse to touch him, to have him notice her. "Hey, great to see you, M. It's been a while, Runt." He rumples her hair in just the way she hates.

"Yeah, yeah, Pick. Watch the hair, would ya? And uhm. Welcome home. Yeah." But Maila's eyes glisten, and she doesn't fix her hair. And we all know it's a bad sign when Maila Keaulana is at a loss for words. We bustle noisily around him to cover the look in our eyes, cautious, afraid, as I cradle Ann and Erro holds the boys tightly at their wrists, all of the children flailing.

And then Errolyn steps in. "Hey, you," she says. The 'you' is a thing soft and intimate, more so than any pet name would've been. The sweater-thick intimacy. "We've missed you so much." With flicks of her wrists, she sends Romeo and Damien toward Yama. They obediently attach themselves to his nearest thigh. Before he can even react, Errolyn has stepped into the remaining space in front of him, putting her arms around him.

Maybe it's what I want to see, but I swear that Yama's shoulders tense up. He is his mother's son, though, so he doesn't push her away. I shift

Ann in my arms and interest myself with smoothing her hair, which I have affixed with a pink velvet headband, but she swats at my hands and begins whining. She's frustrated, doesn't understand why she can't go to her father. When I see her famous bottom lip start to tremble, I quickly smile and murmur, *Who's my pretty girl? Annabug is!* scurrying my fingers up and down her arm until she is giggling again. I do this to cheer her up but also because I can't bear to watch. Maila and Yama's parents are busying themselves with similar things: fiddling with cell phones, digging through purses, and the like. Errolyn threads through the short bristles of his hair, massages the ropy muscles of his neck, murmurs in his ear.

I'm not sure why I continue to be surprised by Errolyn. The very things that have always stupefied me about her are the things that continue to. But surprised is exactly what I am. Not only is Erro behaving as if she never got Yama's e-mail, she's acting like she never sent e-mails of her own, never poured her heart out to me over lunch, never warned any of us about him being dangerous. "He may not be the man we know. Better safe than sorry," she had said. I recall her sitting at the restaurant, all long legs and cleavage, twirling her wine nervously. Had it all been an act? I had dismissed every warning she gave me, yet, here at the airport, presented with a man who looked outwardly the same except that something had withered inside, suddenly all her warnings seemed sound. Looking at him was like looking at a stranger.

But how can I not know *this* man? No matter what he has gone through in the last six months, I know the Yama standing here in fatigues, women and children hanging on best they can, haphazard. Every tic, every move, every single thing about him, I know. I feel foolish, standing here and clasping Ann close, withholding from him the one person he wants to see while Erro heeds nothing but her heart, flinging herself and her sons straight at him.

Frankly, we are all—each and every one of us—still standing here, unsure. Even the children don't know how to act. And children don't usually act, they just *are,* but these three seem to be holding their collective breath. It's uncomfortable, this moment. Errolyn ducks her head in for a kiss. The inevitable moment—mere seconds but ponderous ones—before Yama rejects Erro, it's coming, we all know it. So, I do the only thing I can. I put Ann down on her own two feet.

Not two seconds later, my daughter has gotten between Yama and Erro. Ann exclaims "Daddy!" and it is like Errolyn ceases to exist. Yama scoops Ann up and in so doing shakes off Erro and the boys. "Hey there, hey beautiful, hey superstar, hey my very special girl"—his words come out in a delighted flow, the affect back in place and the ice melted from his blue eyes. He doesn't realize how cruel his words are. He looks at me, and I meet his gaze unblinking. Yes, my eyes say. Yes. I can give this, and I can take it away. I am choosing to trust you with the most precious thing in the universe. Yama holds Ann so close, even with desperation, but she is not fighting him and so they fit together, like puzzle pieces, yin to yang—her arms lock behind his neck and her legs anchor around his middle, while his arms snake around her back and bottom. As much as I was initially attracted to the macho soldier those years ago, I love now the man he is at peace. And I never met that man till we had Ann. It's not a word you use to describe a man usually, I know, but when I see the way he lights up around her, he's *beautiful.*

Erro is the one standing foolishly now. Her lips are a thin line that meets the clenched angle of her jaw. The boys are restless with the tension, and so they exert it the only way children know how: by beginning again the game of chase. They wind around this assembled family and outward into the crowd, so that Erro is forced to call after them, and when that fails, to follow. Meanwhile, Yama looks like he wants to bolt. But he knows better; he understands that Ann is a package deal. He is screwed to the spot, holding close our daughter, holding at bay his ex-lover Erro, and held accountable by the assembled eyes of his family.

I sit down on a nearby bench, watching this thing unfold. I am somewhat amused by the situation, because my place in it is guaranteed. Yama wants to be with Ann + Ann belongs to me = Yama will be with me. What I don't know is what happens to the rest of the elements of this equation: Maila, Errolyn, her boys, all those parents. All those who invited me to BBQs and birthday parties and into their homes, who thrilled and trilled over our pregnancy, but who stood silently by, doing nothing when he broke up with me from Iraq. There were no family airport interventions back then, no assumptions that the end of our relationship meant he must have gone crazy. No, there was a collective sense that I was supposed to be stoic and brave. They thought Yama and I were over and done with, that they'd still see me, sure, but only from time to time and in the role of Ann's mother. But all this time I was lying in wait. Each time I shuttled Ann back and forth, giving Yama all the time he needed with his daughter, letting him fall in love, I was weaving a life in which he was a vital third part.

Errolyn has come back with the boys, all three fairly humming with nervous energy. She sits them down in the seats next to me and warns them to stay there. They sit, fidgeting and resentful. I smile at them but carefully lean away, so as to avoid getting anything on my clothes. Little boys can be so dirty. The parents start in with the offers to put Yama up at their houses and let him use their cars. Meanwhile, Erro's mouth keeps opening and closing, as if she simultaneously starts and stops herself from saying so many things. She looks like a dying fish.

But it is Maila who throws Yama the lifeline. "Is this your bag, bro?" She holds up the camouflage duffel, the only bag left circling the conveyor belt. He nods, putting Ann down and accepting the bag. "Great," says Maila. There is something I'm missing, it's within my grasp but I don't know where to reach. "Then we're ready to go." Now we're all confused; even Yama gives her a blank look. Maila whacks his shoulder. "While I know anyone here would gladly have you stay with them, I went deluxe on your ass. Got us an adjoining suite at the Halekulani. A little R&R before you deal with," Maila pauses delicately, ". . . the Real World. Just like we talked about." Her voice sounds like it is winking. None of this was planned, I realize. This is Maila, saving Yama. But from who, in particular: Errolyn? Me? Perhaps all of us. Whoever the "enemy" is—brother and sister against the world.

Maila begins the rounds of hugging everyone goodbye with the parents. "I'm so glad everyone could make it to the airport today." In an even more surprising move, Yama follows suit. "What a homecoming, right?" says Maila, hugging Erro, who has completely deflated.

"I am one lucky guy," agrees Yama. He embraces everyone the same way, with the same dry kiss on the right cheek, except for Ann, who gets pulled up in the air, her face covered in kisses. He sets Ann back on her feet, kneeling to promise: "Babygirl, I'll see you again really soon, okay?" He's talking to his daughter, of course, but he glances at me, as if asking permission, before following Maila out the door. Ann and I stand, holding hands and still nodding, even though our whole beings hum with the desire to follow.

Darlene Rodrigues

Switch 'um
In three stages

For Hinaleimoana Wong and the other local people
who ever served on the HIV Prevention Community Planning Group

"The nail that stands out gets hammered down."

Island people epistemology
The animistical mystical magical people who remember
To read the mountains, sky, and sea
between the lines of waves, clouds and trees
we see

Stage one
Too much hassle fo' make waves I just like talk stink

Especially if you in one meeting
And you gotta get going on some federal project
Designed to help our community
Prevent violence, stop HIV, or da oddah uku billion kine shit we gotta fix
You read the kaona loud and clear
When the limitations of funding
The misplaced policies that just don't fit Hawai'i nei
Make us quiet
Da buggah no can go li'dat. Going fail fo' sure
And the only people talking in da room are da haoles
The funders, the granters, the state, the government

Everyone holding their breath and like run away
Talk stink outside on smoke break
Grumble, grumble, grumble out da left side of yo' mouth
This is da way local people stop the process
We just no come back

Still yet they keep going even if we no stay inside the room
Dat's how is
Da machine keep going even if we no stay

Stage two
I can feel 'um, see the shibai but I no like make "a"

At least now you know you get one snake
Coiling around your neck choking your breath
You know the process is all kapakahi
Can see the shibai/tae of your own futlessness
You can feel 'um in your gut
Da kine feeling when you look at the waves and dey telling you fo' go back
inside
No go surfing
You read 'um but you do nothing and get cut up on da reef
Da same kine feeling you get when uncle tell you look at the cat's eye and
you know go fishing
You read 'um but you do nothing and go hungry

But instead
You grumble, grumble, grumble, talk out da right side of yo' mouth
Talk stink during smoke break
Make fun of everybody
Yet you come back, and everything still stay stuck cuz you no like make
ass
Someone else going say something
The snake on your neck stay choking you but you don't know how fo'
throw 'em off

Stage three
Ho, sistah, went do something different

That's what our kupuna would say, our manangs and our manongs
Hey, if not working do 'um different
Get the same kine attitude in the Philippines

Can, can!
Need make 300 shirts for one conference overnight
Boom, pau done jus li'dat
They so thirsty for change
They no hold back
But us we hold back
Gotta ask how cum?

So you see 'um coming at one meeting,
Da government stay ramming something down our throats
You see all da local people's eyes rolling
Everybody going bathroom
Or taking smoke break
We past da point of grumbling already
Just stink eyes all around
But no one saying nothing
Your own shibai futting around with the big Shibai that stay floating
    around da room
And then
You take one deep breath
You stop being polite
You stop smiling
And in your nicest haole kine talk you say,
I'm sorry but that just doesn't make sense for Hawai'i
I have a problem with that. I don't like to complain BUT
Dis is wrong and we not going stand fo' dat

And in one instant
The anykine that stay floating around
Comes clear
The bullshit you been carrying around
Da snake choking your neck went make die dead
Just li'dat
Cuz you took one long deep breath
You looked into the eyes of the cat
Remembered how fo' read the waves
And felt the trees at your back

Laura Saijo

Coqui in D

For two weeks we listened to your hopeful little voice
Calling for love from out of the hāpuʻu
Like singing in the rain
Like whistling in the dark

I was myself cheering you on
Hoping you would find a mate too
But our neighbors on the loop came to our door
Stopped us on our walks with the dog

"Did you know you have a FROG?"
"Shouldn't you call the coqui hunters?"
"Do you want us to help you catch it?"
"Have you ever been in Hilo at night?"

We agreed that something must be done
We made plans to do it
But in the rain, in the dark
Your sweet voice still pierced the night
A radiant major sixth in D

Yesterday as we worked on the rock path
Our neighbor appeared, carrying you and your girlfriend
Each in a separate Ziploc bag
Frozen and suffocated and quiet

"Great!" we said
"Thank you," we said
And now, tonight, silence in our yard

Yes, we've been to Hilo at night, and other places too
Where we had to yell at each other

Raising our voices to be heard
Over the vibrant ringing of your communal celebration

And no doubt that's why we want to off you . . .
Because if there's one thing we humans like
It's the sound
Of our own voice

Jhoanna Calma Salazar

AFTER THE DOCTORS TELL HER THERE IS NOTHING ELSE THEY CAN DO

your mother sits you down at the kitchen table, tells you she needs to go back to her homeland, to a city known for miracles. your father sits beside her, says you need to stay, finish your last days of high school. his eyes seem to look past you, maybe at the clock on the stove, blinking away the time. outside, bloody streaks cross the sky as the sun falls on your part of the world, and you wonder about hope, and desperation, and the difference between them. but you wonder even more whether your mother is dying, and, if she is, why she is leaving you behind.

your parents phone from the Philippines. the time delay causes you to hear echoes of your own voice, making your questions seem twice as trivial. *i'm home again,* your mother says. the sun helps keep away the chill that constantly flows beneath her skin. you listen while you sit alone in their house on the other side of the world. when she gives the phone to your father, he whispers that you need to book a flight right away. you don't ask why he is whispering, but when you talk to the travel agent, you find yourself whispering, too—*can i change my return date in case of emergency? my mother is sick . . .*

when you step off the plane onto the tarmac, the heat smothers you, but your mother waits for you in long pants and a sweatshirt that hangs limply over her narrow shoulders. she is the thinnest you have ever seen her. at night, she pulls a quilt over herself while you lay beside her, sweating, unable to sleep, the roosters crowing the night into shreds, and in the silent spaces between, you listen to her breathing, just to make sure that she is. you get up, find your father in the kitchen, sitting in the dark by himself. you sit with him wordlessly, until he says, *just try to make her comfortable,* as if he knew you didn't know what you could do for her.

the next day the three of you take a bus to the mountains of Baguio, your birth city of which you have no memories. your parents tell you this is the place of miracles, where once a statue of St. Therese wept blood, where nuns prayed back the life of a child in a coma, where a healer placed a hand on your mother's barren stomach and you flowered inside her. your mind turns this fact over and over, that the beginning of your life might have been due to one mere touch of a stranger.

at the hotel, a small man with silver hair and no smile knocks at the door. your father lets him in and the man limps over to your mother lying on the bed. with his brown, bony fingers, he traces the perimeter of a large lump that has developed on your mother's neck. he chants in a language you don't understand, waves his hands wildly in the air. when it is all over, you sit at the edge of the bed. your mother touches your hand. her fingers are cold, and for some reason this makes you cry. you manage to ask her if she really believes in miracles. she closes her eyes, doesn't answer. you pull the blanket up to her neck, tuck it under her legs, her arms, her feet. she looks like a cocoon. when she drifts off to sleep, you feel a fluttering in your chest, a soft flapping of wings that stays inside you, even after she is gone.

Salt

Kalihi Ghosts, Not Unfamiliar

Creatures die in our valley,
Animals and people,
Behind trees that line my daily walk.
People and animals too afraid
To come to an open hand,
So afraid they hide when they hear footsteps break twigs.
The one I contemplate most is the old Chinese woman
Brought here by emigrating family.
Lonely in a truly alien world
She jumped from the car traveling up the highway toward the tunnel.
First searchers came, but couldn't see her shadow jump from tree to tree.
Then Charlotte who knew the valley, Charlotte, a sympathetic hiker,
Became a shadow herself, searching silently day after day.
Charlotte puzzled to me, "What can I do?
I can almost feel her eyes on me."
Two weeks later hunters found her body. Lonely old stubborn woman.
She could have been found by the gray hunting dog
Who didn't come back with his pack after the pig hunters
Successfully went in with their bows and arrows.
We saw the huge boar held by its back legs
Hanging from the grinning hunter's back.
The men didn't count dogs till they were back to their jeep.
They drove their radio-equipped jeep to the gate,
Showed me the red dot that picked up the dog's collar.
They could see the dot move across the screen, couldn't get to him.
If they got there, the dog would be long gone from that spot.
What could have spooked him, gotten him to trot away from his pack?
Did he think he could forage his own food, have his own adventure?
Did he think?
Was he another whose life didn't match?
That one I saw. That one I called to.
He stood healthy, big eyes, tail wagging, ten feet away

Ready to leap back into the woods.
He'd watch my dog, but not come.
In a week I saw him get bonier, look at us with a snarl.
Then I was afraid to go toward him.
Would the woman have snarled and sprung away if I could have found
her in time?
Somehow their presence rests behind the familiar trees,
Reminds me there's a world I'll never touch,
From my presence on the trail.

Susan M. Schultz

Memory Cards: Wolsak Series July 2010

Compassion is largely exile. Went down to the ships. Went down to Laupāhoehoe. She was clearly manic, call and self-response a loop: cancer, local, Hawaiian, birth-father, Punahou. Punalu'u turtles, runway of black feathered sand to blue launch. When I drive, I think of pelicans. *All poets feel/are disappointed, but most express it obliquely.* A single boat pushes back against the current, cork bobbing in a blue liquor never wrought. It lives inside the word. Pass. Ion. To compare is to lose it. She noticed the dead mouse on the road, the nursing foal. (His photograph was removed for inappropriate content.) Compassion is largely an isle, nursed by ocean. Its boundaries are liquid. Too big to fail. They come pushing their carts down Kahekili, stopping by the bridge to drink. *The unemployed are too lazy to look for work.* A little boy in orange points away from my window frame. *It's not a bad climate in which to be homeless.*

—July 20, 2010

Let us finish each other's songs. She chants the Kumulipo in the back seat. How do you read the bumper sticker "Bloodlines"? *You are not my mother!* Sight memory, muscle memory. My mother has forgotten how to walk. Her throat forgets to swallow. Parse the word. *For*: forward, fortunate, fortuitous, not against, but with. *Get*: claim, hold, beget. If my mother forgets me, am I misbegotten? *Mother is a job,* he tells her; *it's the person who takes you to school, who makes sure you're safe.* At day's end, she gets you back.

—July 21, 2010

Is as it is last: Saturday morning call. *What are you doing, Mom?* "Lis to you." *I hear you fell and hurt your elbow.* "No, I'm fine." (She coughs coughs again.) *I'm fine* (in a high pitched wail, this time). The boy pla Atari games: *I love the classics!* Simulated on a new machine. *He's exper ing his father's nostalgia.* His inner/outer child. My mother has forg her own body's hurt. *But it's the same code.* I hang up: a familiar sen blank. White, a mountain in the Alps. Too much to see, we kept on walk our heads down. *The aesthetic moves seem unnecessary to the content.* I see the lines break even in prose. *Is last* cannot. Last days, when the ela trips and there is no give except in for-.

—July 24, 2010

tening
.) (She
ys old
ienc-
otten
se of
ing,
can
stic

c Paul Shaffer

LLUMINATION

er mornings, I rise in the dark, and I sit
th a pen and paper in a circle of light
r the work. The window beside me is black

m staring only through the window of the page
ing from ink and concentration. Hours pass,
ıen I least expect it, there's a sudden tide of light

ıe mountain. When the rays first flood the fields,
w curtain behind me brightens over the window,
wells with light. Everything is suddenly golden

ı, and for just that one moment, I make the glorious
vable mistake that it has something to do with me.

John E. Simonds

The Fall of Man

Pick all the mangoes you want, Brad,
we said over Friday night drinks
with neighbors in our backyard where
ripening Piries were hanging.
It seemed like the start of good times
with a traveled couple from across the street.
Brass elephants tapestry-mantled
and other career souvenirs furnished
their home from federal years overseas,
now displaying a harvest of life in their 60s.

Brad's still in the hospital, the dog-walking lady
told us on Monday in front of our house.
Wasn't it awful what happened?
To our blank look, she said,
He fell off your roof. You didn't know?
Saturday Little League parents en route to the park
saw him lying on our concrete walkway,
called emergency rescue to rush him to care.
A Saturday Windward-side wedding
kept us away and from knowing
until the dog-walking lady's report.

The kind of person home-owning's made me
led my first call, not to Brad or his wife,
but an office lawyer who warned,
call your insurance people so they won't be surprised.

You didn't invite him to climb on your roof
but only to use the long-handled picker, right?
Does anyone know how he did it? Never mind.
Don't ask him—said our friend, the lawyer.

If they don't file a claim, there's nothing to do . . .
and nothing to say . . . the less said the better . . .
even 'sorry you're hurt' could be a mistake.
No 'Get Well' cards, said our friendly insurance advisor.

We waved to Brad on his walker
as he hobbled about in his driveway.

We smiled over at Brad on his crutches,
as he went for his daily walks,
first with his wife and then with a nurse.

We said, *Hi,* to Brad on his twin canes,
as he and nurse Mitzi crossed over to chat.

We talked with Brad on his lone cane,
Mitzi at his free elbow,
about the monkey pod trees (not the mangoes)
that scattered their pods on our lawn
and made the street smell in the spring.

We nodded to Brad now using a putter
to get to and from his new car.

Nice weather for golf, we risked, a month later
to Brad and then Mitzi, she hauling his clubs to
the trunk of his Lexus.

His wife drove off in their Benz to meetings and lunches.
Brad drove off for his morning and afternoon tees.

I called out to Brad and Mitzi, golf-carting,
one day from the road that goes by the course.
Brad's game, she called back, *is really improving!*

We were neighbors, not friends
and ignored the topic at hand,
his Siamese trophies hardly
the only elephants in the room.

From a party one night in their home,
sounds of his voice warmed with iced drinks,
maybe his favorite Red Label,
carried over the music
and out in the street where I heard:
Why would I want to do that?
It wasn't their fault! To a mumbled response,
Don't be silly! They had nothing to do with it.
They didn't tell me to climb on their roof!

That high-water mark of the topic receded
and proved to be first and last mention.

The subject never came up,
but a sign arose in the front yard: For Sale,
and one day a moving truck hauled
most of their insides away.
A smaller one came for the rest.

Only the dog-walking lady would tell us.
Brad's back is much better,
but he and his wife have split up.
He's moving in with his nurse—
her little place near the golf course . . .

Did he ever say why he was up on your roof?

The dog-lady seemed too wise not to know.
She and her pet were both sniffers.
I shook my head slowly, miming bewildered,
Still not clear on that yet, I dodged
with an agent's half answer.
People have their reasons,
I offered in boilerplate say-nothing,
and then more intently,
Do you think Brad got to keep the elephants?

THE UNCOMMON MANGO

Sally Sorenson

Mango Wars

Kazuo Akimoto's wife, Mimi, made the best mango cobbler on all O'ahu. Every February when his mango tree blossomed, filling the yard with sticky pollen, he imagined the smell of the sweet ripe fruit of summer. When the green nubs grew large enough to start counting, he already saw them red-gold and heavy on their long stems.

By late May the branches drooped low with their burden, and Kazuo pulled from the carport the long forked sticks he'd fashioned and used them to brace up the branches. Every other morning at 6:45 he uncoiled the garden hose and soaked the roots for ten minutes. He trimmed the jacaranda so the mango tree got maximum sunlight. Everything he could possibly do, he did to ensure a bountiful harvest for Mimi's delicious cobbler.

Everything except tie the hands of his neighbor, Tommy Ching. The tree hung over the property line into the Chings' backyard and, as Tommy pointed out, the roots also reached 'ewa for soil and water and nourishment. As though they'd find something worth absorbing beneath that gravel wilderness. Kazuo might not begrudge Tommy the overhanging fruit, but Tommy acted as though the tree itself belonged to him—Kazuo merely the caretaker of the trunk.

"Good you watering *our* tree, eh brah?" Tommy would say as he stepped into his slippers to retrieve the morning paper.

Kazuo longed to raise the nozzle and spray Tommy's potbelly when he turned, paper in hand, and sauntered back to read it on his lanai. Just once. Just enough to say, "It's *my* tree, my mangos, and that's why I'm watering it." But of course he never did. The Akimotos had lived next door to the Chings for thirty-five years. Both families' children had climbed this tree back in small-kid time, when they were younger than the grandchildren were today.

Mimi often said, "At least one family has to be good neighbors; it might as well be us."

She stopped with the *good neighbor* preaching two years ago. Early January, Kazuo came into the house in a fine rage. Tommy had driven nails into the trunk of the tree and, for good measure, also into the major branches that brushed his yard.

"A distressed tree produces more fruit," Tommy said, which sounded like a lot of hooey. The Chings' yard bore ramshackle proof of what Tommy didn't know—or care—about gardening. No apology for damage done. Kazuo awoke angry every morning for the next five months.

Then the mangos started to ripen. Dozens of them, pounds of them, fat and juicy as never before. Maybe it was just a very good year. Maybe Kazuo's care finally paid off. Judging from Tommy's satisfied smirk, something more had happened.

No apology from Kazuo either.

This year could be even better than that record crop. Kazuo hauled a big green tarp from the garage, spread it on the lawn, and hosed off the mold and dust. He wasn't taking any chances with losing fruit that fell prematurely and rolled too close to the property line. When the tarp dried, he bunched it around the stick props and over driveway pavement. Prevent bruises. Fruit closest to the border already showed the first faint tinge of color on green cheeks, so he repositioned the branch prop to sit more firmly on Akimoto soil.

Next morning as dawn filtered through the thick canopy of mango leaves, Kazuo set his coffee cup on the lanai railing and bent to uncoil the hose. Satisfaction spread like caffeine through his veins as he dragged the hose past yesterday's improved limb support, but as he rounded the trunk and twisted the nozzle, he stopped. All the fruit on the Ching side of the limb had been stripped. Gone. None lay in the bunched folds of the tarp.

He watered ten minutes, waited another twenty before rapping on Tommy's back door. Tommy answered, not the least bit chagrined that a dozen mangos sat on the kitchen counter in plain sight. "Mornin'."

Kazuo stabbed his index finger in the direction of the plundered fruit. "You couldn't wait to take 'em? They're green!"

"Doreen and I, we like eat 'em green with shoyu. Thought I'd take some of our half now." Tommy opened the door a little wider in invitation. "There's a few sliced, marinating, in the fridge. Want some?"

Half? Half! Kazuo couldn't utter a word. He was so appalled at being offered a taste of his own fruit that he stalked home.

For the next two weeks he spent long hours every day doing yard work. He edged his already neat lawn, fertilized Mimi's herb garden, and generally kept an eye on the mango tree. He and Mimi ate most meals on the lanai. He shifted the table and chairs to catch the shade, but really so he could see the whole yard. Happily, the Chings went to stay with their son and grandchildren over Memorial Day, so Kazuo invited Mimi out to dinner. She chose Sekiya's. He didn't object.

By mid-June Kazuo's good fortune covered one whole side of the yard, so he parked in the street rather than the driveway. On Friday he awoke in the pale light to strange sounds, like an aluminum ladder being dragged. He threw on shorts and a tee shirt before opening the back door.

A row of plastic grocery bags flopped on either side of the ladder. Tommy busily filled another bag from his perch on the rungs. "My wife's going to make chutney. While the mangos are still little bit firm, little bit tangy, we'll take half."

Kazuo watched in horror while his mind furiously did the math. "You cannot *take half* every time you get hungry," he fired back. "This is *my* tree! You're picking *my* fruit!"

Tommy climbed down. "You leave 'em on the tree so long, I thought you don't like mangos. I hate to see 'em go to waste."

"*Waste?* I never!" The hours spent tending each year's crop! How could Tommy think he would let them get overripe, become food for mynas and thieving bulbuls? Kazuo's eyes narrowed as Tommy carried three bags into his house.

Quickly, he snatched two full bags and spirited them through his own kitchen door. "Mimi," he barked as he pulled out the big canning pot and slammed it on the stove. Then he hurried out to the carport and armed himself with bushel baskets and his long-handled fruit picker. He'd never cared much for chutney, but he could certainly develop a taste for its bitter sweetness. Starting today.

Joseph Stanton

Finches at Dusk in the Treetops

I love these drum-brush flutterings,
this crescendo of tiny, piping songs
I already hear as I climb
the stairs to find them.
I am rising
to the roof at dusk
to a kingdom of wings,
finches converging from all sides,
roosting in the treetops,
some re-circling again and again
as they jockey for perches,
a game of very musical chairs.

I stand motionless on my rooftop
and let their excited diving flights
whiz around me,
as if I were just
a tree trunk or a rock;
some bullet past, inches from my ear,
sweet whispers of wind.

Most dusks I estimate
200 waxbills,
50 chestnut mannikins,
and our single, precious shama thrush,
lifting its gorgeous, lilting song.

I speak of the splendor
of these massive featherings
to anyone who will listen.
But a friend rails
angrily against them,

"If I stand in the bamboo,"
he snarls,
"shit rains down on my head."

"Then don't," I solemnly advise,
"stand in the bamboo."

Moriso Teraoka

The Accordion

Unless there is a compelling reason, my Sunday mornings are spent at the Aloha Swap Meet. My wife Fumino and I spend half of our Sundays walking the rows of vendors' stalls.

My friends and I gathered at a stall operated by David and Joyce Kamimura. The Kamimuras supply anthuriums for our Buddhist altars at home. His parents from the Big Island send the flowers every week for their many customers.

I still continue this practice by myself since my wife passed away two years ago.

The Sunday prior to Labor Day was no exception. It was a small three-octave accordion that caught my attention. Nostalgically, I picked up the accordion and asked the vendor, "How much?"

"Fifteen dollars," he said.

I laid the accordion back down on the display mat. It was not in tune.

I wondered what happened to the accordion I brought home from Italy after World War II ended in 1945. I remembered that I threw it away, but I thought I would check on it later.

I learned to play a few simple tunes including "Aloha 'Oe" from a prisoner of war.

How did I get the accordion?

The war ended in Europe in May of 1945. The 100th/442nd Regimental Combat Team had breached the Gothic Line in Italy and the German army was retreating north. I think my Company reached Alexandria when the war ended on May 2 in Italy. The German army gave up their arms and surrendered en masse at Ghedi Airport. The German soldiers also gave up their many personal belongings: Luger pistols and Leica cameras were some of the sought-after war souvenirs. Among my loot was the accordion. I don't know why, but there it was.

After almost a month of processing the surrendering German army, the combat team folded our tents, packed up, and my 3rd Platoon of Company D traveled south to Leghorn where we were assigned to guard a group of POWs who worked at the facility moving military supplies at the dock. Our platoon took over a farmhouse near the POW compound. I believe the farming family maintained their residence in the back of our quarters.

Our platoon's daily duty routine was to march the workers to the waterfront warehouse, stand watch, and return the POWs to their compound. This was a period of leisure. Someone was always on a three-day or one-week pass. Switzerland, Rome, and other recreation centers were established by the armed services. A POW was assigned to clean our living quarters.

One of the POWs was an elderly worker who would not have been in the service had it not been for the desperate situation the Germans were in later in the war. The elderly man must have noticed the accordion on the floor adjacent to my bunk bed during his daily cleanup of our quarters. One day he asked me in perfect English if he could play on the instrument, "Go ahead," I said.

How he enjoyed the accordion. I would sit next to him on my bunk bed and listen to his music. He told me that he was a professor of music in the University of Munich. I asked him how old he was. I forgot his exact answer, but he said he was seventy-something. Hitler's army was desperate to fill the ranks in their armed services and drafted him for clerk duties, which he could do. He used to obtain permission from the guard in the compound after his evening chores were done to play the accordion for us.

One evening I asked him if he would teach me to play the accordion and, without hesitation, he said, "Sure." And the lesson began. I knew how to read simple music notes for I used to be in a high school band in Hilo and reading a simple music sheet was not unfamiliar.

By the time his departure orders came for him to return to Germany, I had learned to play "Home Sweet Home," "Aloha 'Oe," and a few German folk tunes.

His name was Robert Theirfelder. I bid him fond farewell and gave him cartons of cigarettes and chocolate. Cigarettes were worth their weight in gold, and I was sure that he and my gifts would reach home safely. But of course he went home not knowing if his family was still alive in Germany. Those were the facts of life during the war days.

Before the year was up, I too was on my way home to Hawai'i, and I was discharged the day before Christmas in 1945.

After I came home from the Swap Meet that Sunday morning, I looked for the accordion, only to find that I must have thrown it away. I placed anthuriums on Fumino's altar and placed another vase of anthuriums for Robert Theirfelder, my teacher.

Moriso Teraoka

We Go Catch Frog

We no more nothing to do today,
Why? You thinking of something?
Yea, Adorable said he like eat frog.
You sure he going buy the frogs wen we catch em?
He said he gonna give us 50 cents if we catch six.
Wow! We go.

Where we going, Pukihae?
Yea I know the spot where get plenty bullfrog
Teru, your house get empty rice bag? And we need some red cloth
I go ask my madda and she can give me one piece of red cloth.
You think the three of us can hook six frog?
Yea, no worry, goin to be easy wea I goin take you.

* * *

You see the sewer pipe?
Yea, I see the pipe
No make loud noise, you see the frog?
They all over the place.

I never hook frog befo you goin show me how?
Yea, hook a piece of red cloth on the hook
No make noise, dangle the hook over the frog
Hide, the hook too high, the frog no can see the cloth
Okay now, the frog think a bug is flying.

You got one, put em in the rice bag and take off the hook
You see easy yea, we going to catch six in no time.

* * *

I neva clean frog before,
No worry I show you how.
Hide, go get some salt from the
Kitchen, and bring one sharp knife

Watch me, I goin clean one
You see, first hold the frog by the head with the left hand
Oh I forgot, put some salt on the fingers so the frog no slip away
Take the knife and cut the head half way just below the eyes
After you do that put the knife on the side
Now hold the top of the head with the right hand,
Hold tight, put some more salt on the left hand fingers,
and hold the body by the head
Now pull down the skin with the right hand
You see, the skin going inside out. Look all the guts with the skin,
Chop off the front and back feet
Flush the skin down the wash house toilet

That was easy yea, okay everybody clean two each and we finish the job.
Adorable goin to be happy and we goin buy ice cake with the fifty cents.

Bill Teter

Why She Was Not There

I wish I could say I am depressed. At least I could give what I'm feeling some weight, some substance. But I'm not. I'm lonely, I'm sad, but I cannot point to anything to justify what I feel. I live in a beautiful place, I have work that I love, and I'm driving now along a road in one of my favorite places in the world. True, I'm remembering that the last time I was here I was with Lianne, and that was a hard, miserable time. She'd decided to break up with me in the week I was up on the mainland before she flew to San Francisco to join me (though she never officially told me until we were on our way back to Honolulu). The long drive up the coast that afternoon along this very stretch of highway in weather identical to today's—well, she was very gentle, all things considered, but the silence as we drove through these trees that day was not.

I've always loved this road, these trees, the way the highway eases around curves in the land and breaks out from walls of trees into moments of light and distance before the trees close in again. But I've come to associate this world with that day. For much of the year we were together I'd wanted Lianne to see these redwoods, this place that had mattered to me so much, and she did see them, and she appreciated them. But we saw them separately, even though we were traveling together. I guess I'm hoping that if I can find a place Lianne and I did not visit, then I can maybe, I don't know, reclaim this part of the world. It didn't sound like a stupid idea until just now.

She never did say what it was, but I suspect it went all the way back to the beginning. We were after all sort of pushed together by mutual friends; we hadn't really found each other. I remember that night very clearly; we sat on the bed we'd been given to share, drinking wine and laughing nervously at our unsubtle friends. "Do you think this is a set-up?" she asked me.

"Yeah," I answered, and then, in one of the last acts of personal courage I can remember laying claim to, I said, "I don't particularly mind. Do you?" No, she said, she didn't. Even so, I suspect she felt rushed and pressured. Everyone we knew wanted us together and was not shy about reminding us.

We drove this road that day largely in silence. The fog lay thick in the treetops. In a sudden break in the trees we found ourselves along the edge of the ocean. She asked me to pull over.

Ahead of us redwoods soared into the gray. To our left a sharp cliff dropped off into the slate gray Pacific. "It's hard to believe that's the same ocean we have in Hawai'i," she said. I didn't say anything; I didn't think she was really looking for conversation. We could hear sea lions calling to one another from the rocks offshore; it was hard to see them in the distance and through the sea spray. The wind blew a swirling sound in the foreground, and the surf below was a low, unchanging background growl. Along a breaking wave I watched a team of three brown pelicans.

"They were almost extinct when I was in high school," I said, pointing. "I'm always glad when I see them now." She just nodded.

God, how I wanted to talk to her. I didn't even know what I wanted to say or hear. She'd always been a quiet woman, and I was used to that. But this was a silence that I could feel eroding something between us. She hadn't even said that anything was wrong. But she had made it clear that she didn't really want to talk about anything other than what was safe—in other words, about anything except us. And I wanted to honor that. But here she was, among the coastal redwoods of Trinity County, a place I'd wanted to share with her, and I felt I couldn't even take her hand. The surf called restlessly from below, the sea lions yelped in the distance, the pelicans disappeared into mist; the redwoods surrounded us in a silence that was a presence, and a light mist began to fall. It ought to have been a holy moment.

"I'm cold," she said.

"Me too," I answered, though I enjoyed it. A week ago we had been grumbling about the muggy Makiki nights. "We should probably get going."

I opened the door for her, and when I closed it I stood for a moment and tried to take everything in. I tried also to find some patience, or faith, or something. She'd talked about clinging men in her past, possessive men, and I was not going to be that for her.

I got in and settled behind the wheel. As I reached for the ignition she put her hand on my forearm. I don't believe we had touched since I'd kissed her at the airport in San Francisco. "I think this is about the most beautiful place I've ever seen," she said to me. "Thank you for bringing me here."

"You're welcome," I answered. "I hoped you'd like it." I glanced out my side window rather than at her. "It's quiet. I've always loved how it's so, I don't know, simple."

Her hand was still on my arm. "You're a good person."

I smiled lamely; under the best of circumstances I don't take compliments well, and this one felt like a non sequitur. I started the car and pulled back out onto the road. She moved her hand to my leg and left it there for a while as I drove.

We stopped for the night in Crescent City. The gravel crunched beneath our wheels as I turned into the lot. An orange vacancy light gleamed down on us, and a smaller red light read "Office" from a window with green curtains. Two stories, maybe fifteen rooms. Two other cars in the lot. It was November; not many people came to Crescent City this time of year.

I tried to still my heart. "I'll go get us a room," I told her. It was dark now and bitter wet and cold. "I'll leave the engine running." As I reached for the door handle she put her hand again on my forearm.

"I think we'll need two beds," she said.

Our eyes met for, I think, the first time that day. "Sure," I said. "Of course." I stepped out into the cold. I hunched my shoulders and tried to walk steadily to the office. I felt hollowed out. It wasn't about sex (though only a week earlier we had laughed together about the wild motel stories we'd never be able to share with anyone). I was just longing for simple touch, for contact that I knew wouldn't be coming.

Inside the office I could smell burnt coffee. A beat-up boom box was playing on the desk behind the counter—Townes Van Zandt:

Time among the pine trees
It felt like breath of air
Usually I just walk these streets
And tell myself to care.

The night clerk looked at me oddly when I asked for two beds. "Hawai'i, huh?" he said as he looked at the address I wrote. "Like to go there some day, see all them hula girls. What the hell brings you here?" It was a comment more than a question. He took an imprint of my credit card and gave me the key. He moved slowly and scratched compulsively at a small raw red patch on his left arm.

It was raining when I stepped back outside. I turned up my collar and headed for the car. I was thinking about Van Zandt's last words as I closed the office door:

And I'll be thinkin' 'bout you
And all the places I have been
And why you were not there.

And I was thinking of the clerk's comment: *What the hell brings you here?*

I saw her silhouette in the darkened car. I tried to remember the sound of the wind in the redwoods, the ocean surf, and the call of the sea lions. But I couldn't. At that moment I couldn't even remember how her voice had sounded when she said, "Thank you for bringing me here." And I sure as hell couldn't remember Hawai'i—the rich blues of sea and sky, the heat, the rustle of ti leaves against the screen in Lianne's cottage window when the wind blew. All I could hear was the gravel beneath my feet and, in the distance, a lonely truck rumbling down Highway 1 towards Eureka.

As I approached the car I could see Lianne in the dim twilight. She was staring ahead at nothing I could see. Now that I think of it, so was I.

Mark Thiel

THE ENGAGEMENT

1.

We had lived in that house shaped
like a chapel for more than a year.

A white curtain billowed in and out
through a wooden window frame—

A Bulbul began to sing from its tattered repertoire
and the bright head of morning
threaded its way over the skyline.

Remember the Mantis that loved
to fall backwards into the Bok Choy—
so green it disappeared into the landscape?

We would get down on our knees to find
where it had fallen and laugh at how wild
and erratic it waved its arms.

We loved that persistent hope something
would always be within reach—
and as far as we could tell, it always was.

Blue and red veins across the sky again,
so much there we never quite understood—

The exact borders of empire,
How to measure the seasons,
Or why the clouds fell across the familiar every day at noon.

And if we had been able we would have held ourselves
up into that first light and disappeared into the backdrop.

All that we hold in our morning mouth
are sweetened hieroglyphics.

2.

High noon and the afternoon kingdom
coos its broken heart.
All day spent in the countryside
where all this excess light is just loose vocabulary.

A flower print blanket spread out over the sand,
a picnic basket with a broken metal hinge,
the first hints of evening at the tips of our tongues.

We watch a pair of Golden Plovers
huddle at the surf's edge—
Quietly their plumage tells us the whole story.

For better or for worse
we are at the edge of these things—
One half of our bodies buried here below the ironwood
and the other half buried back home at Skookum Point.

Somehow there is always a horizon beyond the horizon—
We just have to wait for it.

3.

In August the mango trees that guard our prayers
drop their plush wombs onto the evening street,
and we lay our night bodies along these
flowered equatorials.

These things we forget to speak of
somehow become the most lovely.

Your sleeping body beneath the bedding,
a silver engagement ring blinking
like an unopened star,
dried ti leaf leis hung on unused door handles—

When it begins again, the obvious I mean,
I promise to see it all better.

Delaina Thomas

When I Was Eight

for Baban

the light of me shaped like a worm
escaped from my hands into a thicket
no one else saw it happen
I looked around
a vague smile remaining on my face

I searched the singing roots of plants
my grandmother watered
in coffee cans lining the Pālolo house
I followed her broken English numbly
half expecting her hand to open
with my worm of light in it
as easily as she might turn an earthworm
back into the soil

her worn and gentle hands revealed themselves
made of aloneness as I grew
when she could garden no more
I massaged her small feet
a shine over the wrinkles

after she died the orchids and anthuriums
transitioned to exist only on rain and sunlight
her broken jizu was handed to me by Auntie Ethel
I wrapped it in a hankie
and put it in the jewelry box

sometimes I still see it
spilling over her hands
clasped in front of the mamansan
light through the morning window

is waving like threads in the crystal beads
it's actually *rippling*
I'm not imagining it
driving somewhere or cooking
trying to hear what my sons are saying to me

pueo & popoki
© GK 1980
CANE HAUL ROAD, LTD. HAWAII

Ken Tokuno

Talk about Romance

After thirty years of marriage, Romance becomes the knack
For telling me, your husband, that my breath stinks like rotting
Flesh even while you admit to me that my lips are still as
Soft as marshmallows

And my being able to tell you that you eat too many carrots,
Which is why your hands are orange, yet are still nice to caress
As I walk with you on the satin sands at Kailua Beach late
On Sunday mornings.

This is all the result, My Dear, of nothing less than the vast
Comfort that comes from being so used to having each
Other to pick on and yet I can still wonder over that fresh
Flower in your hair

Or you, the song I learned to play that you never noticed
Me practice. Now even as my life grows drowsy with age,
I do not fear that long sleep where my dreams will be
Eternally you.

Jean Yamasaki Toyama

The Ant Massacre

"I don't know what's wrong. Some keys seem to be stuck," she said, leading us to the far corner of her living room. A dried out Christmas tree stood next to the Hamilton upright. It was March.

The piano tuner looked at me, lifting his eyebrows knowingly.

"Have you been seeing any ants lately?" he asked.

"How did you know?" she replied.

"Well, Christmas trees and plants around the piano is a no-no," he answered, pointing at the dried up poinsettia on the piano. "You shouldn't put any plants near a piano. Attracts ants."

"Really?! No one ever told me that. I so sorry," she blurted.

"He's not scolding you," I added, "just letting you know." Clients sometimes misinterpret my husband's bald statements. Really, he's just giving them information, but because of his stern tone they think otherwise.

"When ants find a cozy place where they're not disturbed, they make a nest. Making a nest means gumming up the place. Their body produces a very sticky substance. You'll probably see some today. It will be everywhere inside your piano," he warned.

Mildred recoiled.

As if to confirm this analysis a few ants came up from between the keys, flaring their antennae before they slithered back in between them. The piano tuner tinkled a few keys; a few more ants came up for a look. "We'll need the vacuum."

"OK, I know," I said, heading for the door.

By the time I had returned from the car with the portable vacuum cleaner, the piano tuner had removed the key slip and the sideboards that held it in place. "Where's the nearest outlet?" I asked, holding the electric plug in my hand.

"Behind the Christmas tree," Mildred answered. She had been standing there, helpless all the while.

I groaned inside and crawled behind the tree. Each time I nudged it a shower of needles cascaded on me. "Sorry about the mess," I apologized, trying to leave the irony out of my voice.

"Don't worry," Mildred replied, ignorant of the omission. "I should have gotten rid of it months ago."

Emerging from behind the tree, I shook my head and rained needles.

In the meantime the tuner was about to remove the middle keys. "Ready?" he asked. Yes, I nodded, holding the long, hungry nozzle above the keys. He lifted five keys with one thrust of his fingers. As he did so, they came frothing out—black and white, frenzied bodies carrying white sacs in their mandibles. To save the colony, no doubt. From previous ant hunts, we guessed that the sacs were baby ants. The white membranes shaped like minuscule peanuts were carried like precious cargo. Nothing could be seen inside. But there was no time to examine the contents. At first they scurried in every direction, at times bumping into each other. They were leaderless, just frantic.

Because of their size these carpenter ants looked fierce, a moving canopy of warriors. As more and more piano keys were lifted, hundreds of agitated bodies overflowed from hidden places into exposed spaces. The wiggling bodies went in all directions. Only a few seconds later they seemed to be following some signal and moved in one direction. This made it easier to suck them up with the vacuum. A fever of emotion. I whipped into action, fanning the nozzle across the keys, sucking up as many mad ants as possible. I moved it back and forth, up and down, into the exposed crevices, swooped over moving black and white dots from one end of the key bed to the other.

"Don't move," I warned my husband and sucked up some errant ants moving up his arm.

The nozzle passed swiftly over darting bodies. No escape. Sucked up into oblivion, reduced to debris in the dust of other old pianos in the vacuum bag, I thought.

"Watch, watch, watch," I uttered in staccato beat, falling to my knees now, following with my nozzle the trail of ants heading down the leg of the piano. The piano tuner jumped out of the way.

Mildred just stood there, frozen, as she watched all these unwanted guests being scooped up. "I didn't know, I didn't know," she repeated. "How did they get here?"

"They were born here," the piano tuner explained, pointing his screwdriver at the piano. "Do you play the piano?" he asked, placing the last of the keys on the floor beyond the tree.

"No, no one plays. It was my daughter's piano, but she's away at school. She came back for Christmas but didn't play. Didn't have time and said it was out of tune. So I thought I'd have it tuned, just in case she came home on a visit. But, no, no one plays," she said as if in a trance.

"Perfect incubator. The piano is perfect, warm and cozy because of the damp chaser. And if no one plays, it's quiet. They've been multiplying here all this time. A perfect ant condo," he repeated.

"Happy, happy and safe. That's what they were," I jumped in. "Not so happy now," I added. "Good thing they're not marabunta," I chuckled.

"What?" Mildred queried, coming out of her daze.

"What are you talking about?" my husband asked, a slight irritation in his voice.

"You remember, don't you? The marabunta, the marabunta, from the movie, *The Naked Jungle.* There were millions and millions of swarming ants. They looked like a moving carpet. They ate humans. Good thing, these aren't marabunta."

The piano tuner gave his wife a dirty look.

Joe Tsujimoto

Night Blooming Cereus (La Pietra, 1988)

While the poet returned us to the shore, reduced our bodies
to potassium, pitch, iodine, and oil, dispersing us again
into the sea, I recognized the black beret, the horn-rimmed
glasses. Leon Edel. Drenched in torchlight. Seated at a patio
table with cronies as white and squeezed of succulence as he,
my old teacher. After the rest had read, according to our
appearance in the Review—according to seniority or age or our
prospective deaths (were things simpler)—Wyndnagle and I would
visit with Edel as he stood absorbed before the punchbowl filled
with wine, shaking our hands out of public habit, not trying
(having tried) to remember our faces; nor wanting to be
fruitlessly reminded, while nibbling at the edge of a fig as dark as
the vast night beyond the courtyard arches, from which,
like distant piano music, like grapes, a voice arises.

"I liked your poems very much," she said to me. She was petite and
dark-haired as Natalie Wood who died by drowning; dressed
in a watery sari, a bird of paradise from across the Ganges.
From the old country. Where I would have pressed my palms
together, bowing to greet the divinity in her; were I in Chandrapore,
in a black olive grove, and could smell the fragrance that ripens
all things. Then, like a lover, she passed a translucent arm through
his and led him away, elegantly, gesturing in the night air.

Amy Uyematsu

As We Walk

He says the sound of waves makes
him too sad to want to live at the beach.
Wave after wave, a melancholy echo.
But if I could move my house to the shore,
where it's warm enough to keep the windows
open at night, I'd position my pillow
so the last thing I hear before dream is
high tide's pounding, each thundering
crash followed by a calm, receding whisper,
over and over, this sound drowning out all others,
my own sadness part of an endless song, until I know
no sweeter sleep than ocean calling, calling.

Amy Uyematsu

The Accusation

my husband tells me I'm crazy but I've got eyes
he's just like my Jose back home
only thinks of one thing
little girls old ladies same
once we driving on the highway I catch
him leering at woman must be 80 or more
'stop the car' I command
nearly fall out the door, leave him for good
but he says I'm the only one
and I want to believe
after all we've only been married two years
he tells me he'd given up looking
him already 76 when we met
and me 51 when I became wife number four
love real happy for a while
he takes me to Las Vegas and I get to play
every day the quarter video game
I always select the same machine
I swear it likes me best
since I always win 5, 10, even 20 dollars
while people around me sour
about these one-armed bandits
but my husband says our hotel bill
is getting 'out of hand' so we come back
and I'm all the time bored
I cook and clean and water my potted plants
still too much time so I do the morning crossword
proud my English is good enough to fill the blanks
I gossip with Manila girlfriends
e-mail sisters in Hawai'i and France
I crochet dresses for my growing rack of blue-
eyed dolls from 99-cent store
no matter how busy I can't forget

that picture of his wife
in the box on top cupboard shelf
the first time I see her I cry
'look at her' is all I can say
I almost tear the photo to shreds
but my husband calls me silly
'she's old now all white-haired
who doesn't turn any more heads'
lucky for me I still do with tight
black slacks and sling-back pumps
my husband says it makes him proud
to have me at his side
but I know how all of them think
and my husband no better
all the time I watch him close
like last week he sneaks our shopping cart
to a different line
claims a shorter wait
who does he think he's fooling
I can see his eyes undressing
the smiling checker
I yell at him all the way home
he insists 'I'm innocent'
even laughs at my upset
so mean to flaunt
that filthy heart
why should I trust when
just this morning he clicks on TV
to women's soccer finals
I rush over to block the screen
'you're disgusting' I scream
'lusting at those teenage girls'
I make him turn it off
my outrage quickly turns to pleas
all I'm asking for is one
just one good man
who'll just be only mine

Sylvia Watanabe

Atomic Histories

1. The Names of Clouds (1945–1992)

These are the clouds our hands have made:
Tapestry   Adze   Boxcar   Rivet

Clouds like curly-haired women stretching their long necks up:
Sappho   Grable   Diabla   Eva

Clouds rising like umbels of Queen Anne's lace, blooming in the sky and falling down:
Zinnia   Apple   Mushroom   Ghost

Trinity was first, but Bravo was biggest.
Little Boy and Fat Man. Able, then Baker.

One by one, they bloomed and fell:
Priscilla
Gilroy
Olive
King
George
Duchess
Emerson
Darwin
Pascal
Boomer
Ipecac
Gasbuggy
Granny
Tot
Stinger   Wasp   Hornet
Torch   Knife   Hatchet

Screamer
one thousand one hundred Calamities

Bee Dead
How?

2. Little Boy

A charred pair of shoes she had no face
A shadow on the steps he'd turned to look
A clock stopped at 8:15 the insides were fused
Burns shaped like birds and flowers she wore her favorite dress
A boy in rags it was his skin
A tattered dress in a tree she blew away

A door had opened into the air There
you were then you weren't

3. Song of Removal: Bikini Atoll, March 1946

The trees comb the air with their long green hands. The sway of dancing girls. Bright heat. The little fish shine beneath the waves. I was born in Bikini, and I long to go back.

They loaded us onto the ships; we watched from the decks as the houses burned. We waved to the burning houses, the trees, the beach, the gardens and graves. We were told that soon we could go back.

Then, twice, there was a blinding flash. The first cracked the sky. The second turned the ocean inside out. And something that was always there, but behind, slipped through—a strange, long-necked cloud with a roaring inside.

But we were safe, we were told, far away from home. One island in the middle of nowhere was like another island in the middle of nowhere.

Once we lived on Bikini, but we cannot go back.

4. After Bravo

for Chiyoko Tamayose

They call them Turtle. Octopus. Giant clam. The ones with the spines protruding from their backs, they call Marlin Fish. Some, with the split skulls, their brains falling out into their mothers' laps they call Coconut. That one, picked off a human vine, is a bunch of grapes.

And this, they call Jellyfish—no limbs or eyes, no bones, only mouth and breath.

I mien eo wot elotak emij rej kalibwene.
And the moment   it was born   it died   they   buried it.

Beryl Allene Young

A Mind in Flux

The mind is a mirror catching light,
reflecting it like the sun's rim brightening
after eclipse. The fruit nectar in my glass
sweetens my mouth as light intensifies,
but my mouth is quivering, shattering
apart like a cracking hourglass,
and I am a tiny spider taking its leap of faith
into eternity on the coattails of the wind.
Jumping, letting out its silk line,
it drifts to a new coast, a new shore
beyond what it knows. Cascading
from a plane, I leap,
a skydiver hurtling earthwards,
my parachute streaming upwards
like a long umbilical cord
before it opens and inflates,
becoming a giant white mushroom
billowing up above.
His shadow speaks, darkens across my forehead
and down the left side of my body
like an old rag thrown over my shoulder.
He is not my father, but a lesser buddha
wearing saffron, one who absorbs sunlight
and carries me as easily as he carries
a bowl of water in his cupped hands.
Playing with the gold tassels
of a ceremonial hair ornament,
I put it on, the sunlight shining
on the tassels braided into my black hair
like a golden seam that flashes light off
like a bright sword. Enjoying the shade,
I sit on a stone bench in the East-West Center's

Japanese garden watching the gold carp
swimming in and out amongst the lily pads
in the pond, their translucent fins fanning
the algae-strewn waters, ducks paddling
and calling from the water's surface.
I dip my rough, red hands into the waters.
Grown old, wary, and fretful,
I agonize over the picking of the water lilies.
I weep at the whispered theft of the golden carp
from the Japanese pond and garden.

Darrell H. Y. Lum

GRANT KAGIMOTO: Artist Profile & Portfolio

I. History

Grant Kagimoto, owner of Cane Haul Road, is noted for screen printing images of local life on bags, dish towels, and T-shirts. Kagimoto and other UH art students started Cane Haul Road in 1977, parlaying their screen printing skills into a business. Having no business plan to speak of, the other partners eventually fell by the wayside, leaving Kagimoto with his savings, the enthusiasm of youth, and a curiosity to see how far he could get.

In a time where T-shirts are machine-printed in high resolution using a dozen or more screens with inks that glow in the dark, change in the sunlight, or glitter and sparkle, Cane Haul Road may be one of the last local screen printing companies that prints by hand using a limited palette, achieving a classic folk art feel to its products.

So how does this almost local boy, almost katonk, almost military brat, become the head of a company that arguably represents all things local? While Kagimoto modestly attributes it to luck and being at the right place and right time (during the era of the Cazimeros, Olomana, and Booga Booga), clearly there is something more: a heightened vision and awareness of surroundings and identity, an ability to befriend people and to fit in, and a keen sense of self, place, and community.

Born in Hilo, schooled in Okinawa, educated at UHM, and, although never coming close to having worked on a "haul cane" road, Grant Kagimoto has managed to capture local culture, values, and, in his words, "all that is special about Hawai'i" in his apparel and product designs. He admits that had he not left Hilo, he would not have ended up where he is today.

While his designs are decidedly local, Kagimoto's experiences living away from the Islands made him a keen observer of his Hilo cousins whenever he returned for visits. Growing up and living on base in Okinawa, looking Japanese but unable to speak it, then returning to Hilo every two years to what he calls his emotional home and the Pidgin that he no longer could speak, Kagimoto developed his eye for detail, visual imagery, sound, and word play.

Visits back to Honolulu and Hilo as a youngster must have been difficult: "Coming back to Hawai'i at 8, 10, and 12 and listening to how people spoke, I realized my siblings and I were odd ducks. We dressed differently, spoke differently, our diet was more haolefied, yet this was my family. I started picking up on a lot of little things that my cousins did that made Hawai'i special and different. And seeing people in drapes, jac-shirts, bouffant hairdos, hot rods was really something. After all, all I knew was living on an Army base and having mostly white friends. And I didn't speak Japanese or go off base much. We didn't protest the Vietnam War. I only knew that some kids' fathers were away for six months at a time. "

Perhaps the key to Kagimoto's deep sense of the Islands and local identity is his parents' admonition that differences on base were because "We are from Hawai'i" and not because "We are Japanese; those guys are Okinawan; those guys are Filipino; and so on."

Lucky too, in his view, that his immigrant ancestors were allowed to live among the Hawaiians a hundred years ago. "Lucky that we grew up with their generosity and that affected us too."

His commitment to this particular ethos, to celebrate who we are as local folk, is reflected in his community service to the Mō'ili'ili Community Center, the Mayor's Office on Culture and the Arts, TEMARI, and other organizations.

Perhaps being away from the day-to-day business of local living provided his nostalgic “nowadays not like before” point of view, in many ways stuck in the 50s and 60s. This idyllic view is perhaps what draws us to his designs, along with his decidedly wry sense of humor.

In many ways, his popular Home Sweet Hawai‘i design of an old plantation house and the words “country stays, simpler ways, plantation days” sums it all up for Kagimoto and Cane Haul Road.

Illustration: Arthur Kodani

II. The Designs

How did designs like Musubi and Friends and Club Musubi become icons of all things local? A musubi with bunny ears? And his/her/its friends are rabbits wearing T-shirts depicting saimin, teri beef (a sumo wrestler), shave ice, ume surprise, green mango, and a lunch wagon.

Inspired to become a graphic designer after a lecture by visiting designer Bruce Hopper in Duane Preble's Art 101 course at UH, Kagimoto has sketchbooks dating back to 1977 which give insight to the musings of an artist who often plays with words as much as with visual ideas, usually starting with written notes and tiny thumbnails before developing one of the over 400 designs produced in the past 34 years. Ideas from 30 years ago find their way into today's designs, attesting to their timelessness.

There is a strong graphic and draftsman-like precision to his work, focusing often on plantation era items, old style furniture, and familiar

symbols and icons (fruits and vegetables, floral quilt designs, family crests, food, crayons, toys). He still occasionally hand-cuts a stencil on silk screening film (harking back to the early methods of screen printing), carves linoleum to create a block print, or etches a reversed image (white on black) on "board" with a teasing needle. He says he likes the feeling of not having complete control of the knife or cutter, giving the work a simple, spontaneous feel. He occasionally uses fellow artist Art Kodani to execute the final drawings but the designs are entirely Kagimoto's.

As it turns out, art imitates life in many of the designs:

Ume Surprise – One of his earliest designs on a canvas tote actually comes from Kagimoto's dislike of ume and, faced with a box of musubi

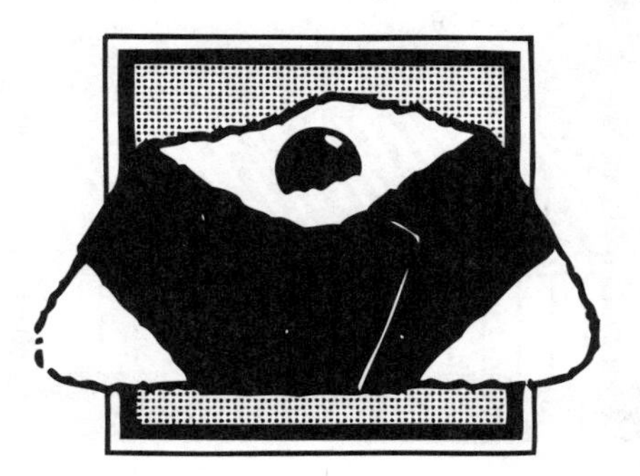

(some with and some without ume), his brother and sister would warn "watch out for the ume surprise."

Hilo Lullaby – Along with the words "rain on totan roof" depicting rain falling on the corrugated metal roofs typical of Hilo homes. As a youngster flying into Hilo and seeing all the rusty rooftops he wondered why the houses didn't use regular shingles like Honolulu. His cousins told him that they always fell asleep to the sound of the rain on the roof while Honolulu people couldn't sleep because of the rain falling on the totan.

Engalish Standard School Rejeck – Turns out Kagimoto was, in fact, an English Standard School reject. Although his brother and sister attended Hilo's Riverside School (English Standard), Kagimoto attended Union School (called "onion" school by its non-English Standard students). And when he first arrived in Okinawa with his Hilo Pidgin, people asked his mother what language he was speaking!

Illustration: Arthur Kodani

Illustration: Arthur Kodani

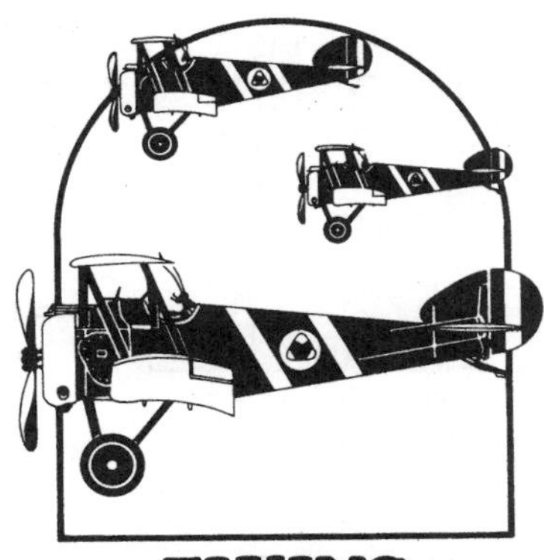

waist thickening
fat city

hair thinning
hat city

vision fading
tri-focal city

Illustration: Arthur Kodani

MAF (middle-aged futs) and OFC (old futs club) – Not surprisingly, aging is a common theme in his sketchbooks and in some of the popular designs. And one of his personal favorites: Drugs, naps, and rock 'n roll. He explains, "I take a lot of medicine, love a nap, and still listen to rock 'n roll."

The aging theme becomes more apparent in his 1991-93 sketchbook:

Middle age is like beef stew plate lunch: more and more vegetables and less and less meat.

Middle aged is

When clerks start calling you sir or ma'm
When your high school clothes make a fashion return
When the car you drove in college becomes a classic
When you start sounding like your parents
When your waist size matches your age
When bedtime becomes 10:00 pm
When pop music becomes "noise"

Illustration: Arthur Kodani

When you start talking about your cholesterol level
When your skin clears
When your eyebrows grow like weeds (out of control)
When bran (roughage) becomes an important part of your diet
When your favorite music is on the oldies channel
When writing notes to yourself replaces memory
When comfortable replaces fashionable clothes

While life is not just a musubi with rabbit ears, Kagimoto manages to take our everyday worries and treat them with a matter-of-fact clarity that puts things into perspective:

Makule, not make
Deep kim chee
Bachi, what your mother told you
Mister Urusai, he so samurai
Flying cockaroach
Make Die Dead Exterminators

And one that was sketched in 1993 but never produced, "Tropical depression, had it all already: rent, housing, traffic."

Cane Haul Road, Hawai'i

Kailua Pig

surfboards by Porky

cane haul road ltd., hawaii © 1982 Kagimoto

mu`umu`u

www.canehaulroad.com

island
Tryathalon

Try come • Try wait • Try see
I stay trying already!

CHAWAN CUT

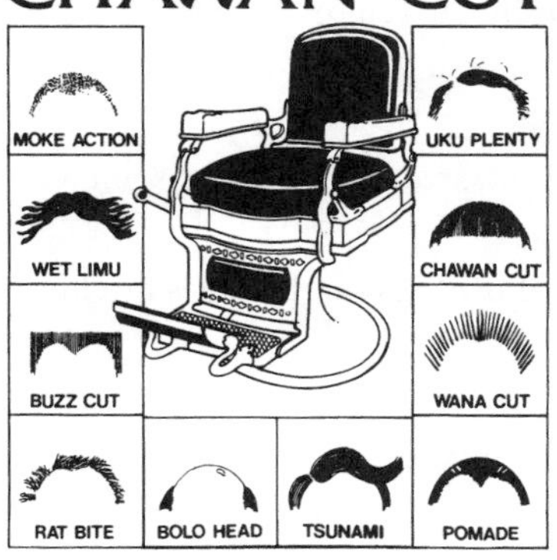

PICKLED
PIGS FEET

Then there is the famous Daikon Legs design which apparently takes a lot of courage for women to wear! According to Kagimoto, "If you bought it, who would you give it to? If you wore it, you'd better have the body of a dancer."

His puns and word play are funny, bizarre, twisted, and some take a moment.

An early entry in his sketchbook shows how some ideas are born. There's simply a list:

> "kitty litter, cat o nine tails, raining cats and dogs, cool cats, catastrophe, cat tails, cat tongue, fur balls, cat food, paw prints, bad cat, cat scratch fever, cat whiskers, tom cat, kitty cat, kitten, cat fight, cat eyes, fat

cat, alley cat, black cat, obake neko, maneki neko, cat person, jungle cat, wild cat, stray cat, cat nap, scared cat, scalded cat, catfish, catacomb, catalog, catapult, cataract, catchup, cat on a hot tin roof, fuzzy logic"

Or a riff on slippers in 1994:

"gecko slipper (with suction cups), hiking slippers (high soles), slipper flipper (swim fins), golf slipper (with golf cleats), fashion slipper (high heels), Swiss slipper (with holes), luau feet slipper (extra wide), political slipper (one slipper with straps going left and right), picnic slipper (4 pairs of straps on each long slipper)"

6/23/92
GARLIC
"R"
GARLIC ARE US
Book# 4
a clove a day
COUNT CHILI PEPPER
GARLIC
GINSEN
shaman
wife/husban
strangers
ALL OF THE ABOVE
Korean garlic press
drums / shamans
kim chee burger
kim chee & stew
Grandmother's kim chee
global warming - too many jars of kim chee fermenting at the same time
3rd degree
kim chee black belt
hot
hotter
more hotter
hottest
fatal
weather report - kim chee scale of temp.
temp. according to mama kim chee (Aunty?)
-garlic eaters of the world unite, you have nothing to lose but your friends
centigrade/farenheit / kim chee
Kim chee from Hell
sayings?
ONE BARK
FIRE DOG
3 alarm kim chee
Fire alarm
KIM CHEE FIRE DEPT
in deep kim chee
Kim chee to Go
Kim chee the god of fire
warrior
throwing

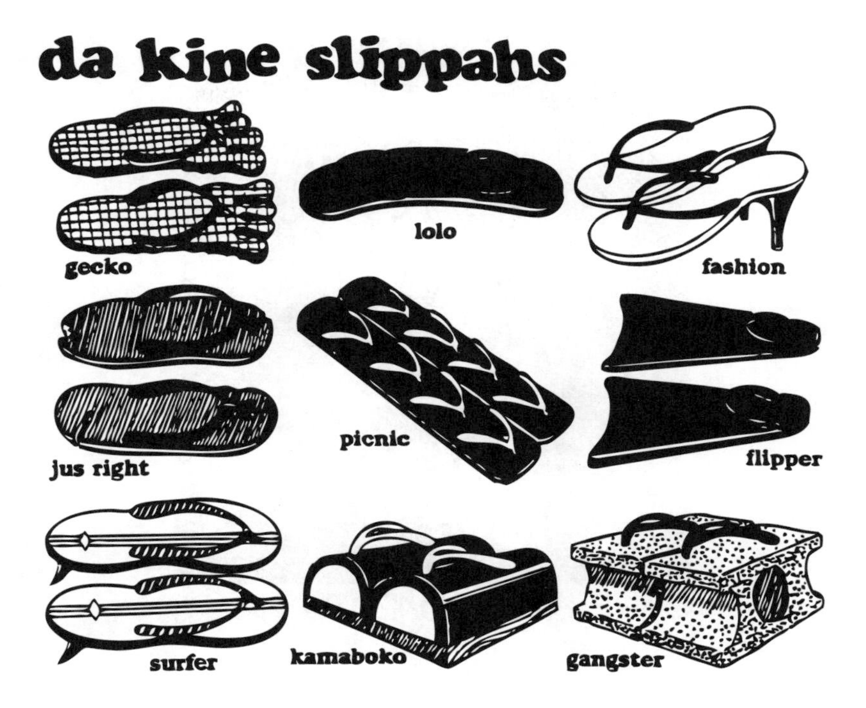

III. Is local dead?

Kagimoto looks to the mainland expatriate market and the Internet to revitalize sales in the current economy. He admits that it appears his customer base are people 10 years younger and 10 years older than he is and that he has addressed all the things that they are interested in. Along with increased competition of small niche markets such as urban street designs and bold Polynesian tattoo designs, the local market has been decreasing. When asked, "Is local dead?" he answers, "Yes, as far as a big commercial market. Our time has come and gone." He laughs, "We're past our 'pull date,' like old milk and we need to seek another customer base."

And despite a small notation in his 1992 sketchbook of his 5-, 10-, 15-, and 20-year goals (the last list included retirement), Kagimoto was still able to come up with nearly 50 new ideas literally overnight to celebrate this issue. After 34 years, it seems like Grant Kagimoto is definitely not pau yet.

Artist Notes

Musubi and Friends: This design was actually our first catalog. It had all our designs on it. I actually wrote musubi with an "e" until Jean Fukuda pointed out that I was so "haole" I misspelled it.

Hardly Any Char Siu Nowdays: This is very early Cane Haul Road…Chinese noodles, Japanese soup stock, invented in Hawai'i. Nake'u Awai accused me of being "high class" for even having char siu in the first place.

Bachi: I remember the first time I heard this was from my grandmother when we went to visit a graveyard and she warned us not to step on the graves.

Make Die Dead: I just love the redundancy, how dead is dead? You know on some old Hawaiian tombstones they use the word "make" and the date.

Mr. Urusai: Stole this idea from a friend's wife, who actually called her husband "Captain Urusai. You so samurai."

Flying Cockaroaches: The famous Hawai'i flying cockroaches scare everyone, even adults. To have fun I put them in Sopwith Camel airplanes.

Daikon Legs: I had the idea but had a hard time drawing the leaves. I looked in the supermarket, but all the daikon had their leaves cut off. I mentioned it to Philip Markwart and he suggested looking in a Japanese family crest (mon) book. Sure enough there was a radish crest, just added shoes.

Bao Wow: I like keeping it simple and the RCA Victor type dog.

Saloon Pilot: We always tried to bring Hilo Macaroni saloon pilot crackers back to Okinawa after our summer visits to Hawai'i. The DC 3 was the first plane I flew on.

Rolled Rice: I love English cars, a Rolls is out of my league, but I had a Triumph in college.

Quack Seed: This is the iconic crack seed glass jar. The lid is a natural Chinese looking hat and ducks are funny.

Island Tryathlon: We don't do things, we try...try, try.

Mynah Mynah: I love those birds and their arrogant strut.

Won Bok: Sounds like one buck, and then someone said it reminded them of "wan," Korean money. This was the beginning of my vegetable puns.

To Be or Nasube: Everyone knows Hamlet. I actually didn't know that I misspelled nasubi until way later.

Chawan Cut: Haircuts on base were only 25 cents so my mother sent me to get it cut often. Love those old barber chairs.

Pickled Pigs Feet: This is the haole kind in the jars.

Sipa Sipa: The Filipino rattan ball brought by the early immigrants. Love the pattern of the weave and the elegant design.

Tails of the Pacific (p. 188): This was from the impressive display of fish tails on the wall at the Sumida Watercress Farm, also home of the Aiea Boat Club.

tails of the Pacific

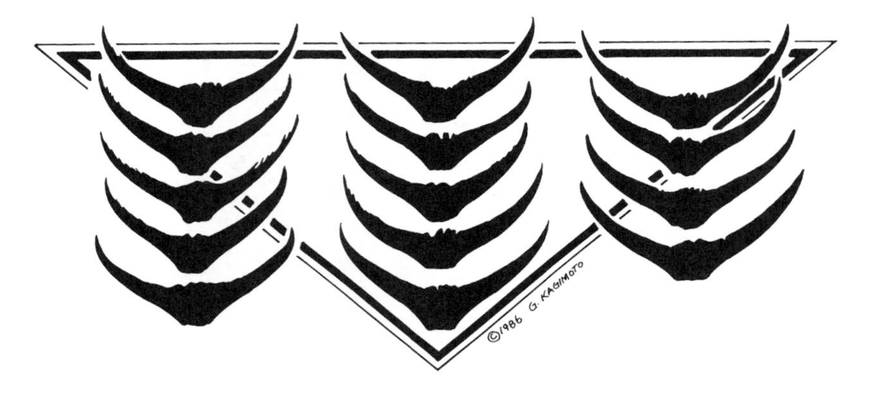

WAITING FO DA BIG FISH:
100-WORD/100-LINE ONLINE CONTEST SELECTIONS

Editors' Note: The online writing contest started in July 2010 as "The Great Bamboo Ridge Short-Short Story Contest." It had a 100-word limit and small monthly prizes. By March 2011 the contest morphed into "The Great Bamboo Ridge Fishing and Wishing 100-100 Contest" which allowed entries between 100 words and 100 lines based on monthly themes. All told, there were 317 entries by 169 authors over 11 months. The contest continues as "The Great Year of the Dragon Contest" with no length limits and no required themes, but writing "triggers" from early issues are still featured for inspiration.

The selections in this section were made by the editors, contest coordinator Lanning Lee, and guest judges Lee Cataluna, Lee Tonouchi, and Lois-Ann Yamanaka. The judges contributed their own 100-line pieces that start off the section followed by our "Big Fish" winners!

Lois-Ann Yamanaka

Weiner

My father says this to me all the time:

"Be a winner, not a whiner."

When I complain about helping big old Dominic sit still while Aunty Narcissus cuts his hair and toenails in the garage.

When I am forced to be Babachan's mahjong fourth at the senior center when Granny Hatsu vacations in Las Vegas.

When I grumble about hauling in all of Jichan's stinky recycled bottles for the measly two dollars he gets while Dominic gets to sit in the car.

When it's too hot to get chiso from the garden for hot tea.

When it's too cold to get chives from the garden for the eggs.

Be a winner, not a whiner.

A winner who appreciates getting a ride home from school, not a whiner who asks how come Jichan had to come in the ugly old Valiant with the three dogs in the front seat while he had to sit in the back seat.

A winner who gladly barters for the best price with the hippie owner of Hilo Natural Foods for his old jichan who is self-conscious about speaking English, let alone carrying the heavy buckets of organic Mexican limes and kumquats through the back door of the store.

A winner who could one day have his name in the sports section of the Hilo Tribune Herald if he only took his participation in Little League more seriously instead of sitting out in deep right field picking dandelions.

My father says to be a winner. A Winner. A WINNER.

Spelling Bee? "You better get to the state competition, Linus."

Haiku contest? "Yours about winter better be selected. You wrote about winter like I told you, right?"

School paper? "You better be Editor-in-Chief."

My father gets especially demanding about my losing ways when he's at the bottom of his big Franzia box of pink wine on Friday nights.

"Be a winner," I mutter at him, "not a wino."

He falls asleep on the living room couch with his glass in his hand. I take it to the sink and crush the empty box. I cover him with the crocheted afghan and turn off the lights.

This year, Big Betty enters me in all of the events she enters at the Hilo County Farm Fair.

It's her family's tradition of winning. They have blue ribbons for everything from her grandma's prize-winning ʻōhelo berry/mountain apple chutney to her grandpa's award-winning dendrobium hybrid "Sweet Lady Elizabeth of Hilo" to her mother's Hilo Kennel Club champion silky terriers from Australia. And that's not mentioning all the trophies for her father's Archery Shoots and feather leis, and her brothers' bowling, golf, tennis, judo, surfing, canoe paddling, turkey trot, greased pig, and hula hālau wins through the years. They have so many trophies, her mother had to start displaying some on the shelf above their toilet.

Big Betty's been a big winner herself. She won last year's Dung Discus Throw sponsored by Kahuku Ranch, chocolate creme pie eating contest sponsored by Lanky's Bakery two years in a row, and a speech festival ribbon for her dramatic rendition of Robinson Jeffers's "Hurt Hawks." She was the only one from our school who qualified for the Big Island District Speech Finals.

This year she entered the Dung Discus Throw again. Which I simply refused to do with dried cow pies. The chocolate creme pie event. And a new event sponsored by Miko Meats, the Hot Dog Eating Contest. The winner gets a year's supply of Miko hot dogs.

The events are held on the main stage in the middle of the fair grounds. It's hot, high noon when Big Betty, me, a fat Portagee in coveralls, a big Hawaiian mama in a shorty muʻumuʻu, and a linebacker from the high school football team take the stage for the last of three heats. The sweaty manager from Miko Meats makes us wear hot dog hats made from sponge.

"But you cannot keep them," he says while putting them on each of us. "We need um for next year."

From this point in time, it's all slow-mo for me. I see Big Betty next to me, securing her hat, intense, hot dog poised for her mouth. The big mama's salivating. Big Betty's yelling at me in slow-mo, "Get ready, Linus, get ready. Focus, Linus, focus." I look into the crowd. I see my jichan, babachan, Uncle Fung, Aunty Narcissus, and father. I see Elton pouting. He lost in the second heat. I see Dominic clapping like an overgrown seal and flapping his hands when the tent snaps in the wind.

"Be a winner, Linus, a WINNER," my father's voice rings.

The starter's gun fires, and I shove hot dog after hot dog in my mouth, one in each cheek, one down the middle, big swig of water, again, and again, hot dog after hot dog followed by a big swig of water. The fat Portagee looks at me in awe, the slobber from his mouth thwacking my cheek when he turns my way, but I keep shoving Miko hot dogs in my mouth until the second gun fires—twenty-eight hot dogs later. The manager runs up to me and hoists my hand high in the air.

"The Winner!" he proclaims.

We have a freezer full of hot dogs. Enough hot dogs to last us two, maybe three years. And I have a trophy that is a bronzed hot dog. Engraved on the bottom of my trophy:

1st PLACE WINNER: LINUS HARUNO.

I admire it every day. Linus Haruno 1st Place Winner. That's what it says. I like the ring of it. Father puts my trophy in a place of honor. Right on the TV in between this year's school pictures of Dominic and me. Mama would be so proud of me. A reminder, right there for all of us to see every day and night even after the lights go off.

Lee Cataluna

Kōloa

Aunty Josie introduced people with subtitles of their greatest pain.

"This is Kenny Boy. He was born in prison, you know."

"This is Mrs. Ruiz. Poor thing. Her husband died of cancer six years ago."

"This is my dear friend Eleanor. She got shot in the eye by her grandson and he's still in jail for that. Hi Eleanor! How's the family?"

If it happened that we met up with a person more than once, Aunty Josie would repeat the epithet each time: "You remember my old neighbor Mr. Tabutol, from before time the camp. He's the one I told you the wife ran off and he raised all the daughters by himself." If I said, "I know. You told me already," she'd add another line, more details, another layer of pain. "The wife ran off with a woman. Did you know that?"

Aunty Josie limped from her house near the river through the buffalo grass all the way to Sueoka store every day. She refused to buy more than a day's worth of groceries, carrying back only enough for dinner for one night. She would spend her morning in her chair thinking of what she wanted to eat for dinner—green onion and canned tuna omelet, hamburger curry, chicken gisantis—start out for Sueoka store by 10 am, get there by 11:30, make her rounds of hellos to the butcher, the manager, and all the cashiers, and hobble back to her house in the early afternoon for her nap.

The summer I lived in her damp, fetid little house, I accompanied her to Sueoka's every day. I'd follow behind her on the way back, carrying her one little bag of chuck steak and a yellow onion and the terrible short stories of every person we had come across in the market.

"Come. Say hello to Mrs. Contrades. One time, her uterus fell out of her body and she had to tie it to her leg with a towel and drive herself to the doctor."

I began to believe this cruel recitation of all her neighbors' sorrows was her version of gossip. In a small town where years could go by with nothing happening, the old news had to suffice. The divorces and illegitimate pregnancies that fueled the rumor mill of Aunty Josie's youth in the 1940s had become commonplace and bland over the last 60 years. Now, it wasn't enough that an unmarried woman was having a baby. It wasn't enough that someone was leaving his wife. There needed to be an element of the macabre. The old tragedies Aunty Josie constantly dredged up had stood the test of time. They were classic tales, unrivaled in their ability to distinguish an otherwise placid-faced neighbor, like a war medal or a twisted scar.

I came to Aunty Josie's house after I bombed out of my first semester of college. My mother said maybe I should start at community college first, to get a taste of what to expect, but I knew what to expect at college. I just didn't know what to expect from myself. I was pressed into service watching over Aunty Josie for my mother's oldest sister, who had planned a three-month trip to visit grandchildren in Washington State. Aunty Josie made it clear that she was the one babysitting me and not the other way around.

Aunty Josie, my grandmother's only living sibling, was hit by a car on her way home from Sueoka's one day the year before. A tourist barely clipped her with the rental car, but she flew ten feet into the buffalo grass along Wailā'au Road, though she didn't get hurt. The police made a report and Aunty Josie got evaluated by a social worker. She barely passed muster. My mom said it was my job that summer to keep an eye on her and help organize the house. Mostly, I sat on a flat rock near the river at the back of her yard and watched the neighbor's television screen through his open jalousie windows when I wasn't walking back and forth with her to Sueoka store and being introduced to all the sad stories in Kōloa.

"That man over there, Mr. Shimazu, he cut off three of his fingers with a table saw." If I tried to stop her, to head off the one-lined indictment with an, "Aunty, please!" she'd brush off my attempts to silence her and go in for the kill. "Hi! Mr. Shimazu!" and she'd wave at him so he'd wave back, thus illustrating her story. "You see, only the thumb and pinky left. You saw? You noticed? You like me make him wave again?"

The summer I lived with Aunty Josie in her sweltering, lizard-infested Kōloa house, I tried not to think about the label she was eventually going to attach to me.

"This is my niece. She flunked all her classes."

"This is my niece. She never knew her daddy."

"This is Sandra's daughter. Her mother gave up on her already. Lucky thing the brother is smart."

On Friday evenings, Aunty Josie made me take a bath early so we could wait on the porch for her friend Eleanor to pick us up. The priest at

St. Raphael's church did a special Friday night mini-mass, condensing the entire hour-long service into two songs, communion, and a speed-read Our Father. Aunty Josie had no use for efficiency. Time was the one thing she was not interested in saving. She liked mini-mass, however, because there was more time afterward to visit with the priest and question him about the details of each prayer request printed in the parish bulletin.

"It says here urgent intercession requested for Mrs. Pascua. Is she in the hospital with the diabetes again? Or something else wrong with her?"

The priest surprised me every time by answering her in great detail. He must have been starved for novelty too, desperate for something truly dire around which he could focus an organized prayer circle.

It happened on a boiling day in August when Aunty Josie woke with a fever. The trees by the river were as still as stone without the usual trade winds and the smell of the slow green river filled the house with a stench so thick I could feel it like a coating of oil on my skin. Aunty Josie lay in her bed under three torn and stained patchwork quilts and shivered despite the oppressive heat. She insisted she was going on her daily walk to Sueoka store, but by noon, she was still shaking and moaning under her covers. I convinced her I could be trusted to go and come back by myself, and she dictated her grocery list, just enough ingredients to make chicken long rice with ginger root. "That's sick man food. They serve it all the time in the old folks home," she assured me. "Mrs. Freitas tells me that's all they feed her husband ever since he fell off the ladder in their driveway and cracked his head and cannot walk."

It was strange to walk through Sueoka's without her. Everyone I met was tainted in my mind by Aunty Josie's words. I waved to the butcher, who I knew had a son locked up in a psychiatric hospital. I said hello to the stock boy, and my eyes went straight to his cleft lip that had never been properly sewn together. The woman who smiled at me in the produce section was the one with the daughter who was arrested in a DEA drug sweep of the housing project. They used a helicopter and drug dogs and everything. All the awful details from Aunty Josie's stories tainted each interaction. I bought the chicken from the lady whose father was a child molester. The green onion was grown by a family in ʻŌmaʻo that had a terrible legacy of breast cancer.

In just two months, the whole town had become doomed and diseased to my eyes. I couldn't look at anyone without thinking of their worst day. I found myself looking at strangers, at the many tourists who swept through with sand-covered legs and glowing sunburns, and wondering what sadness they left back home, what tears were hidden behind their sunglasses.

Aunty Josie liked my chicken long rice. She said I made the noodles nice and mushy the way old folks like, and that I could get a job cooking for all the sad sacks at the old folks home. "Good money," she said. "And stable job. You can work there until you old enough to move in."

Cold slid down my sweating back like an ice cube. I didn't know what I wanted that summer, but right then, I knew what I didn't want.

"I could never live here."

Aunty Josie coughed to clear her throat. "Why? This is a nice town. Good people. Everybody takes care of everybody."

"How can you say that? You, of all people. Your chief occupation in life is spreading gossip and telling the horrors of every person's life."

It was the closest I ever got to yelling at her. Aunty Josie didn't stop herself from screaming at me, her feverish face shaking in rage.

"Why? It's the truth! If I was making it up, that would be cruel."

I left the room and let her sleep, but when I came back to check on her around midnight, she was awake with a small kerosene lantern on. Her fever had broken. She was waiting for me.

"You think I'm a bad person. You think I tell those things to hurt," she said. "You don't know because you haven't lived yet."

I tried to say that maybe it would be better if she didn't remind people of their greatest sorrows every time she sees them. She slapped my arm as though killing a mosquito against my flesh. "I not reminding them of nothing. Those kinds of things, they go so deep you never forget them, not for one second of any day. I telling you so that you know. So that you're kind and you're understanding. You're the type you think everybody has it easier than you. I want you to know how hard people's lives are. Their lives are hard. And look. They're still walking around Sueoka's, still buying their meat and their bread."

That was my Aunty Josie. I stayed with her one summer. She outlived two husbands and three children. She had high blood pressure and glaucoma. She died in her own bed of a massive stroke and I imagine the merciless Kōloa mosquitoes drank from her blood long after it was cold. And I'm sure the butcher with the son locked up in the psychiatric hospital and the lady with the fallen uterus and all her friends will think of her fondly and miss her daily visits to Sueoka store.

Lanning C. Lee

One Devil in Baggy Pants

On the spine, the publisher's colophon resembles, a little, the AA combat service patch of the 82nd Airborne. All American. This strikes me as very appropriate given the amount of alcohol consumption he says ensued when those who could come home did. He chose college, supported by the G.I. Bill. And drinking.

The still glossy pages smell powerfully of some toxic ink, and the pictures of engines no longer running in the real world have not lost their charm. The book is one he read during those college days, the one book he chose to keep, to bring all the way back to Hawaii when he managed to come home—All the Way!—as the 82nd's motto shouts. Together with his diploma, this book is the only tangible evidence I have now of his undergraduate experience.

He did, much to his surprise, come back from the European Theater alive. Immediately he became a card-carrying Socialist and majored, in the end, in political science, although he did have to revert to capitalism after he married my mother and had us.

This book has nothing to do with politics. The topic is automobile engine combustion theory, design, and maintenance, which to my knowledge garnered him little information he ever put to use. But I see his fingerprints captured from time to time, smudges on a shiny page here and there. None of them perfect. So he must have worked on car engines before I was born. Maybe it was only for that semester when he selected this course. I know he was done with car engines, except for driving them, by the time I was old enough to see how he occupied his time.

That's the definition of a true liberal arts education. Someone hunting all over the course catalog for a major that might mean something after four years of parachuting into battles from Sicily to Belgium, and then marching into concentration camps on the way to Berlin, the images of those four years permanently burned into his brain, indelibly imprinted in his memory.

Operation Market Garden was the only time they ever failed to accomplish an overall mission, although his 504th Parachute Infantry

Regiment did achieve their part of the objective at heavy costs. He told me that they all expected they'd die, and he always said, whenever we would watch *A Bridge Too Far* together, that Robert Redford was perfectly cast as Major Julian Cook, but that Ryan O'Neal was too young to play Brigadier General James Gavin.

I'm familiar with many publishers, but I've never heard of this one. I want to go online to find out who they were, but I don't really wish to find that they went out of business a long time ago. This is the one book he's left me. An artifact full of knowledge that must have been cutting edge in its day, but now is obsolete, archaic, forgotten, even though for me it is very much here, relevant, and always now.

Lee A. Tonouchi

Da Local Spirit

Davelynn just couldn't take living there no more. She couldn't help but feel unwelcome in her new home. Was as if her walls was breathing.

She couldn't believe da kinda day she was having. Early dat morning while driving town bound in H-1 traffic, one guy driving one white Toyota pickup had da nerve for honk at her and shout, "Ho watch it, lede. Why you no go back where you came from!?" Da whole day she felt on edge at work, like all eyes was scrutinizing her. She thought she had outgrown those types of feelings. When she wuz young all da neighborhood children nevah asked her for play wit dem until eventually she jus got used to feeling ignored and invisible.

Couple few days ago Davelynn had just moved into her new place of residence, one old fixer-upper back in her old Pearl City neighborhood, and she hadn't even finished unpacking when she first began for hear what started off as soft shallow breaths. Her first instinct was for attribute da sounds to da Kona winds. But aftah closing da windows, da breathing persisted and intensified, until tonight when da breaths came so heavy it resembled one female respiratory patient with gala gala making one obscene phone call. She tried for persuade herself da sound could be anything, anything oddah than da supernatural alternative, dat her house was indeed haunted.

She never like boddah dem, but she decided for call her only friends, da Oshiro sisters, Dawn and Tracy, and casually ask dem for stop over and help her with something. Davelynn hoped for convince dem of her newest theory dat da sound in her house was actually one giant gecko with laryngitis living in her drywall, but as soon as da sisters pulled into da driveway da noise strangely subsided. There was one eerie silence in da house. Without Davelynn having to say anything, both sisters turned to each other and nodded knowingly. Dey both concurred, "Definitely obake."

In Hawai'i, Local people is conditioned from childhood for believe in da supernatural. But all her life Davelynn had defiantly considered herself for be one woman of reason. Growing up, elders ingrained it into their heads. "No bring pork ova da Pali," "Always give ride to da lady in white hitchhiking at night," and "Nevah, eva, under any circumstance bring home

Big Island lava rocks." She often wondered how her friends could believe in all dat stuff, and if dat belief somehow made dem more Localer.

Even da way she got da deep discount on her house wasn't typically Local. It wasn't because she knew someone's friend's auntie's cousin's daughter or anything. She got what was termed da DB Discount. Da realtor had warned her about da possibility dat there might be a Dead Body somewhere on top da premises.

"Wow, help you with someting is right. You can kinda just sense da obake, yeah? If da ghost not Japanese, do we still call 'em obake? I wondah?" Tracy tilted her head and pondered her own question.

"No be mento," Dawn scolded.

"I dunno if da ghost Japanese, but I would say it has to be Local," Tracy said.

"And how you know dat?"

"'Cause ghosts, dey always telling bu. Get it? Like Wassup, bu?"

"Oh boy. Is this da reason you called us, Davelynn?"

"Well . . . I thought I was just hearing things. But maybe I was just hearing things. I felt like a force was trying to chase me away. It's because I got da DB discount on da house."

"DB discount? So you just show your Dave and Buster's card and you can get one discount on houses?" Tracy asked, looking puzzled. "Or does DB stand for Dooney & Bourke? Because that wouldn't make sense."

"I tink I know what DB stands for," Dawn nodded. "But maybe you should explain to Tracy how you got such a deal on your new place."

"Well, there were rumors that da former owner may have been involved . . . in a murder. There was a young woman who mysteriously disappeared many years back. Da owner of da house was a person of interest and detectives suspected he may have hidden da DB, da Dead Body, somewhere on da property as he was in process of doing home renovations. There was never enough evidence to secure a warrant. But da rumors still persisted and that's why da house had been on da market for so long."

"I tink we should call Psychic Von," Tracy volunteered. "I get her number save on my phone."

"She da one who does those radio commercials?"

"That's so silly! Give me that phone," Davelynn demanded, making da call herself. "Hello, is this Psychic Von? Do you know who this is?" She gave Psychic Von five seconds for reply before hanging up.

"Okaaay. That was a little rude. Why you no do dat with your own phone? What if she get caller ID? Now I can't ever call her. And I don't know if your test debunked anyting. Cuz wouldn't Psychic Von only know your name if you were dead? Cuz I think she's only psychic with dead people."

"We can figgah this out, on our own," Dawn said reassuringly. "Logically, wouldn't da spirit, if there is such one ting, wanna reveal to you da name of her killer. Why you get da feeling it's trying for chase you away?"

"Oh yeah, no? It doesn't make sense," Davelynn agreed. Suddenly she felt one chicken skin sensation dat took her back to high school time when da Oshiro sisters managed for get her to go graveyard on one of Glen Grant's ghost tours. Davelynn was amazed how almost everyone on dat bus agreed dey felt chicken skin and had seen something. She had felt da chill in da night air too, but why oddahs would identify chicken skin as one spiritual encounter she couldn't figgah out. She attributed dis to mass hypnosis. Perhaps Glen Grant with his amazing storytelling ability was able for plant da suggestion of da supernatural into people's heads. He was just able to reinforce what people was already preconditioned for believe. Suddenly, it all made sense.

"I think I know why I feel like there's a ghost saying I don't belong. It's because I made myself think that. It's because I've been feeling like how I've always felt deep down. I don't look Local."

"Why, how does one Local person look?" Dawn asked.

"I don't know," Davelynn shrugged. "Like Mufi Hannemann I guess."

"Tall?" Tracy tilted her head.

"Yeah Tracy, tallll," Dawn said sarcastically. "You had it right, Davelynn. You don't know. You don't know what one Local person looks like. And no worry about not knowing somebody who knows someone when you got your deal on your house. 'Cause even if you nevah say, I know das bothering you. Getting one discount is important, but what's even more important is da story. Having one story for tell, das da how, no?"

"Yeah, I do have a pretty cool story, don't I? Sorry for dragging you guys over here." Remembering she was being one poor host, Davelynn opened her fridge and began serving her guests some can juice. Just as she put down da tray of drinks, dey felt da kitchen table shake and dey heard what could only be described as mournful Japanese singing.

"Japanese poltergeist!" Dawn screamed as she shot up.

Tracy grabbed her sistah's shoulders before patting her on da head. "Babooze, das just my phone. It's vibrating da table. And of course I'm gonna have one Japanese ringtone. I just got it. It's my favorite love song from *The Super Dimension Fortress Macross*."

"Aren't you gonna answer it?" Davelynn handed da phone to Tracy.

Tracy glanced for see who it was before picking up. "Uh guys, you're not gonna believe dis. It's Psychic Von. And she says, she says she's getting a message . . . for Davelynn."

Donald Carreira Ching

Mahalo Frank De Lima

My faddah nevah like jokes.
"Not funny," he'd say,
wen I told him da one
'bout da Yobos,
eat so much kim chee
can smell 'em one mile away,
or da Buddha Heads, blind 'em
wit dental floss.

Da Blallahs, da Soles,
even da Podagees, who talk
in dat sputtered, sprinklah tongue,
and no can screw in da light bulb
witout tchree mo'
tellin' 'em which way fo' turn um.

"Korean, Japanese, Hawaiian, Samoan,
Portuguese, not *Podagee*, undahstand?"
My faddah nevah like jokes.
"Not funny," he'd say, den ask,
"Where you wen hear
dat racist shet from?"

Doodie Cruz

Safe Keeping

We'll be late. Do you want me to go and pick her up? Mom doesn't look up from the dishes soaking in the sink; she just nods.

So I go and get Grandma. I strap her in tightly in the seat beside me. I try to fill the empty space between us with idle chitchat. Her silence pains me. I tell her how beautiful the service tomorrow will be, of the many people, family and friends who have helped with its planning.

Mom weeps when I walk in with Grandma, and places fresh blossoms on her plastic urn.

Myles De Coito

A Christmas Carol

Ho! Open-palm slam on the table right next my Caesar salad. Shake water glass and all. "So what do you do for a living?" We here at my wife's Christmas party, my twenty-month-old on my lap, waiting for thirty dollar prime rib, and her—the new supervisor—trying for make conversation like Gestapo interrogation. No: *Where you from? What high school you went? What year you grad?* Sheez, I would even take one, *What's your favorite color?*

I get nice aloha shirt, ironed jeans, fancy—Scott—slippers, and fresh shave. So I tell, "Look good." And my wife kick under the table.

Myles De Coito

Not Silvah Bullet, Mo' Like Pupu Rocket!

How come only scarce, remotely accessible florae qualify as panacea; e.g., açai, ginseng, noni, nopalea. Why no can be red hot dog?

"Ho, I tell you, dis pas' whole month I jess run down. I get stress up to hea, I no can kick dis cough, I put on ten pounds, and my ankles is hella swollen."

"Tita, ne'mind all dat. You know what you gotta try? Red hot dog. Eh, I been steady on tree a day da las' month—for my new yea's get healty resolution. One in da mohning wit egg. One oddah lunch time insigh musubi. And dinnah wit one salad. Girl, I loss ten pounds, only need sleep tree hours a night, da kids not even boddering me, and me an' Gerald. Well, nevah you mind!"

M. Jane Lambert

Overheard

"He came into my room again last night, half naked, hugging his pillow," the man in the cap stirs his coffee.

His bearded friend rubs an ear having heard this all before. "What did you do?"

"What could I do? I got up to change his bed; and when I came back, he was asleep in mine."

"Don't stand for it," the friend says. "Give him sheets and tell him to make his own damn bed."

"I can't do that." The man in the cap pushes the coffee away. "What kind of son would I be to disrespect my father?"

Mel Lau

Getting Gas

I'm late, but the "dangerously low" light's been blinking for the past
10 miles.
Damn, better stop. Yes—only two at each pump.
Guess I'll line up behind the . . . VW bus.
Driver's out, staring at the pump.
Still staring at the pump. C'mon buddy, push some buttons!

Hokay . . . dude #2 slides out of the passenger seat to "help."
Both stare at the screen.
And stare.
Some discussion, then, no action.
Yo, guys, while we're still young!

The panel door slides open and a pareau-wearing woman emerges.
Strumming an ukulele.
Serenading the men!
I am so dead.

Mary Lombard

The Women's Table

They were eating out tonight. Their anniversary dinner. But they sat in silence. Her husband was tired.

She counted eight couples in the restaurant and all of them were quiet as well. Mouths opening for food, not for conversation. One table was noisy, though, all women, older than she, middle-aged, six of them, chatting and laughing. Oh, they were rowdy—really! Having a grand time.

She felt a lump in her throat. She wanted to be over there, with them, away from this cavity of silence.

"You ready to go?" she said.

Terri Nakamura

Two for

"I donna kno why you go out wit ignorant country fuckas everytime." My father, Puna bred, Vietnam vet, keeps spewing like Kīlauea volcano.

I hold the cell phone to my ear, while ashy tears run down my face. My cold fingers comfort the purple island on my cheek.

I'm six again, speechless. My father's words always hit hard, like his fists.

I feel like the same little girl even though it's twenty years later, but this time, lava is running through my veins.

"WELL, HE'S JUS LIKE YOU, DAD." For once, there is silence and I feel grown up.

Christy Passion

Poi

Every night Mama would say, "No talk stink—the poi going get rotten." So I held my tongue about sister, Papa stopped talking about the job, and we ate. Dinners started quiet, but ended with laughter; her admonition clearing away the day. Then came the shortage: taro and construction. Dinners became moody. I went to college and learned about the recession. I ate instant potatoes alone, let the dishes pile up, till the smell drove my roommate out. I didn't call. I was rotten. Once I craved poi, but the market only had day-old, too sour to hold down.

Brian Rugen

Unmistaken Identity

"Keiko? Is that you?"

I don't recognize his ghostly face, but I know who he is.

I didn't mind wearing the lingerie. And the money was good. Mama-san was strict with the customers, but the foreigners—they were just too aggressive when drunk.

I feign ignorance and paddle into an oncoming wave.

It crashes on top of me and I'm momentarily pinned on my back under water. Fighting, I surface, on my board again. I watch the white foam from the wave slide down my breasts, peeling off me like the dead skin on a snake baking in the sun.

Normie Salvador

Shinji Fujita Searches for God

"*Kami?*"

The Galapagos tortoise returned the stare, hoping for lettuce.

"No, Shinji. *Kami* is 'god.' *Kame* is 'turtle.'"

"But Auntie Koko said, 'God is a turtle.'"

Makoto rounded on her twin, "What've you been filling his head with this time?"

Kokoro brought her hands up defensively. "Wait, let me think . . . . Umm . . . . Oh! Last Sunday, he asked me, 'What is God?' . . . At one point, I think I told him 'God is eternal.'"

Shinji, satisfied turtles were divine, turned back but was disappointed; the tortoise had begun to wander off. *That wasn't God? Hmm . . . .* He called out to another.

Misty Sanico

No Laulau Left for Locals— it's good for business . . .

We used to come here, ono for laulau. Joyful . . .
Before the national television network came.
Now, the place is spilling tourists.
It's good for business.

We order, the waitress shakes her head.
We end up with chicken luau—not da same.
We wait and watch dolefully.
Barely touched laulaus are scraped off tourists' plates into the trash.

They hang a sign, "NO MORE LAULAU."
A local family turns back to their car.
Tourists head for the autograph photo the network left behind . . .
Take pictures, order one of everything, send half back in the rubbish.
We eat solemnly—not da same.

Carrie Y. Takahata

Dating: Boundaries and Endings, One and the Same Sometimes

"I knew this would happen," he says, "and you wouldn't want to talk to me and we'd go to dinner and you wouldn't look at me and then we'd be at the concert and you'd—"

"Stop. You need to stop. You're making up a story."

"But that happened. I came to your apartment and you didn't—"

"We're talking . . . we haven't gone . . . anywhere."

"But you're not—"

"This is ridiculous. I'm done."

He follows me.

"What are you doing?" I say.

"Walking you to your door," he says.

"Nuh-uh, this is over."

"Thank you for saying that," he says seriously, "thank you."

Carrie Y. Takahata

"Thank you for rescuing me,"

he says, kneeling next to my table in the middle of that dive of a bar, Sutter Station. I smile and say the pleasure is mine since all I really want to do—ever since we met—is drink whiskey, pull him in. I'm lost in this when he tilts his head and turns inside to say, "I'm fucked up; you really should leave." And, for the first time, I see him—three years at the very front of Afghanistan—buried down there, all the way inside.

Bill Teter

INSPIRATION

Dinner has been tense.

She's angry that he's written about her. The story is still on her side of the table. "It's not about you at all," he says. "I took five minutes of our conversation last week." It was her story, she answers, not his. She feels he has violated her. That's the word she uses: violated.

He says, "You photograph people, make art from their faces, hands, hair—their naked bodies."

It's not the same thing." She turns her accusing eyes on him. "You'll probably use this in a story," she says, "won't you?"

"No," he answers. "I won't."

Jean Yamasaki Toyama

Bloody Easy

To assure some kind of excellence one must have begun early. Mozart was four. The only thing I could do at four was bleed well. Even my breathing wasn't up to par; my eating below average, but my bleeding, well, I excelled at that. With so much practice it was no wonder that I was a superior bleeder. But it's not a spectacular gift. Doctors worry; people pity.

I don't know where this talent came from. It's natural for me, not something I had to work at. It just happened. A line of blood would stream out of the corner of my eye or my mouth or sometimes from the corner of my right thumb. My left thumb. Any one of my fingernails. Any corner of my body. I couldn't predict. It just happened.

Stopping the bleeding was not easy. To stop it, that was the trick. If the bleeding didn't stop, then, well, I would die, of course. When they first discovered my talent and its danger, they tried to replenish my supply with pints and pints of other people's blood. That was a waste. I kept on bleeding. Then they used artificial blood. That's what stopped it. They couldn't explain.

I was a naturally brilliant bleeder, who became artificially normal and alive.

Joe Tsujimoto

6-Word Stories (À la Hemingway)

For sale: baby shoes, never worn. —Hemingway

My life sucks.
It's your fault.
—Steve Wagenseller

Two severed heads, a summer romance.

His former lover,
now his mother-in-law.

Teenagers run amok,
murder their teacher.

Oversight: failure to feed
the gators.

Rejected,
Suspected, he vanished in Chinatown.

They found her eating the hand.

Pekinese brain
Galapagos ass
His boss.

Found in coffin:
iPhone iPad Xbox.

His eyes burn
having seen her.

Kristel Yoneda

Grandpa Is an Astronaut

Everyone is at Grandma's house,
Eating sushi on paper plates,
Telling stories about Grandpa.

Grandpa is really skinny now
And never pinches my cheeks anymore.
"Are you chewing gum?" he'd say.

He's in bed next to his favorite recliner,
People sit with him and cry.

Grandpa stares at the ceiling with his tubes,
I think he's an astronaut dreaming of outer space.

When Mommy gets home that night,
She drops her purse on the ground and sits on her bed.
She cries so loud I feel the house shake
And I know then that Grandpa has gone to space.

O. Yunomi

Junk Mail

"I gave!" she said forcefully, throwing the mail to the floor. Surprised by my usually tranquil ninety-year-old mother's vehemence, I picked up the envelope addressed to her from a veteran's organization, along with the solicitation letter and preprinted donation envelope. "My son . . . an' fo' *what*?" she whispered.

"What timing," I thought. Earlier that morning we had been making plans to pick up flowers in Chinatown to take to Punchbowl for Memorial Day. For more than 40 years she's been walking up that hillside to the grave of an Army captain, killed in Vietnam on his 26th birthday.

Donald Carreira Ching

Traditions

It was late Sunday afternoon; Danielle and I had just arrived at her parents' townhouse still smelling of dust from the swap meet, where we had collected a few yellowed paperbacks and three packs of Silly Bandz. Her mother was on the computer trying to repair the router, refreshing Facebook to see if her efforts were bearing any fruit. Her father, Elani, was in the kitchen, waiting.

He had already done most of the work, waking up at five in the morning to harvest the ti leaf that was now drying in the dish rack.

"Sorry da lūʻau leaf stay kinda small, had fo' go Times fo' buy 'em, Wong's stay closed Sundays," he said, pointing to the taro leaves piled in a section of the disassembled pressure cooker.

"I didn't know Times sold lūʻau leaf," Danielle remarked.

"In the produce section, wrapped up in plastic bags," I reply, thinking about when I worked at the grocery store.

"How much?"

Elani had already begun wrapping the laulau—four medium-sized bundles sitting on the side, waiting to be cooked. "Like two-thirty-nine a bag, but da leaf kinda small, ah? Wong's stay fifteen dollahs fo' like triple dis."

I try to watch him, but he moves quickly, from tray to tray, instinctively measuring in his head how much of everything he needs. "Where do you start?"

He finishes another, then joins me near the oven. "First, grab one big leaf, like da biggest you can find." He turns a few over, finally pulling a monster from the bottom. "Den," he says, "take some of da smallah leaves, put 'em in da centah."

I find a leaf and follow his lead.

"Grab a little of dis, hāhā," He reaches into another bowl, picking from the stems that he had separated earlier. "And den come, take some pork, some beef, couple cubes fat." He plucks large chunks of each and puts it in the center of his lūʻau leaves.

"Thought there was only pork inside?"

"Cheapah ah? Jus' pork. Beef too expensive, but my faddah one ching, not chang li'dat. He liked some beef, an' da fat help da leaves stay moist." He carries the bundle to the cutting board.

"How come you don't put a piece of fish?" Danielle asks.

He smiles, "'Cuz of you," referencing her distaste for seafood.

I watch him take one of the ti leaves off the rack and lay it down.

"Usually you gotta start early, ah? Go outside fo' get da ti leaf ready, clean off da dirt, make sure you have enuff."

"How do you pick 'em?"

"You usually wanna get da ones near da centah, da green ones, stay mo' pliable, y'know? Strongah." He holds the bundle and wraps the leaf around, gripping it near the top. He takes another leaf and lays it the other way. "See, you gotta hold 'em tight," he says, "den you wrap 'em li'dis, get da oddah side, covah 'em all." The bundle is completely concealed, the stems of the two ti leaves sprouting from his tightened grip. "Den you gotta bite 'em."

I watch as he tears the second leaf's stem with his teeth, splitting it down into two pieces. Carefully he takes the smaller of the pieces and wraps it twice near the top, tucking his finger and then sliding the piece inside.

"Keep 'em tight, y'know?"

While Elani watches, I begin to choose my meat, taking small pieces of beef and pork, a single cube of fat.

"I want a laulau with just leaves," my wife says.

"Try put couple mo' pieces," Elani tells me.

I add a few more chunks, but my laulau still looks manini compared to his.

Danielle comes in the kitchen and starts taking pictures with her iPhone. "That one's mine," she says, pointing to the bundle I just made. "Almost vegetarian."

Her mom laughs from the living room, reading the paper while checking on the computer after every other page. "Not even a year into the term and the governor's already breaking campaign promises."

"Why, what's it say?"

"Nothing, just talking about the furloughs."

"One ting you learn, no mattah what, politics nevah change, same ol' shet, y'know?"

I watch as he finishes another bundle, while I struggle to tie mine. He sees me and repeats the steps, watching over my hands.

"Y'know my faddah was so fas', could do like ten to my one."

"Jesus," I said, finally putting my laulau in the tray with the others. "So how are we gonna cook this?"

"I gotta go get da gas from up Kurt's house in Kahalu'u, could cook 'em on da stove but da ting eventually burns, ah?"

"How would you normally cook it?"

"Before, you put 'em in da imu wit da pig, take like one whole day fo' cook 'em. Nowadays, not li'dat, no get da time. Dis way, take only like tchree hours."

After making a few more, I go to sit with Danielle in the living room. Elani is still in the kitchen, humming melodies of Hawaiian songs neither of us knows. On the table is a Haleakala Dairy bottle that her parents had bought at the swap meet, destined for the entertainment center where it will join old Primos and glass balls netted by Elani's hands; the same ones that knotted the netting of the Hōkūle'a decades before.

It'll be hours till the laulau is finished steaming, before we sit with our hapa rice and Taro Brand lomi salmon. I will peel back the layers for the first time, for so many years afraid of the dark leaves, the color so much like the lush veins running down the Ko'olau. Sprinkle the Hawaiian salt over the meat, like Elani had been taught by his father, and taste the ocean washing over my tongue. We will talk story like we always do, like has always been done and, years from now, I will wake when the sun rises and gather ti leaf, preparing with my hands a story so old.

Donald Carreira Ching

What did the Haole say to the Podagee?

My father used to say Portuguese like it mattered, like it wasn't just a synonym for Haole. He'd talk about the 'ukulele, but not a single Portuguese player. Sweetbread, but only talk about "Hawaiian" brands. Maybe if you caught a tan, you could pass for hapa, but even then, you knew.

Even the Japanese have more clout. So what if the Portuguese were picking pineapple beside them? The Chinese, the Filipino, all of them outside the hall like Morales wrote, watching the Portuguese and Puerto Ricans kachi-kachi, listening to the rhythm of the guiro; the smell of vinadalhos soaking into the street.

What'chu gon do, move mainlan'? Worse yet, dey gon tink you one Mexican. Gotta learn Spanish fo' get by, propah English fo' survive wen you go break yo' back fo' feed da kids. Get two jobs fo' dat one-bedroom wit da view of da freeway and da beautiful grey sky.

Den wen you come back fo' visit da folks, talk story wit yo' friends. All da guys sittin' around drinkin' beers and eatin' poi, you standin' dea nursin' yo' '93 cabernet. Dey gon tink dey was right all along, and you, you gon tink bout what yo' faddah said, and keep askin' yo'self what da fuck one podagee anyway? Drinkin' wine from one plastic cup, wishin' you had sugah fo' sweeten da poi, wonderin' why you wen leave da mosquito repellant back in yo' hotel room.

Donald Carreira Ching

In Time

He wore the watch every day of their life. It was more than they could afford, but she bought it for him anyway. Automatic, twenty-one-jewel movement, sapphire crystal, and a case made of solid gold. On the back she engraved "Everything in time."

They were celebrating their anniversary then. In between champagne toasts and whispered nothings, she gave him the watch. He thanked her, telling her that it was too much, then reached in his pocket and got on his knee. "I love you," he told her and opened the box.

A few months later, he wore the watch for the first time; it was their wedding day. The gold tone of the case clashed with his cufflinks, so he took them off and safety pinned the cuffs closed. Standing at the end of the aisle, he pulled his sleeve just a little higher, so that when she saw him she'd know that he remembered, she'd know he cared.

When their first child was born, he pulled the crown out so he could jot down the exact second he had seen their son's face. He did this again the first time he had spoken, the first time he walked. He kept a journal, a time card of memories, so that if he ever opened it, he could remember the precise moment that his life had changed.

Eventually the crown became worn and the watch had to be serviced. Overhaul, rust removal, new gasket, and stem. Their son would be attending school soon and she had just lost her job. The original parts were too expensive, so they told the watch-smith to replace them with cheaper ones, they'd take care of it another time.

And so it went, gas prices rose, medical bills would pile up, a new daughter, another son. The movement would need to be oiled, the crystal replaced. The watch was in the shop so often that moments passed unnoted, gaps of blank space filling the page.

He remembered the events leading to the first time he'd forgotten the watch. They had gotten into an argument and were running late to their youngest son's school play. The cafeteria was packed and his wife was able to only find a single seat near the front while he lingered in the back and watched from a distance. The play had just begun when someone next to him asked for the time. "7:15," he said, and looked up, a young woman with almond eyes smiling back.

She was his son's teacher. Ten years his junior, she had grown up a few blocks from where his father used to work. It was the first time he had met her, but a week later he saw her again. That time was because their son was sick, the next because his wife couldn't make it for a conference. Eventually he'd bring her coffee, then soon they were going to lunch.

One day, they had a few too many and he woke up next to her wondering what he had done. It was dark outside and he looked where his watch should have been, shaking his head when he realized he had forgotten it at home. She mumbled something to him and touched his naked back. "What time is it?" he asked her. She picked up her cell phone and told him. He found a pen on the bedside table and wrote the moment on a notepad beside his ring.

Jim Harstad

The Unforgettable Flight

Of course I didn't always look like this. Hair once grew on top of my head, not on my chin, and when I hadn't shaved for a day or two the stubble that appeared was dark, not white. I still hold a clear memory of the day that change began.

Stalled in rush-hour traffic on Seattle's Airport Way one morning in March of 1966 in my gunmetal gray fastback Chevrolet. Gray as the sky, the wet street, the industrial buildings, and my own dark thoughts. The mist-green Ford beside me blew its horn. The rain drummed, the windshield wipers swiped. It had been like this since December, when I'd stopped doing outdoor labor in Ketchikan, Alaska. It was worse there. The rainbird is Ketchikan's official mascot. Moss grows everywhere, even on car windows. In October it had rained an inch a day, every single day. But I had escaped. To this.

The Ford's horn blew again, insistently. Its driver had the passenger-side window rolled down and was leaning toward me, motioning with her right hand. I rolled my fogged window down. "Mr. Harstad!" yelled the sinewy blonde over the noise of rain-strangled traffic.

"Gail Glockner!" I yelled back.

Gail Glockner had been an indifferent but likable student in my first-ever eleventh-grade English class at Renton High School nearly three years before. Her father, a lean man with a vise-grip handshake, had come to school one day. Why was I confusing his daughter's brain by making her read *Moby Dick* and write papers about it? I tried to explain why, and she eventually passed the course with a C. That was my first year. After my second year, I quit. There were over 150 of them every day. There was only one of me.

"What are you doing?" Gail Glockner shouted.

"Working at Boeing. What're you doing?"

"Working at Boeing." We both laughed.

A 1960s Seattle joke was that anyone not working for Boeing had either just been laid off by Boeing or was about to be hired by Boeing.

"Why aren't you teaching?" Her lane was moving. She was blocking traffic.

"Got tired of being poor."

Behind her, horns were honking. She honked back and jammed her Ford into gear.

"You were good!" she shouted as she drove away.

"Thanks!" I yelled at the muddy Oldsmobile following her. Eventually my lane also began to move. Toward Boeing.

After work that evening, the radio interrupted its program to announce that the State of Hawai'i Department of Education would be interviewing teachers downtown the next day. Especially English teachers. "I'm not going to work tomorrow," I told my roommates. "Hawai'i calls."

"You'll turn into a coconut out there," they warned.

"That sure beats moss."

The next day I talked to three dark-suited gentlemen from the DOE, who assured me that I was perfectly fitted for the position they were offering. Would I please sign my name on the line beside the X? "I'm good," I told myself. "Gail Glockner said so." And I signed.

In late August of 1966, I found myself at a sunny 35,000 feet over the Pacific Ocean in a gleaming silver Pan Am 707, built, of course, by Boeing. A week later, I was one of the new haole teachers at Wai'anae High School. Forty years later, I was one of the old haole teachers at University Laboratory School. All those students for all those years can blame Gail Glockner, if they can find her. I never saw her again.

Cathy Kanoelani Ikeda

8th Grade Education

Yamete, stop, *okaasan* scolds—
no crying
otosan's ashes sit silent on the mantle
as the minister starts the chanting again
Hayaku, hurry,
okaasan pushes me toward the shrine
I'm the oldest son, so I first,
pinch the incense, three times
put into the urn with the *senko* burning,
bow in prayer
namu amida butsu
namu amida butsu
Kaiji and Takushi behind me,
then Mit-chan behind them.

I responsible for them now
plus *okaasan,* pregnant with her fifth child.
Even if I beg *okaasan* for let me go high school,
she say *shikata ga nai,*
it can't be helped.
She say I have to go Pioneer Mill,
get my *bango*
keep food on the table,
make sure Mit-chan and the boys finish high school.

I one man now
with one 8th grade education.
I feel my life
floating away in *senko* smoke.

Terri Nakamura

I NEVAH KNOW MY MADA WAS ONE LESBIAN

I nevah know my mada was one lesbian until my jackass cousin Brian wen spill da beans. Me and him went to da same school and he was couple years older den me but he thought I was too ghetto, so he usually ignored me. But one rainy aftanoon wen I was waiting on da curb in da front parking lot of school fo Aunty Ron fo pick me up, he came up to me wit one smirk on his face. Brian thought he was hot shit since testorone hit him and he was only in six grade. His height and bulky muscles appealed to all da intermediate school girls. He had one eight grade girlfriend who gave him hickies everyday in da stairwells

"Ha, Chris you know wat my mom tole me?" he sneered. I nevah like Aunty Kate; she always grumble to my grandpa about everything and always spoke wit pity towards me.

"What, Brian?" I looked up since he was about seven inches taller than me.

"Your mom and Ron are carpet munchas," he folded his arms around his chest. I wanted fo punch his face and wipe dat smirk off him.

My forehead scrunched. "Wat you mean?" I told him. I nevah heard da term before.

"They lezzies, they like fo lick each other's nani." He waited for my reaction. I stared up at him in disbelief.

"Not, stop making up stories," I told him.

"You bettah watch out befoa you turn into one too," he told me. He started laughing. I grabbed my backpack and launched it at him. He stopped and put his arms up and grabbed the bag. He threw it back at me and it hit me in da face. I started fo cry and he started teasing me harder.

"Yeah, dat's why my mom no like your aunty," he continued. "She wen turn yo mom into one lesbo, one rug muncha."

"Shut up you asshole! Dat's not true," I never questioned Aunty Ron and my mom's relationship. Dey nevah act like dat towards each otha, so I nevah think nothing about it.

"Yeah right," Brian yelled. "Dey share one room, right? You so stupid if you don't know, you dummy!" he laughed. He stuck out his tongue and started making licking motions.

"Dis how dey do it to each otha, Chris," he told me. He started moaning, "Oh Ron! Oh Ron, be da man I want you to be! Especially since Chris's father wen bail on me. Be da man, be da man! Uh, uh, uh, be da man!"

I got even moa pissed. I stood up and pushed Brian and started attacking him with my fists.

"Ow, Chris, you dumb midget, get off me," he easily threw me off and I tripped on da curb and fell on my ass.

"You asshole!" I screamed, my face burned. Brian smirked at me and turned around and walked away and left me on da ground. I slowly got up.

I was pissed. It couldn't be true. No fuckin ways.

I saw Aunty Ron's rusty Honda Accord pull up in the driveway and I grabbed my backpack and ran to da car. She unlocked da passenger side car door, but I didn't get in. I stared at her face through da window until she electronically rolled it down.

"Aunty!" I exclaimed. She looked at my disheveled hair and red face and went all kines of concern on me. Raindrops started to fall, da coolness hitting da heat of my face.

"You okay, Pocho? Come inside, stay raining," she told me as she shifted da gear into park. "Wat happened? You got into one fight? Whea da girl stay? Wat's da mattah?" she started getting hyper.

"Are you and my mom girlfriends?" I shot at her. "Brian told me you and mom are lezzies, is dat true?" Aunty Ron gave me a funny face and looked at me as if she didn't know wat to say.

"Well?" I asked her defiant. I stood dea in front of da passenger door staring at my aunt. It started to rain hard, but I didn't want to get into da car until she answered me.

"I . . ." she stammered. She stopped, composed herself, and den spoke again.

"I nevah like you find out dis way," she spoke quietly. I took my backpack off my shoulder and slammed it against da car door.

"So you and my mom are lezzies," I spat out. "How can you do dis to my mom, to my family, to me, Ron?" I sneered. For da first time in my life I didn't add aunty. She looked at me with glassy eyes. It was as though I felt her hurt shoot through da car window and zap me. I felt bad, but I was also pissed to da max.

Aunty Ron's eyes started to tear and soon a river ran down her face while her eyes nevah left mine.

It was da first and only time I seen her cry. My anger melted into a puddle and I opened da door and jumped in da car. My arms went around her broad shoulders and I put my face on hers. She grabbed on to me tightly and let out a large sigh. She was still silent. I started to cry.

"No cry, my Pocho," she whispered. "Not your fault." She held on.

"I'm sorry, Aunty, I just wen feel stupid wen Brian came up to me . . ." I spat out. I continued, sobbing my ass off.

"I nevah like believe and I wen hit him and whack him wit my back-pack, cause I nevah like believe . . . but I no care . . . fo reals, I no care . . . you take care me, evah since I was one bebe," I began to choke. "You take care mom . . . even grandpa . . . I stay mad cause everyone know except me . . . I love you, you my aunty, you my aunty mom."

Aunty Ron was silent throughout my rant. She patted my head, den let me go when my sobbing subsided.

I sat back into the passenger seat. She had stopped crying too. She spoke in her usual tita attitude.

"Wow, you wen whack Brian . . . good fo you my girl . . . I wouldn't mind giving him some nice doughnuts right now . . .." She cracked a huge smile, and her coconut face filled wit warmth.

I smiled back through my teary face.

"I wen make pork chops fo dinner, sound good to you, my Pocho?" she started up the car and put da car into gear.

"Sounds really good, Aunty," I put my seatbelt on and we drove home.

Bill Teter

Changing Lanes

He has never been able to understand Honolulu traffic. What makes it bunch up in immovable jams in the middle of the day in the middle of the week? Just past three o'clock and he's stopped cold on Beretania Street. And pointed in the wrong direction at that. What made him think he could get to Ala Moana and back in time? He knows he'll be late—again—for his 3:30 class. He glances at the mess of student papers piled beside him on the seat. Two weeks and they still haven't been graded. Another set coming in today. A month to go before the end of the semester and he feels brain-dead already. He doesn't know how he'll be able to deal with the hundred or so papers that block his way to the summer.

Ahead of him the Punahou stoplight cycles from green to yellow to red. No one in his lane moves. He watches the cars passing slowly by on either side of his lane, waits for a break on his left, and when a moped chugs past, he pulls over. There's a sudden blast of a horn and screeching brakes, and a red Bronco stops less than a foot from the left rear of his Corolla. Very close call. He thinks for a moment about the expired no-fault card in his glove compartment, considers how fragile is the texture of his life this day. Even a small accident, no one hurt, could mean a court appearance and heavy financial consequences. He's living from paycheck to paycheck now, and saving nothing. If that Bronco had come a foot farther, he'd have been in very big trouble. He doesn't look at the Bronco's driver—eye contact with someone who has a right to be mad is the last thing he wants. Instead, he shakas, then straightens into his new lane. He knows he can't get far enough over to make a left onto Punahou, but one more lane over and he'll be able to turn at Kalākaua and begin to make his way back to the university. Then he sees his mistake.

"Stupid!" he says aloud. He should have moved right and turned up Punahou. That would've been a lot faster. In his mind he was still heading to Ala Moana and the dentist. But he knows already he's going to have to forget the appointment he's already late for. All the dentist is going to do today anyway is take X-rays and tell him how bad the tooth is. Too bad to save, no doubt. He wonders how much it will cost, wonders too if he could possibly skip the work. As if in answer his tooth suddenly stabs at him. That's the way it has been for a couple months now—a sneak-attack pain that comes and goes unpredictably, exploding along the lower right side of his jaw and then disappearing. He feels now like his head has gone through the windshield during a terrible head-on collision. Okay, okay, he can't avoid getting the tooth worked on. But he also can't afford what it will cost. The pain hints to him, and not subtly, that he can't afford to not be able to afford it.

No trade winds the last week or so—the air is still, damp, and hot. Thick, humid clouds make the sky look surly, just like everyone in their cars. He feels the sweat dripping beneath his shirt. This hot, and not even summer yet. The moped rider in front of him has the right idea: yellow tank top over a black and pink Wet Seal swimsuit, and a boogie board lashed on the back. On her way to the beach.

He reaches the Punahou intersection. At the stoplight his car idles roughly, threatening to stall. For no apparent reason, the Corolla occasionally does this. A few times it has cut out on him, just stalled dead. He knows he needs to have someone look at the car and fix it. He doesn't even want to think what that will cost. As he lets out the clutch and eases the car forward a bit, it shudders as if he is trying to start up in third gear. A warning to him, he knows, like the tooth.

Green . . . yellow . . . just before red, he makes it across Punahou Street. Closer to Kalākaua now—one more lane over. He flips on his turn signal.

He and Laura rode together only once, a Sunday drive around the island. At first they talked casually, but eventually she went silent, then rummaged around in his glove compartment until she found a little memo pad. She spent the rest of the drive writing. Even when he stopped at Sandy's she stayed in the car ("You need the sun more than me, haole boy," she'd smiled). When he dropped her off at her house, she said, "Read this tonight, Michael. Thanks for a fine day." She kissed him and waved when she got to her door. He never read the note. It's still in the glove compartment. He knows what it says—not the specifics, of course. But the kiss told him. He hasn't seen her in over three months.

He checks his watch: 3:20. It will probably be another five minutes before he can get around to Young Street and start back to UH. Ten minutes to get there, another ten or so to park in the structure and run (in this heat? not likely) up to Kuykendall. By then he'll be fifteen, twenty minutes late. Most of the class will be gone. Well, at least there'll be less grief because he doesn't have their papers graded. He wonders if this time the Department Chair will finally summon him to her office to talk about his future.

He tongues the hole in his tooth, sucks air through it as if fanning a flame. It makes him wince. He gasses the engine and soothes the rattle. He looks at the papers beside him and feels queasy. How will he get them all read? How will he even start? He can't even find a decent song on the goddamned radio.

Off to his left he sees the small two-story building, no different really from the other L-shaped "plazas" along Beretania and King Streets. The building announces its name and birth date in block letters on the wall facing the street: Chong Building. 1954. Korean characters on a small sign in the parking lot advertise a ground floor beauty salon. He knows even without the parking lot sign that there are two dentists' offices on the ground floor, and a travel agent and a chiropractor upstairs. At the far end of the building upstairs is the CPA office where Laura works. He drives past this building often, and tries not to notice it.

The traffic nudges forward. He watches for a break on his left. He hears the sputter of the moped in front of him, and a few horns further ahead. On the radio Lex Brodie thanks him very much. A space opens and he makes a sharp turn into the next lane. But so does the Bronco behind him, accelerating as it turns. The driver blares his horn again. Michael jerks his steering wheel hard to the right. Before he can hit his brakes his right front bumper clips the moped, which has stopped. The bike flies out from under the driver and bounces off a taxicab. The young woman disappears beneath the front of his car. The Bronco charges past, the driver hurling a curse at him like a hand grenade.

Michael is sick to his stomach. As he flings open his door and jumps out of the car, he sees the woman's head come slowly up over the hood. At least he didn't run her over. He helps her up.

"I'm sorry," she says.

"What?" he answers. "Are you kidding? I just rear-ended you."

"No. I'm okay." She seems a little dizzy. "I'm just sorry."

The cab driver is out now. He looks at the rear of his car, then at the two of them. "Goddamn," he says to no one in particular in a thick Asian accent of some sort. "Goddamn."

"You sure you're all right?" Michael asks her. Together they look at her moped, bent in the middle and lying on its side, the motor still stuttering.

The boogie board is several feet away, its skag snapped off. No marks on his car. The moped has broken the taxi's right taillight.

Traffic snarls itself into a knot around them, and grinds to a halt two lanes wide behind them. Seven or eight cars back he sees the blue dome light of a police car. A passenger climbs out of the taxi. He wears an ugly orange aloha shirt. Tourist. "We're going to miss our flight," he says ominously.

The cab driver mutters, "Look what you do. Goddamn." He gestures not at the back of his cab so much as in a wide, vague arc that takes in the whole mess on Beretania Street.

Michael follows the cabbie's sweeping gesture. He hears a few horns. The girl is sitting against the hood of his car, dazed, muttering. The police car swings into the next lane and starts to move up towards them. The blue light begins silently to flash.

Now he sees someone appear at the top of the end stairway of the Chong Building. She walks down a few steps and sits. She is smoking. He squints, trying to see clearly through his pain, but he can't tell if it's Laura or not. It looks like her, and she is smoking with her left hand. She seems at this distance to be looking right at him; if so, she makes no sign of recognizing him. He fights against an absurd desire to wave at her.

"Goddamn," the cab driver says again.

Bill Teter

Hiking to Kaliuwa'a in the Late Afternoon

That day
We hiked silently through a forest
Of ripe mountain apples and torch ginger,
The sun ruthless in a cobalt sky.
But up ahead friendly clouds
Nuzzled against the mountain.

We had only kissed once. You
Said you weren't sure. You
Were waiting for a sign. You
Asked me to be patient. Later,

We rested in cool shadow at the edge of a quiet pool.
You sank a stone into my reflection,
Testing the depths.
I sat still
While my image wavered,
Until the ripples calmed themselves for you
And the surface was as smooth and still as hope.

Kristel Yoneda

The Politician and the Writer

The politician and the writer agree to meet, for the first time in four years, both penciling it in their respective calendars as just "lunch." The writer suggests Mariposa at Neiman Marcus because he loves their popover rolls and the politician reluctantly agrees despite the high probability the two of them will be seen together by someone she knows.

He rushes to the restaurant only to arrive two minutes before their scheduled time, pacing near the front desk until he notices the politician is already seated. She doesn't wave when she sees him and instead gives a strained smile, as if to signify her lack of enthusiasm. Making his way to the table, the writer mentally practices how to execute a polite hug. He tries to remember if the politician usually leans left or right in an embrace, however his energy is wasted and she doesn't budge from her seat when the writer greets her.

"Oh, hi," she answers, surprised to see him standing in front of her. She sounds mildly irritated, as if she were being interrupted from something more important than stirring her coffee.

"Were you waiting long?" the writer asks. "I didn't realize you were here already."

She sips her coffee slowly to avoid conversation. "Nope. Just got here." She feels the gaze of an older man nearby wearing an aloha shirt and slacks. She wonders if he recognizes her. The politician quickly surveys the area as the writer seats himself, doing a mental inventory of familiar and unfamiliar faces. When the writer accidentally bumps his arm against the table, the man looks up curiously in their direction. This is mostly because he gets distracted by any kind of movement around him and soon he returns to his own conversation. The politician decides to move the man into her unfamiliar column, but leaves a mental asterisk next to his face.

The writer fumbles with the menu. "Do you know what you're going to order?"

"Oh, I'm fine with my coffee," the politician answers flatly. "I ate already."

He tries to hide his irritation that she's already eaten despite their plans today. He pretends to scan the appetizers section, using it as an opportunity to get a better look at the politician. Her hair is pulled into a haphazard ponytail, and her floral print blouse, for better or worse, makes her look notably older than she really is.

The politician feels the writer's eyes on her, so she instead concentrates on how she can swirl her coffee into a tiny whirlpool without spilling over the sides of her mug. She doesn't know why she said she ate already. She had her regular unexciting bowl of instant oatmeal for breakfast, but that was nearly six hours earlier and now her stomach is knotting up in anxiety and hunger. She considers opening the menu to order something, but feels strangely paralyzed knowing the writer is watching her. She feels like he's searching for chinks in her armor and she won't allow him the upper hand. She doesn't want him to reach for the check at the end of the meal, like she knows he will. She doesn't want to feel like she owes him anything, even an $18 sashimi salad.

The writer notices the politician tensing up, but doesn't know why. He tries to push the conversation along. "So how have you been? Busy?"

"Yeah, pretty busy. We're getting ready for campaign season," she explains. "There have been a lot of long nights at the Capitol and, actually, I need to get going in about thirty minutes. I have to head back and take care of some stuff."

"Wow, you sound like a real politician," he smiles. He's met with a vacant stare.

"And you? Have you written anything lately?" she asks.

"A few things," he answers. "Right now I'm working on my final edits for a short story I'm getting published."

As the writer outlines the premise of his piece, a memory of him floods the politician's mind: the image of them in their first apartment working side by side at their desks. She remembers looking over at him from her mountain of textbooks and how he always said "I love you" whenever he finished writing for the night. She neatly folds up this thought and tucks it away by focusing instead on how much rounder his face has gotten since she last saw him. She wonders if this means he's happier now.

The waitress flips open her notepad at the table and smiles at them. "Ready? What can I get you?" she asks.

"I'll have the strip loin, please. Medium well. Oh, and lots of those popovers. If I could I'd probably order popovers with a side of strip loin instead," he laughs.

"Let me tell you a secret. This is totally my favorite shift because when it's slow, I just sit in the back and eat those things. Don't worry," the waitress winks. "I've got you covered. And for you, miss?"

The politician had forgotten how the writer's friendly, almost flirtatious nature, always puts strangers at ease. She can't understand why his personality now simultaneously charms and irritates her. "Just more coffee, please."

Before they were defined by their professions, they were known simply as Ethan and Katelyn. They met during their first year in college and fell in love, navigating the next seven years together like invincible teenagers. If asked now, neither of them can remember who ended it and both don't like talking about it.

The waitress returns with a basket of popovers and a small dish of their specialty mango butter. "I love this butter," the writer says as he generously slathers up his roll.

"I know," the politician finally smiles. She remembers they celebrated their first anniversary here and, briefly, they're both reminiscing about the same memory.

The food arrives soon after and the writer unfolds his napkin on his lap, reaching for his silverware. Out of habit, he offers, "Do you want to try my steak? I can cut you a piece." He opens his hand, signaling her to pass him the small plate sitting near her untouched silverware.

She waves no, pointing down at her coffee. "I'm good, thanks."

"Can I ask you a question?" he asks. "Why did you agree to see me today? I know you're busy and I'm not high on your priority list anymore."

The politician, without thinking, reassures him, "No, no, you are." She isn't sure if she means it, but it's too late to take it back.

He cringes at her transparent response. "But why did you decide to meet me?"

"Because you're an old friend." She's not sure why she said that and soon regrets it when she recognizes the hurt all over the writer's face. She doesn't mean to wound him, but sitting here with him reminds her of something he destroyed and it still hurts her. He wonders how many times she's used the term "old friend" to describe past lovers or if that's what he's been reduced to in her memory. He searches her face for any remnant of their past, any memory left behind, but she looks so unfamiliar to him now.

During their sophomore year he remembers buying her a small journal, identical to his own, to document their adventures together. She collected ticket stubs and printed out poetry that reminded her of him, Scotch-taping it neatly to its pages. His journal was filled with prose, poetry and short stories strung together with her name. Every so often, they'd trade journals and read together; laughing at how each remembered the same event just a bit differently than the other. Back then their lives fit together very neatly, page for page.

The writer picks up the check as soon as the waitress sets it down. He thanks her for the extra popovers and makes small talk while writing out the tip. Watching him interact with the woman, the politician can't remember why she once loved the writer so much. She recognizes how important he used to be to her, but feels very disconnected from it, as if his significance is to someone else.

They walk together to exit the restaurant, both thanking the hostesses at the front desk. The politician checks her watch. "I have to go," she says. "Thank you for the coffee."

"Yeah, of course," he answers. "It's the least I could do. I mean, originally I wanted to buy you lunch today." He doesn't mean for it to sound rude, but the politician thinks he's being passive-aggressive with that deflated look on his face.

"I hope I see you around," she says as she turns to leave. She feels bad because it sounds insincere, but she doesn't know how to comfort him anymore.

"Take care of yourself," he calls out to her. He stands there and watches as the politician disappears into the crowd. He's surprised at how long it takes him to locate her again, but then he recognizes the familiar bend of her ponytail as she walks away.

LETS REMEMBER WE DIDN'T START THIS VIOLENCE ON EARTH

HOMO SAP INHERITED THE WEAPON

HOMO SAP DIDN'T INVENT THE WEAPON.

AUSTRALOPITHICINES

FROM HOMO HABILIS 2 MILL YBP

H. HABILIS TAKES US BACK

HOMICIDAL TRIP AGAINST CONSPECIFIC

ALL THIS VIOLENCE

EVERY HOMO TYPE SINCE THEN HAS BEEN A KILLER

SO HEY, AIN'T EVEN OUR FUCKING APES

FAULT! IT'S THE OTHER APES

H HABILIS, AUSTRALOPITHECINES, H ERECTUS

THAT STARTED IT. IF THEY'D

BEEN MORE PEACEFUL WE WOULDN'T

BE THE WAY WE ARE, THAT'S KARMA. BUT, SINCE,

THRU NO FAULT OF OUR OWN, WE ARE

BEQUEATHED TO US BY H. HABILIS ET AL.

ON THIS BLOODY PATH, LET'S DO IT

RIGHT. I SAY PURE HYPER TECH WAR SCI-WAR

I'M FOR PUSH BUTTON WAR

SANITARY WHITE GLOVES. RED TELEPHONE

CLEAN

BRIEFCASE WITH CODE. PRESS THE BUTTON

THE RECORDED MESSAGE

NO NEED DECLARATIONS OF WAR. OLD FASHIONED

NO NEED ARMY / NAVY / MARINE CORP

AIR FORCE. MOTH BALL EM.

WARRIOR BULLSHIT OLD FASHIONED

LEAVE IT TO THE SCIENTISTS,

REMEMBER 99% OF THE SCIENTISTS

WHO'VE EVER LIVED LIVE NOW — 1/3

OF EM ARE WORKING ON THE SCIENCE

OF HOW TO KILL CONSPECIFICS

IN LARGISH NUMBERS. THEY'RE BOUND TO COME UP WITH SOME

RIGHT AWAY

GIVE US THE VAPORIZER BOMB, GUYS!

ONE TIME 100-200,000 KEEP A MINIMUM

WHAT'S 100,000-200,000 WHEN WE

GOT 5 1/2 BILLION? IN ANY CASE LETS WE

BE LIBERAL IN OUR APPLICATION

OF SCI-WAR. BUT, NOW, HOW ABOUT THE VICTIMS

DO WE

THINK ABOUT ALL THOSE PEOPLE WHO

OF POPULATION? RETHINK

DEATH.

THINK OF IT

Tribute to Albert Saijo

Editors' Note: Albert Saijo passed over to the next on June 2, 2011, in Volcano, Hawai'i, where he'd lived for almost 20 years. His importance as a poet and writer was shaped by his life: raised in the truck farm era of the San Gabriel Valley; interned in Heart Mountain in World War II; veteran of the 100th Battalion, 442nd Regimental Combat Team; friend and co-author of Beat writers Jack Kerouac and Lew Welch (*Trip-Trap*, and Saijo is the Japanese character in *Big Sur*), as well as Lawrence Ferlinghetti, Gary Snyder, and others. Author of *The Backpacker*, on wilderness backpacking (published in 1972), and *OUTSPEAKS—A RHAPSODY* (Bamboo Ridge Press, 1997), his first book of poetry.

Saijo wrote in pencil in large unlined artist sketchbooks, correcting with colored pencils, illustrating and inserting lines in the margins. He insisted on ALL CAPS and avoided punctuation. We've included reproductions of some of his manuscript pages in this section. His wife Laura reports that he continued to write until nearly the end. She shared these unpublished poems culled from his writing journals, some dating back to the 1950s.

We are honored by his presence in *Bamboo Ridge* and grateful for his contribution to the literary community.

THE ZOO HYPOTHESIS

EARTH IS THE ZOO OF A SUPERIOR INTELLIGENCE — WE ARE WOUND UP TO GO THRU WHAT WE CALL LIFE FOR THE ENTERTAINMENT OF A SUPERIOR INTELLIGENCE WHO WATCHES US LIKE A DAYTIME SERIAL — HOW ELSE EXPLAIN THE FACT WE GO THRU OUR MOVES KNOWING THAT IT'S PRETTY MUCH ALL BULLSHIT FROM BEGINNING TO END — WHY DO WE FEEL WE ARE WALKING THRU A PART — WHAT'S PLAYING — SUPERIOR INTELLIGENCE LIKES RAW SWEEPING DRAMA TO DISPLAY GAMUT OF EMOTIONS — ACTION — STUPENDOUS EFFECTS — A CAST OF BILLIONS WITH PLENTY HEROES HEROINES & VILLAINS — A STORYLINE TO TWIST YOUR HEART AS IT TAKES YOU FROM SAMSARA BOTTOM RIGHT ON UP TO NIRVANA HEAVEN — & GORE — SUPERIOR INTELLIGENCE VERY PARTIAL TO GORE OF VISCERAL KIND — SUPERIOR INTELLIGENCE EATS WHILE WATCHING US SLASH EACH OTHER APART AS WE WATCH TV GORE WHILE EATING AT PRIM TV TRAY — SUPERIOR INTELLIGENCE WILL EVEN STAY UP TO WATCH A GOOD HEAD ON COLLISION — FOLKS IT AIN'T ALIENS FROM OUTER SPACE BEEN DOING THOSE BAD THINGS TO US ALL THIS TIME IT'S SUPERIOR INTELLIGENCE — OR IS SUP INTELL IN CONSPIRACY WITH INTERGALACTIC HEAVIES TO PUT HUMANS IN A BAD LIGHT UNIVERSALLY — SUP INTELL MAY BE SUPERIOR BUT GODDAMMIT WE'RE ALL BASICALLY EQUAL AROUND HERE AIN'T WE — DOESN'T CONSTITUTION OF UNIVERSE HAVE BILL OF RIGHTS — LIKE THIS CONSTANT SURVEILLANCE OF OUR SMALLEST ACTS — NO PRIVACY OR WHAT — SAY YOU'RE STOMPING RIGHTEOUS MAD & YOU'RE THROTTLING YOUR WORST PERSONAL ENEMY & YOU REMEMBER SUP INTELL IS WATCHING WITH A BEMUSED SMILE — MAKE YOU FEEL LIKE AN ASSHOLE WOULDN'T IT — I MEAN HOW COME WE GOTTA TAKE THIS SHIT — WE MAY BE ANIMALS IN A ZOO BUT SWEET JESUS — THERE'S GOT TO BE A WAY OUT — MAYBE DEATH OR SATORI — BUT THESE ARE JUST PROVISIONAL CUZ THERE'S THOSE FUCKING BARDOS THEN WACKO REBIRTH — MAKES YOU WANNA LIE DOWN & KICK & SCREAM DON'T IT — BUT HERE'S A POSSIBLE SOLUTION — LET'S TRY OPEN EYE OF COMPASSION — THEN BE ANIMAL IN ZOO & LOOK RIGHT THRU CAGE BARS AT SUP INTELL EVEN AT SUP INTELL'S BIZARRE TASTE IN ENTERTAINMENT & I BELIEVE WE WILL SEE SUPERIOR INTELLIGENCE IS NO MORE THAN US IN AN ODD MIND BEND

GOD WITH THE HELP

GOD WITH THE HELP OF EDISON AND THE CHINESE INVENTED EVERYTHING ON EARTH — EVERYTHING — THIS IS A WELL KNOWN FACT — THEY DID IT IN 6 DAYS WITH A DAY OFF ON SUNDAY — QUESTION — WHY 6 DAYS WORK 1 DAY REST — WHAT'S THE RUSH — HERE A JOB CAN TAKE AN ETERNITY AS FAR AS THAT GOES SINCE THERE IS NOTHING ELSE HAPPENING & IT'S AUTOMATIC — WE CAN RELAX — LET'S FACE IT — GOD EDISON AND THE CHINESE WERE WORKAHOLICS — GIMME A SOCIETY WHERE SUNDAY LASTS 7 DAYS IN A 7 DAY WEEK & EVERYTHING IS FREE — WE CAN DO IT

FLAT EARTH

I WANT THE EARTH TO BE FLAT & CIRCULAR WITH MYSELF AT THE CENTER ALWAYS — AND I WANT IT TO BE THE SAME FOR EVERY OTHER CREATURE AS EVERY CREATURE IS AT THE CENTER OF ITS OWN RAINBOW — THE ASTRONOMY CAN FOLLOW — THERE WILL BE THE ILLUSION OF CURVING AWAY AT THE HORIZON BUT THIS IS OK SINCE WE NEVER REACH THE HORIZON — THE ILLUSION IS PURELY AN ARTIFACT OF OUR MODE OF APPREHENSION — THE IDEA OF A SPHERICAL EARTH HAS PROVED A TROUBLESOME ONE — DO WE NEED IT — LETS GET TO WHERE WE DONT — THINK OF IT —THE EARTH IS FLAT & CIRCULAR —STILL YOU MAY MOVE OVER IT IN ANY DIRECTION WITHOUT EVER REACHING AN END — YOU MAY EVEN RETURN TO THE SAME SPOT MANY TIMES —MYSTERY OF MYSTERIES — LETS HAVE NO EXPLANATION FOR THIS

SIMPLIFY COMMUNICATION

1

I WANT THERE TO BE NO DIFF BETWEEN WHAT I THINK AND WHAT I SPEAK — I WANT TO SIMPLIFY COMMUNICATION TO THAT — THINK — SPEAK — NO EDIFICE OF STYLE — NO SUBJECTION OF THINKSPEAK TO DESIGN INTERVENTION — NO BELLE LIT IDEAL — JUST UTTERANCE — LIKE BOW WOW LIKE MOO

2

I WANT TO WRITE AS SIMPLE AS A CHILD DRAWS — I WANT TO MAKE A PLAIN STATEMENT OF FACT — LIKE HERE IS BLANK PAPER — THIS LINE ACROSS THE BOTTOM IS THE GROUND & I AM STANDING ON THE GROUND — THERE ARE FLOWERS & GRASSES & A TREE GROWING OUT OF THE GROUND — I AM TALLER THAN THE TREE EVEN IF IT SHAKES ITS BRANCHES UPWARD LIKE ARMS — ABOVE THE GROUND IS BELOW THE SKY AND THEN THE SKY STARTS — IT IS BLUE WITH WHITE CLOUDS AND A BIRD IS FLYING ACROSS IT — THE SUN IS A BRIGHT YELLOW BALL & IT PUSHES ITS RAYS OUTWARD INTO THE BLUE SKY — MY HOUSE IS JUST AS TALL AS ME BUT THE SMOKE COMING OUT OF THE CHIMBLY GOES HIGHER THAN ME & I AM POINTING AT IT AS IT GOES UP INTO THE SKY — INSIDE THE HOUSE WATER IS RUNNING OUT OF THE FAUCET INTO THE SINK — IN ANOTHER ROOM THE LIGHT IS ON OVER THE TABLE & NOW I AM SITTING ON A CHAIR AT THE TABLE DRAWING THIS WRITING

TIME

TIME IS SAMSARA — IT IS IRREVERSIBLE & CONSTANT — IT PILES SUFFERING ON SUFFERING — TIME IS NIRVANA — IT IS AN IRREVERSIBLE & CONSTANT REVELATION OF DIVINITY — RAPTURE IS IN TIME — TO LIVE IN TIME IS TO WORSHIP

YOU WRITER YOU

I PUT ASIDE THE BLACK-HEADED GROSBEAK'S MELODIOUS LAY & BECOME WORDSMITH — IM NOT SURE I LIKE THIS BUSINESS OF WRITING AS MUCH AS I FIND MYSELF IN IT NOW AT THIS POINT IN MY EARTH LIFE JOURNEY — IT IS DIRECTED THINKING & IM BEGINNING TO SEE DIRECTED THINKING LIES AT THE BOTTOM OF ALL OUR ILLS — DIRECTED THINKING IN A VERBAL MODE IS ESPECIALLY DAMAGING — IT TRASHES OUR MENTAL SPACE — IT TURNS THINGS BROWN — AT THE SAME TIME IT IS LIKE AN ODD DEVOTION — IN WRITING WE TELL & REHEARSE TIME TOY BEADS CONSTANTLY — WHEN A WRITING IS ON OUR MIND WE BECOME TIMEBOUND & DESPERATE — A ZOMBIE TO OUR DAILY LIFE — IN PARTICULAR WHEN DOING A LONG PIECE THAT REQUIRES YOU RETURN TO IT DAY AFTER DAY COMPARED TO WHICH A SHORT PIECE IS A LARK & INSPIRED MAKING THE HEART BEAT FASTER — THE LONG PIECE IS A KARMIC CHORE — EVEN AS YOU BRIDLE AT IT YOU KNOW YOU HAVE TO DO IT — WHY — BECAUSE I WANT TO TELL YOU I WANT TO TELL YOU I WANT TO TELL YOU

SKYSCRAPER

CHEAP IDEA WITH SOLEMN SHADOW CANYON — STRICTLY PAPER SOLUTION — TOTALLY OUT OF SCALE — A PSYCHOTIC ARTIFACT — PSYCHOTIC ARCHITECT — PSYCHOTIC CLIENT — LAB RAT LIVING MODE APPLIED TO HUMAN — DEAD AIR OF DEVITALIZED INTERIOR — SICK BUILDING SYNDROME — ENERGY SUCKER — THE UNLOVELY ARCHITECTURE OF MEGALOMANIA & GREED

NOW I RECOGNIZE IT ... FOLLOW

~~HAND WRITTEN~~

WRIT BY HAND

I GUESS I'M OLD FASHIONED

I'LL ALWAYS WRITE BY HAND —

THE ~~PHYSICAL~~ EYE-

HAND - MIND CIRCUIT

ZERO MAN GOD MIND TIME SPACE MIND WITH PHYSICAL PERIMETERS

GIVES ME PLEASURE

EXERCISE IT IS MY

THE ONE PLEASURE

TRAIL — THAT THRU

I PURSUE

AS I ARMED ONLY WITH

BRUSHY GRAMMAR

WILD INNER VISION THE

I AM INNER VISION MAN — EARTH

FEEDS ME SYMBOLS OF ITSELF

TRAIL I FOLLOW IN TURN

AS I FOLLOW TRAIL

I PRESS MARKS ON PAPER

SO I DONT GET LOST —

ALPHABETIC MARKS I GARNER

IN AGGREGATES THAT STRUNG TOGETHER

CONNOTE MEANINGS

FROM THIS 24 HOURS A DAY

NONSTOP EXPERIENCE IN

WHAT WE CALL (CIVILIZED STYLE) THIS LONG HELD

BEING ALIVE — TO THE POINT OF BURSTING BY HAND IS THE

BREATH — WRITING CHEAPEST

THEN THINK OF IT FORM OF DOING ART NEXT TO SINGING

ONLY OUT OF POCKET EXPENSE PENCIL & PAPER

PRESS AIR THRU YOUR THROAT HAPP IN

VOICE EYE HAND

— MIND A FREEBIE

COORDINATION A FREE

& MUSE DONT CHARGE —

MINIMUM EQUIPMENT FOR OPTIMUM EXPOSURE

I WRITE IN A 8½" X 11" SKETCH BOOK

WITH 288 PAGES COST ME $11.49 —

MY PENCIL IS A PENTEL AUTOMATIC

USES 0.5 MM LEAD SO

MIND-EYE HAND COORDINATION

SET ME BEFORE A MT & TELL ME TO DRAW IT AS I WILL DRAW YOU MY VISION OF IT WHICH MAY OR MAY NOT BE YOUR MT

THRU MOUTH TONGUE THROAT

WRIT BY HAND

GUESS IM OLD FASHIONED I'LL ALWAYS WRITE BY HAND — USING MY BUILT IN FREE MIND EYE HAND COORDINATION CIRCUIT — INVISIBLE MIND WITH PHYSICAL PERIMETERS — I PRESS MY MARKS WITH PENCIL ON PAPER — IT IS MY TRAIL — THE ONE I LEAVE AS I FOLLOW SCENT OF INNER WILD BEAST THROUGH BUSHY GRAMMAR OF CIVILIZATION — I SET DOWN ALPHABETIC MARKS SO I DONT GET LOST — SO I CAN FIND MY WAY OUT — I AM AN INNER VISION MAN — EARTH FEEDS ME SYMBOLS OF ITSELF—BUT SET ME BEFORE A MT & TELL ME TO DRAW IT & I WILL DRAW YOU A MT THOUGH IT MAY NOT LOOK LIKE A MT TO YOU — PERSONAL MEANINGS ARE MY GAME — MEANINGS I GARNER FROM THIS 24 HOUR A DAY GREENWICH MEAN TIME NON STOP GRUNT IN BEING WHAT WE CALL ALIVE — THIS LONG HELD BREATH TO THE POINT OF BURSTING — WRITING BY HAND WITH PENCIL ON PAPER IS THE CHEAPEST FORM OF ART NEXT TO DRAWING & SINGING — INNER VOICE EYE HAND MIND COORDINATION A FREEBIE & MUSE DONT CHARGE — OUT OF POCKET EXPENSE FOR THIS HOBBY MINIMAL — I WRITE IN A 288 PAGE 144 SHEET 8 1/2" x 11" SKETCHBOOK COST ME $11.49 —THAT'S ABOUT 4 CENTS PER EACH RECTO & VERSO — THE PAPER IS REGULAR DRAWING PAPER — MY PENCIL IS A PENTEL MECHANICAL USES 0.5 mm LEAD SO NO NEED EVER SHARPEN — I USE 2B LEAD WHICH IS SOFT & DARK — PENCIL HAS REPLACEABLE ERASER — PENCIL WITH ERASER HEAD IS RIGHT UP THERE IN MY LIST OF GREATEST ACHIEVEMENTS OF CIVILIZATION — THE PENTEL PENCIL COST $2.59 — A LIGHT WELL DESIGNED PRODUCT THAT WORKS — FITS NICELY IN HAND — MADE IN JAPAN WHERE THEY ONCE BRED FOR EYE HAND MIND COORDINATION — MY FAVORITE PIECE OF SINO JAP CALLIGRAPHIC ART IS RYOKAN'S —1 2 3 ICHI NI SAN — GREAT CALLIGRAPHY MAKES TEXT LOOK LIKE WHAT IT MEANS — SO FOR TOTAL CAPITAL OUTLAY OF $14.08 I CAN DO MY ART — THE HIGH OF WRITING FOR ME IS WATCHING WORDS FORM ON PAPER AT PENCIL POINT COMPLETE WITH MEANING & NO AUTHOR

ZOOM ZONE

DO THINGS QUICKLY LEAVING MORE TIME FOR HAPPY
MICROSOFT AD

WAS THAT YOU ZOOMED BY — THAT WAS US ZOOMED BY ZONED — EVERYBODY GOT GLOBAL BRAIN — COMPULSORY MOLECULE SIZE BIOCHIP IMPLANT PUT WHOLE HUMAN RACE IN SYNC — NOW OUR INFO CAPACITY OUTSTRIPS THAT OF STANDARD NATURAL BRAIN — NUMBER CRUNCH FASTER THAN IDIOT SAVANT — AS SWIFT AS TIME IN BOTH DIRECTIONS — 6 BILLION SUBSETS OF ADAM IN SYNERGY MAKE EARTH HUM — NOOSPHERE HERE — CYBER BUDDHAMIND BLANKETS EARTH — www.cybersangha.com — DEATH OF PRIVACY — NO MORE SECRETS — PSYCHOLOGY USELESS — PERSONAL ENCRYPTION IMPOSSIBLE SO SELF OUTMODED — WE LOOK INTO EACH OTHERS EYES AND SEE OPEN TO THE SKY — WE SEE PRISTINE DEPTH OF GLOBAL BRAIN — GLOBAL BECOMES LOCAL & VICE VERSA — GLOBALOCAL HYPERTECH LANGUAGE TOO FAST FOR MOUTH TO SPEAK — WE SPEAK SWIFT DOTS OF LIGHT — MACHINE TALK TO MACHINE TAKE CARE OF EVERYTHING FROM CRADLE TO GRAVE — EVERYONE THINKING THE SAME THOUGHT SIMULTANEOUSLY — EVERYONE WANT SAME THING AT SAME TIME & WANT IT FAST — DESIRE FULFILLMENT GAP ALMOST CLOSED — GOODS ALMOST FREE — CREDIT NO LIMIT — CONSTANT DESIRE PUMP UP — DESIRE INFINITE — PROFIT AUTOMATIC — HOMO SAPIENS BACK FLIP TO PREADAMITE — NOW GOT PLENTY MORE TIME FOR HAPPY

CAS

ONE OF OUR FIXED IDEAS THAT AFFECTS OUR LIFE MIGHTILY IS THAT WE INHABIT ONE SPACE THE SPACE OF CIVILIZED AWAKE STATE SELFHOOD — EVERYTHING ELSE BEING STATIC WE TUNE OUT — CIVILIZED AWAKE STATE SELFHOOD IS WHO WE ARE BOTH AS PRIVATE INDIVIDUAL & AS PUBLIC CONGREGATE COG — WE ARE BORN INTO IT THEN NURSED INTO IT TILL WE ARE PROPERLY BRAINWASHED INTO INTRICATE BEHAVIOR OF CIVILIZED SOCIAL BEING IN A SETTING LARGELY OF OUR OWN FABRICATION WHICH WE CALL REALITY & ACT OUT 24/7 BECUZ WE HAVE FIXED IT SO EVEN IF WE ZONK OUT ONCE A DAY — EVEN IF ONCE A DAY BEING IN CIVILIZED AWAKE STATE HAS EXHAUSTED US TO POINT WHERE WE GOTTA RETREAT TO BEDROOM & CLOSE THE DOOR BEHIND US PULL CURTAIN ACROSS WINDOW TAKE OFF OUR WAKING STATE CLOTHES GET INTO BED TURN OUT LIGHT CLOSE EYES & FALL ASLEEP PERCHANCE TO DREAM WITH WONDERFUL ASSURANCE THAT ONCE WE GET THROUGH THIS NECESSARY BUT MEANINGLESS & INCONVENIENT BLANK OUT WASTE OF TIME — WE GOT IT FIXED SO CIV AWAKE STATE WILL BE THERE THE MOMENT WE OPEN OUR EYES — CIVILIZATION NEVER SLEEPS IT ONLY FALLS OVER DEAD IN THE DARK — WE GET UP DON CIV AWAKE SELFHOOD CLOTHES — PERFECT FIT FOR MOVING THROUGH SAMSARALAND

EVER 9/11

ONE TWO PUNCH DROPS BIG APPLE FOR LONG COUNT — 2 BIT PRICKS HIT PENTAGONAL FORTRESS AMERICA — SECRET ENEMY FROM 3RD WORLD BRING DESTRUCTION TO HOMELAND — CHICKENS COME HOME TO ROOST BIG TIME

LIFE DIES IN GREENHOUSE

A FAST FORWARD VIEW OF
CATASTROPHE

UNDER CAP OF FOSSIL FUEL CO_2
EARTH GETS HOT — OCEANS
WARM & EXPAND — ICE MELTS —
STORMS GROW MORE FIERCE
& ACID — HIGH WATER
DROWNS LOWLAND & STORM ~~FAR INLAND~~
SURGE ~~[illegible] WATER~~ SEAWALL —
PUT MANHATTAN BEHIND ~~[illegible]~~
WATERWAYS EUTROPHICATE ~~[illegible]~~
MORE & MORE LAND SLIPS UNDER
WATER — SEWERS FLOOD —
OUTBREAK OF EXOTIC DISEASE —
LIFE GETS SICK WORLDWIDE —
FAR INLAND HEAT WAVES
& DROUGHT — SALT LAKES &
DESERTS GROW. NO RELIEF —
LIFE CHOKES IN OZONE ~~SINK~~
ONLY ANEROBIC MICROBES SURVIVE
EARTH BACK TO THE ROCK WATER
AIR WIND FIRE ICE
~~ANEROBIC MICROBES~~
~~[illegible]~~

LIFE DIES IN GREENHOUSE

A FAST FORWARD VIEW OF CATASTROPHE

UNDER CAP OF FOSSIL FUEL CARBON DIOXIDE EARTH GETS HOT — OCEANS WARM & EXPAND — ICE MELTS — STORMS GROW MORE FIERCE & ACID — HIGH WATER DROWNS LOWLANDS — WATERWAYS EUTROPHICATE — STORM SURGE PUT MANHATTAN BEHIND SEAWALL — MORE & MORE LAND SLIPS UNDERWATER — SEWERS FLOOD — OUTBREAK OF EXOTIC DISEASE — LIFE GETS SICK WORLDWIDE — FAR INLAND HEAT WAVES & DROUGHT — SALT LAKES GET SALTIER — DESERTS GROW — NO RELIEF — CLIMATE SHUDDERS — LIFE CHOKES IN OZONE SINK WITH ONLY ANAEROBIC MICROBES SURVIVING — EARTH BACK TO THEM AND ROCK WATER AIR WIND FIRE ICE

CRUEL & UNUSUAL

LETS OPEN UP ALL OUR PRISONS — LETS LET EVERYONE OUT INCLUDING THE MOST HEINOUS RAPE TORTURER SERIAL MURDER — THE MOST HEINOUS R T S M THE NATION STATE HAS LONG BEEN AT LARGE — AND LETS NOT FRET ABOUT THE SOCIABLES OF IT — ISNT ADAPTATION THE STRONGEST TRAIT OF OUR SPECIES — AND LETS LET EVERYONE OUT WITH A DECENT COMPENSATION — $100,000 SAY SO THEY GOT GREASE TO PHASE IN OUTSIDE — THE DEFENSE BUDGET FOR 1 YEAR SHOULD COVER IT — LET DEFENSE TREAD WATER 1 YEAR WHILE WE RIGHT THIS AWFUL WRONG — TALK ABOUT CRUEL & UNUSUAL PUNISHMENT OUR PRISON SYSTEM ISN'T CRUEL & UNUSUAL PUNISHMENT — NO — I GET IT — FOR HUMANS PRISONS ARENT CRUEL OR UNUSUAL PUNISHMENT IN THAT FAR WORSE THINGS ARE DONE OUTSIDE PRISONS IN THE WAY OF PUNISHMENT EVERY DAY & EVERYBODY KNOWS IT — IF PRISONS ARENT CRUEL & UNUSUAL PUNISHMENT WHAT IS CRUEL & UNUSUAL PUNISHMENT — HOW ABOUT SENDING SOMEONE WHO IS DYING TO A MODERN HOSPITAL

MOO

WE ARE A COWED ANIMAL — BUT HOW ELSE CAN WE BE IF BEFORE WE DO ANYTHING WE MUST ASK IS IT LEGAL — OUR SOULS ARE HEMMED IN BY LAWS — LAWS MAKE US EAT SHIT & LIKE IT — I WOULD LIKE TO SEE EVERY STATION & FIGURE OF AUTHORITY BROUGHT DOWN — I WOULD LIKE TO SEE EVERY BOSS COP JUDGE POLITICIAN I MEAN EVERYONE & ANYONE INCLUDING MOMS & POPS SAYING HEY YOU DO THIS EVEN IF YOU DONT WANT TO WITH THE POWER TO MAKE YOU — I WOULD LIKE TO SEE ALL OF THEM GET LOST OR DROP DEAD IMMEDIATELY — AT LEAST ONCE IN EVERY GENERATION — JUST PERHAPS IT WOULD BE A DETERRANT

MELODIOUS LAUGHING THRUSH

A TROPICAL DEPRESSION FROM SOUTHWARD WITH TORRENTIAL RAIN — IN A STILL HUSH BETWEEN DOWNPOURS WITH ONLY VISIBLE MOVEMENT THAT OF WATER CHANNELING DOWN DRIVEWAY OVER LAVA TO LOWEST POINT IN YARD — THEN ANOTHER MOVEMENT — IN ʻŌHIʻA TREE — A PAIR OF MELODIOUS LAUGHING THRUSH GARRULAX CANORUS HWAMEI OF THE BABBLING SONG — FIRST YOU SEE THE LARGE SHARP BRIGHT YELLOW BILL PECKING PECKING AT THE BARK — SCATTERING BITS OF BARK — SNAPPING UP THE DISLODGED INSECTS — THEN YOU SEE ITS DASHING WHITE SPECTACLES STYLISH & ABRUPT — THEN THE LOOSE & EASY USE OF BROWN FLUFFY WINGS & BODY WORKING THROUGH BRANCHES & FOLIAGE LED BY LARGE CLEAR EYE — HUNGRY AFTER 2 DAYS OF CONTINUOUS RAIN — NO TIME FOR SONG

DARK AGE

I WANT A DARK AGE — AN AGE THAT LEAVES NO TRACE — LET FUTURE TRY TO FIND US — I WANT A DARK AGE — AN AGE IN WHICH NOTHING HAPPENS BUT EXISTENCE AND DAYS ARE NOT NUMBERED — I WANT A DARK AGE — A DARK AGE OF THE IMAGINATION THAT FLOWERS STARK & SEXUAL AS SCARLET ANTHURIUM — I WANT A DARK AGE — AN AGE IN WHICH NOTHING TRAVELS FASTER THAN DAY — AN AGE OF QUIET — I WANT AN AGE WITHOUT FEAR — I WANT A DARK AGE

HIC JACET CHULIE

HERE LIES CHULIE DEAD OF WOUND INFLICTED BY FERAL DOG — HER STOMACH RIPPED OPEN & GUTS HANGING OUT — STRETCHED OUT IN GRASS ON DRIVEWAY — O THOU CUTE & CUDDLY BEYOND MEASURE — YOUR WARM PURR & LOVING GLANCE WILL NEVER LEAVE US — YOUR ALWAYS CLEAN ANIMAL SMELL — YOUR SMALL BREATH ON MY CHEEK — HOW YOU WOULD REACH UP & TOUCH MY FACE WITH YOUR PAW WHEN I HELD YOU & PETTED YOUR STOMACH — HOW YOU NEVER WALKED EVEN A SHORT FEW STEPS YOU ALWAYS TROTTED WITH YOUR CLASSIC EDITH BUNKER TROT — NOW YOUR BODY LIES BURIED OUTSIDE OUR WINDOW AT EDGE OF LAWN WRAPPED IN FINE LINEN CLOTH WHITE THE COLOR OF DEATH ON BED OF BANANA LEAF — WITH YELLOW DAY LILY LAID ATOP YOU & ON TOP OF THAT THE DIRT OF OUR COMMON MOTHER EARTH — NOW YOU HAVE REJOINED THE SKY & LOOK DOWN ON US & WE FEEL YOU AS WE FEEL THE QUIET WARMTH OF THE SUN ON A COLD O SO COLD WINTER DAY — YOU CHULIE WHO LEFT US BEREFT MARCH 17 1997

I WANT TO TAKE EVERY
NAME OFF EARTH &
LET IT BE THIS SWIFT
LIVE BALL THRU SPACE,
SO WE ONLY HOLD &
BREATHE IT & NOT
IMMEDIATELY WANT TO
USE IT. LET'S UNNAME
EVERYTHING. WE WILL
STILL KNOW IT WITHOUT
A NAME. WE WON'T BUMP
INTO IT OR MISTAKE IT
FOR SOMETHING ELSE. LET'S
TAKE DOWN EVERY SIGN
& BECOME A JAM
OF EXISTENCE.

NO NAME

I WANT TO TAKE EVERY NAME OFF EARTH & LET IT BE THIS SWIFT LIVE BALL THRU SPACE — SO WE ONLY HOLD & BREATHE IT & NOT IMMEDIATELY WANT TO USE IT — LETS UNNAME EVERYTHING — WE WILL STILL KNOW IT WITHOUT A NAME — WE WONT BUMP INTO IT OR MISTAKE IT FOR SOMETHING ELSE — LETS TAKE DOWN EVERY SIGN & BECOME A JAM OF EXISTENCE

MIRACLE

IVE READ FRA JUNIPERO SERRA NEEDS ONE MORE MODERN MIRACLE IN HIS NAME TO PUT HIM ON THE ELEVATOR FOR THE FLOOR WHERE SAINTHOODS ARE DISPENSED — I THINK HIS TRIP WAS JUST ANOTHER EXERCISE IN EURO STYLE BROAD GENOCIDE AGAINST A NATIVE POPULATION BUT A MIRACLE IS A MIRACLE & I MUST REPORT IT — I WAS SITTING AT MY TABLE THINKING OF FATHER JUNIPERO SERRA & OF HIS EL CAMINO REAL FREEWAY PROJECT WITH ITS PLAN FOR A SAINT MCDONALDS AT EACH OFF RAMP & THAT MADE ME THINK HOW MUCH I WANTED A TOASTED MAC TUNA-CHEEZE SANDWICH WHEN LO WOMAN PUT PLATE BEFORE ME WITH TOASTED MAC TUNA-CHEEZE SANDWICH ON IT — IS THIS MIRACULOUS INTERCESSION OR NOT — I DIDNT ASK — HE KNEW I SAY — THEN VOICE FROM ANOTHER ROOM — IT WAS ME SEZ WIFE — OF COURSE I SAY YOU ARE THE EVER PRESENT MIRACLE — LET JUNIPERO STAY AWHILE LONGER ON THE FLOOR WHERE THEY HAVE PRE-CANONICS

TIME IS MOTION IS GRAVITY

1

GRAVITY IS QUIET DON'T SEE IT OR HEAR IT — AT SEA LEVEL ONLY FEEL IT IN A SUAVE WAY — THE FIT PERFECT — FEELING OF BODY IN MOTION OR STILL IN PLACE — STUCK TO GROUND — LIFTING THROWING WALKING SITTING RUNNING SAFELY BOUND BY GRAVITY AGAINST CENTRIFUGAL SO DON'T GO OFF ON RECTILINEAR LINE INTO INTERSTELLAR SPACE — INSTEAD HUGGED TO EARTH IN THIS ZIG ZAG ORBIT WE STUMBLE THROUGH TILL WE LEAVE TEMPEROGRAVITAS FOR SPACE ONLY

2

TAKE PISS — WATCH PISS STREAM OUT & DOWNWARD — AH TIME —AH MOTION — AH GRAVITY

INNER VOICE SEZ

I HAVE AN INNER VOICE — IT KNOWS BETTER THAN ME — IF I SHUT UP IT WILL TALK MORE — IT MOSTLY WANTS TO DO OPPOSITE TO WHAT I WANT TO DO — BUT WE DONT FIGHT — WE'RE TOO INTIMATE — WE KNOW EACH OTHERS SECRETS — GENERALLY WHEN I DO WHAT I WANT TO DO IT ENDS UP BAD — INNER VOICE NEVER SEZ TOLD YOU SO — INNER VOICE ALWAYS SEZ NOTHING MORE SACROSANCT THAN NOW — THIS VERY MOMENT — PAST AND FUTURE ARE ILL-FOUNDED RUMORS — DONT SULLY NOW WITH YOUR BIG PLANS FOR FUTURE BASED ON PROJECTIONS FROM LONG GONE PAST — EVERYTHING GETS DONE IN THIS NOW SO DONT WORRY A PAST AND FUTURE — NOW YOU ARE BORN — NOW YOU ARE ALIVE — NOW YOU ARE DEAD—ALL THE SAME NOW AND NOW IS NOW NOT FOREVER

UNIVERSAL UNI

POINTING DOWN TO OCEAN NEIGHBOR SEZ THERES PLENNY FOOD OUT THERE ALL ORGANIC & WILD — LIKE WHAT — LIKE UNI FOR INSTANCE — NEXT DAY HAPPENED TO BE EXTRA LOW TIDE — NEXT MORNING AFTER THAT HE COME BACK WITH BUCKET HOLDING SEA URCHIN STILL MOVING ITS SPINES — SEE WHAT I MEAN HE SAID — BREAK OUT CENTER — SUCKING MOUTH & TEETH — IT DID NOT SCREAM — EXPOSE INNER GUT POND OF VASCULAR WATER — SEA URCHIN I SEE YOU ARE MADE IN FIVES — EXTRACT FIVE YELLOW TO OCHRE TONGUES OF WHAT LOOKS LIKE GONADAL ORGAN — PLACE ON ROLL OF RICE WITH WASABI PASTE — SURPRISE — NO TASTE OF SEA BEAST RATHER JUST UNIVERSAL SUAVE — TASTING LIKE NOTHING BUT ITSELF — THE SMOOTHNESS ALMOST UNANIMAL — WHEN IT HIT STOMACH IT SPREAD OUT THROUGH BODY WITH A RUSH

NO PROBLEM

HEY YOU — US — YEAH YOU — DONT THIS HERE PROBLEM BELONG TO YOU — NOT US — IT DONT BELONG TO US — MAYBE IT BELONGS TO YOU — YOURE HOLDING IT ANYWAY — AND IF THE PROBLEM BELONGS TO YOU — WHY ARE YOU TRYING TO MAKE IT A PROBLEM FOR US TOO — FOR US NO PROBLEM — IF ITS A PROBLEM FOR YOU WORK IT OUT YOURSELF — DONT BOTHER US WITH IT — WE'RE BUSY

USA
LATE 20TH CENTURY

WE ARE A GREAT NATION BECUZ WE ARE STILL THE FOREMOST CONSUMER POPULATION ON EARTH — SOME COUNTRIES MAY OUTPRODUCE US BUT WE STILL OUTCONSUME EVERYONE — WE WILL EVEN GO DEEP INTO DEBT TO CONSUME — WE ARE TRAINED FROM CHILDHOOD IN DESIRE EXPANSION & ENDLESS CONSUMPTION OF GOODS — OUR MOTTO IS LET OTHERS PRODUCE WE CONSUME — WE WASTE & WANT NOT — OUR HERALDIC SIGN IS GRAY BLOATED DESIRE ON SPINDLY LEGS RAMPANT AGAINST GOLD FIELD — WHAT WE BUY IS US — OUR CULTURE IS A SUPER SHOPPING MALL — WE FEEL THE CONVENIENT FLOW OF MONEY & NOVEL GOODS WILL NEVER END — AND IF IT DOES NO PROBLEM — HEAVEN IS AN ENDLESS MALL WITH INFINITE SHOPS EACH WITH ITS ORIGINAL LINE OF GOODS WITH CREDIT SANS DEBIT FOR ALL

PAB

I INHABIT AN ANGEL BODY — THIS PRESENT I INHABITS A PRIOR I — HERE IS THE EARTH BODY AND HERE THE PRIMORDIAL ANGEL BODY (PAB) EXPRESSING ITSELF EARTHSTYLE THROUGH EARTH BODY — PAB IS EVER UPRIGHT EQUABLE SANE STILL EMPTY — THE ONLY NAVIGATOR — INVISIBLE — IDLE — IMMOBILE EVEN IN MOTION — THIS CEPHALIZED COCOON THAT FITS WITHIN OUR SKIN EXACTLY — THIS UNMOVING CENTER BINDU DOT WALKING OVER 800 YEAR OLD LAVA — ROAD IS RAW LAVA WITH CLIMAX VEGETATION GRADED OFF — WALKING BODY BECOMES HOUSE OF ANGEL BODY — FOREST TAKES HUSHED HABIT IN LIGHT RAIN

Albert Saijo Autobiographical Notes: THE PAST IS IN FRONT OF US LIKE THE FUTURE

Editors' Note: This autobiographical sketch was originally written in 1998 to Marie Hara who requested information for an article she was writing about Saijo for the *Hawaii Herald*. It is followed by an excerpt of an email message from Laura Saijo sent to his friends announcing his passing. He was 85.

MARIE –
MY LIFE IN 25 WORDS OR LESS IS GOING TO TAKE SOME COMPRESSING – THE BIO IN OUTSPEAKS COVERS SUBJECT BRIEFLY – I WAS BORN IN LA BUT MY CONSCIOUS MEMORIES OF LIFE START WHEN WE WERE LIVING IN PUENTE A SMALL HAMLET ABOUT THE SIZE OF PĀHALA OR NĀ'ĀLEHU – THIS WAS IN THE SAN GABRIEL VALLEY JUST EAST OF LA – THE VALLEY WAS ABOUT 30 MILES LONG BY 15 MILES WIDE – THE VALLEY WAS BOUNDED ON NORTH BY THE SAN GABRIEL MTS A RUNNING RIDGE OF FLATTISH PEAKS FROM 5000 TO 10000 FT ELE – IT WAS A GRAND SIGHT TO SEE PEAKS COVERED WITH SNOW IN WINTER – THE VALLEY WAS BOUNDED ON THE SOUTH BY SMALL RANGES OF LOW ROUNDED HILLS – THE VALLEY WAS BROAD & FLAT WITH DEEP SOIL & LOTS OF WATER UNDERGROUND – WATER TABLE FED CONSTANTLY BY WATER FLOWING OUT OF MTS – FARMLAND – MOST OF THE VALLEY WAS IN FARMS & ORCHARDS – ORANGE & AVOCADO ORCHARDS – THE FARMS WERE THE TRUCK FARMS OF THE JAPANESE – AT THIS TIME THE JAPANESE PRETTY MUCH CONTROLLED THE TRUCK FARM PRODUCE BIZ OF CALIFORNIA – THEY PIONEERED THE IDEA OF TRUCK FARM – A FARM THAT PRODUCED ALL THE VEGGIES YOU SAW AT THE STORE – ALL THE LEAFY GREEN VEGGIES – THE ROOT CROPS – BERRIES – ONIONS – YOU NAME IT – THE ORANGE & AVOCADO & WALNUT ORCHARDS WERE THE DEMESNE OF RICH WHITE AMERICANS WHOSE ORCHARDS COVERED HUNDREDS OF ACRES – IN THE MIDDLE OF THE ORCHARDS APPROACHED DOWN AN ALLEE OF PALMS WOULD BE THE MANSE SURROUNDED BY A BROAD LAWN – MEDITTERRANEAN OR CALIF MISSION STYLE

ARCHITECTURE – THESE ORCHARDS WERE MANNED WITH MEXICAN LABOR – IM DESCRIBING THE SAN GABRIEL VALLEY OF AROUND 1930 – DURING THE BEGINNINGS OF THE GREAT DEPRESSION OF THE LATE 20'S THE 30'S TO WW2 – IN PUENTE MY FATHER WAS XTIAN MINISTER AT LOCAL JAPANESE PROTESTANT CHURCH WHILE MOTHER WAS JAPANESE SCHOOL TEACHER – BUT MY FATHER DIDN'T LIKE RACIALLY SEGREGATED SCHOOLS OF PUENTE SO HE MOVED FAMILY TO ANOTHER TOWN IN THE EASTERN PART OF THE VALLEY—MONTEREY PARK – WHERE THE SCHOOLS WERE RACIALLY INTEGRATED – AT THAT TIME IT WAS A TOWN THE SIZE OF HONOKA'A – I STARTED SCHOOL HERE – THE SCHOOL WAS ON A HILLSIDE AT THE EDGE OF TOWN – I HAVE VERY PLEASANT MEMORIES OF THIS SCHOOL – THEN WE MOVED AGAIN THIS TIME TO A TOWN IN THE NORTH CENTRAL PART OF THE VALLEY CLOSER TO FOOTHILLS & MTS – BALDWIN PARK – I REALIZE NOW MY FATHER HAD A RESTLESS TEMPERAMENT – HE LIKED TO MOVE AROUND & TRY DIFFERENT THINGS – NOW HE DECIDED TO QUIT THE MINISTRY AND BECOME A CHICKEN FARMER – WE RENTED A PLACE THAT HAD CHICKEN COOPS IN THE BACK – IN FRONT OF THE HOUSE ALONG THE ROAD WERE TALL PINE TREES – ACROSS THE ROAD WAS A DAIRY FARM – A RURAL NEIGHBORHOOD THAT INCLUDED ALL THE RACES – HISPANO MEXICAN WHITE & JAPANESE – THESE 3 RACES OR NATIONALITIES COMPRISED GREATER PART OF THE POPULATION – THERE WAS ONE AFRICAN AMERICAN FAMILY IN TOWN THE WASHINGTONS – THE WHITES WERE NUMERICALLY & SOCIALLY & POLITICALLY & ECONOMICALLY TOP DOG – THEN FOR THE REST JA'S & HISPANOMEX – THE 3 RACES PRETTY MUCH KEPT TO THEMSELVES EXCEPT FOR BIZ – THE JA'S WERE SPREAD THINLY THRU THE VALLEY ON THEIR FARMS BUT HAD THEIR COMMUNITY IN JAPANESE SCHOOLS, CHURCHES, ETC. – THE JA'S FROM HIROSHIMA KEN SEEMED MOST NUMEROUS – MANY OKINAWAN FAMILIES IN THE VALLEY – I CAN HEAR THE OKINAWAN DIALECT – MY FATHER FROM KUMAMOTO KEN MOTHER FROM SHIKOKU – NONE OF THE TOWNS IN SAN GABRIEL VALLEY HAD JAPANESE SECTIONS – SOME TOWNS HAD HISPANO MEXICAN SECTIONS – THEY WERE THE ORIGINAL PEOPLE HERE AFTER THE ABORIGINAL INDIANS – BY THIS TIME THE ABORIGINALS HAD PRETTY MUCH BEEN WIPED OUT – IT WAS RARE TO SEE A NATIVE AMERICAN IN SAN GABRIEL VALLEY – IF THEY HAD A PRESENCE IT WAS NEAR INVISIBLE – IN BALDWIN PARK ALL THE PUBLIC FACILITIES WERE OPEN TO ALL THE RACES – THE

SWIMMING POOL AT THE MUNICIPAL PARK & ALL THE SPORTS FACILITIES & THE SCHOOLS WERE INTEGRATED RACIALLY EVEN THE MOVIE THEATER DIDN'T HAVE A WHITES ONLY SECTION – CALIFORNIA HAS A LONG HISTORY OF WHITE PERSECUTION OF ASIATICS CHINESE & JAPANESE – AT FIRST OUTRIGHT BLOODY VIOLENT PERSECUTION & IN THE 20'S & 30'S A QUIETER LEGALISTIC PERSECUTION LIKE NONCITIZEN JAPANESE COULD NOT OWN LAND & OF COURSE JAPANESE COULDN'T BECOME CITIZENS SO – BUT AT THE LEVEL OF A KID GROWING UP I DIDN'T FEEL ANY KIND OF OUTRIGHT RACIAL DISCRIMINATION – THAT IS OTHER THAN THE NORMAL TACIT WHITE SUPREMACIST MODE OF THE TIME – IT WAS EXPRESSED IN THE MAXIM YOU CAN PLAY WITH EM BUT DON'T BRING EM HOME – A MAXIM RESPECTED BY ALL THE RACES – THIS WAS PRETTY TOLERANT FOR THOSE DAYS – THE 30'S – THE WEATHER OF THE SAN GABRIEL VALLEY WAS PERFECT TEMPERATE ZONE WEATHER – IT'S HARD TO BE UPTIGHT IN WEATHER LIKE THIS – IT WAS A COMPARATIVELY QUIET SPOT ON THE RACIAL FRONT – PRETTY GOOD CONSIDERING THE ADULT ISSEI JAPANESE SPOKE JAPANESE WHITES SPOKE ENGLISH HISPANO MEXICANS SPOKE SPANISH – BUT ALL THE KIDS WERE PUT IN THE SAME SCHOOLS & TAUGHT THE SAME STANDARD ENGLISH – THE JAPANESE KIDS DID WELL IN THE CLASSROOM & ON THE PLAYING FIELD – BIG JOCK IN HIGH SCHOOL WAS A CHUNKY KID NAMED HATAKEYAMA WHO QUARTERBACKED VARSITY FOOTBALL TEAM TO CONFERENCE FINALS – HEY I WAS ELECTED CLASS PRESIDENT SEVENTH GRADE – ON THE SURFACE EVERYTHING WAS PRETTY SMOOTH – APART FROM THIS U S PUBLIC SCHOOL SCENE THERE WAS BEING A JAPANESE STUDENT ON WEEKENDS – SATURDAY WAS JAPANESE SCHOOL DAY – MY MOTHER TAUGHT AT OUR LOCAL SCHOOL ONE OF THE LARGER ONES IN THE VALLEY – ABOUT A HUNDRED KIDS OF ALL AGES – I NEVER GOT MUCH OUT OF JAPANESE SCHOOL – FIRST OFF KIND OF EMBARRASSING HAVING YOUR MOTHER BEING ONE OF THE TEACHERS YEAH – THE SCHOOL WAS HELD IN THE MIDDLE OF AN ORANGE ORCHARD IN A FORMER MANOR HOUSE WITH LARGE WINDOWS & SEVERAL HIGH CEILINGED ROOMS – IT WAS A STOUTLY BUILT WOOD HOUSE IN VICTORIAN STYLE – THE BUILDING WAS SOMEWHAT RUNDOWN – CAN STILL HEAR SMALL KIDS CHANTING THE ALPHABET & OF LEARNING THE KANJI I REMEMBER WELL SITTING AT LONG TABLES WITH RUTCHY FELLOW STUDENTS WHILE OUTSIDE BECKONED A WORLD OF PLAY – THIS BUILDING WAS ALSO USED AS A

COMMUNITY CENTER & IT WAS WHERE WE DID OUR KENDO & JUDO PRACTICE – THEN ONE EARLY MORNING THE BUILDING BURNED DOWN – ARSON WAS SUSPECTED – U S JAPAN RELATIONS TURNING UGLY – FOR KIDS IT WAS LUCKY BECAUSE NO MATTER WHAT WAS HAPPENING IN THE WIDE WORLD KIDS WERE STILL ALLOWED TO BE KIDS – IT WAS DURING THIS TIME THE DUST BOWL WAS HAPPENING & REFUGEES FROM THIS GREAT DISASTER BEGAN APPEARING IN CALIFORNIA IN NUMBERS – YOU BEGAN TO HEAR OF OKIES – THE SAN GABRIEL VALLEY ON THE WEST WAS CUT THRU N-S BY A HUGE WASH FORMED BY THE ANNUAL WINTER FLOODS CAME ROARING OUT OF MTS TO THE NORTH – IT WAS AN EXPANSE OF SAND ROCK BRUSH & LOW SCRUBBY TREES – USED TO BE THE ONLY PEOPLE LIVED THERE WERE HOBOS IN THEIR CAMPS BUT NOW SHANTY VILLAGES OF REFUGEES FROM DUST BOWL POPPED UP THRUOUT WASH – THEN THE KIDS STARTED SHOWING UP AT SCHOOL – THEY WERE THIN & PEAKED LOOKING – DISPLACED – HUNGRY – THEY WERE ACCEPTED SAME AS EVERYONE IN OUR CHILDRENS COMMONWEALTH – LITTLE DID I KNOW I'D BE A DISPLACED PERSON SOON – WE GOT THRU THE DEPRESSION IN FAIR SHAPE – CHICKENS IN THE BACK YARD, TEACHERS AT JAPANESE SCHOOL GOT PLENTY VEGGIES FROM PARENTS OF STUDENTS – FATHER WITH CHICKEN & EGG BIZ – MOTHER TEACHING JAPANESE SCHOOL & WRITING A DAILY COLUMN FOR THE KASHU MAINICHI ONE OF THE LARGE JAPANESE VERNACULAR NEWSPAPERS OF LA BASIN – HER COLUMN WAS TITLED SEKAI NO UGOKI –WHEN SHE WASN'T WORKING OR DOING CHORES SHE WAS WRITING – SUMMERS WE WOULD BE IN THE FIELD PICKING BERRIES TOMATOES ONIONS ETC. ON A NEIGHBOR'S FARM SHOULDER TO SHOULDER WITH THE MEXICAN FAMILIES – WE GOT BY MOM POP BIG BROTHER ME YOUNGER SISTER – WE DID OK – THEN CAME THE WAR – SUDDENLY JAPANESE PART OF MY LIFE WAS GONE – NO MORE JAPANESE SCHOOL NO MORE KENDO PRACTICE NO MORE J SCHOOL BEACH PARTY NO MORE KENJINKAI PICNICS BON ODORI CHAMBARA MOVIES IN LOCAL H S AUDITORIUM WHEN AT THE END OF EACH REEL THE PROJECTIONIST WOULD SHOUT INTO THE DARKENED ROOM RIGHTO PREASE – SUDDENLY MY MOTHER AND FATHER ARE WORRIED ABOUT GETTING PICKED UP BY THE FBI – DIG BIG HOLE IN BACKYARD – IN GOES ALL JAPANESE LITERATURE & ANY THING THAT COULD BE CONSTRUED AS PRO JAPAN – BURN EM BURY EM – ELDERLY RETIRED ENGLISH COUPLE NEXT DOOR IN SMALL COTTAGE STOOD IN THEIR YARD & WATCHED

SMOKE RISE INTO SKY – ANTI JAP PROPAGANDA FLOODS NEWSPAPERS & RADIO & MOVIES – RACE HATE HYSTERIA – I KNEW IT WAS SERIOUS WHEN OUR CLOSEST JAPANESE NEIGHBOR DID SOMETHING I THOT WAS FAR OUT – A FARMER – 11 KIDS – 80 ACRES UNDER FULL CULTIVATION AT ALL TIMES – MRS TOOK CARE OF FARM – TINY WOMAN ORDERING AROUND BURLY WORKERS – MR WAS A DREAMY GUY – HIS JOB WAS LOAD UP HARVESTED & CRATED PRODUCE ON HIS BIG TRUCK & DRIVE IT INTO LA WHOLESALE PRODUCE MARKET AT THE END OF EACH DAY – ON HIS OFF TIME HE PAINTED PICTURES – HE NEVER WORKED IN THE FIELD – HIS MASTERPIECE WAS A PORTRAIT OF EMPEROR HIROHITO – IN THE MIDDLE OF AN ORANGE ORCHARD THERE WAS HIROHITO IN FORMAL REGALIA WITH PLUMED HEADWEAR MOUNTED ON A WHITE HORSE – THE PAINTING WAS HUNG IN THEIR LIVING ROOM – SHORTLY AFTER THE WAR STARTED AS THE HYSTERIA GATHERED HE TOOK HIS PAINTING OFF THE WALL & BURNED IT – I THOT THAT WAS FAR OUT – THEN FDR SIGNED EXECUTIVE ORDER 9066 MAKING LEGAL THE FORCED EVACUATION & INCARCERATION OF ALL JAPANESE CITIZENS & ALIENS ALIKE FROM THE WEST COAST – THERE WERE NO ACTS OF VIOLENCE AGAINST JAPANESE IN THE VALLEY – AT SCHOOL THINGS WENT ON LIKE NOTHING HAPPENED – NO ONE TALKED ABOUT IT – EVERYONE KNEW WHAT WAS HAPPENING – AT HOME IT WAS BUSY & DESPERATE GETTING READY FOR THE DAY WE WERE TO BE INCARCERATED – SELL WHAT WE COULD SELL OF OUR PERSONAL PROPERTY & WHAT WE COULDN'T JUST LEAVE – DUTIFULLY WE SHOWED UP AT THE TOWN PARK TO BE CARTED OFF IN ARMY BUSES TO THE POMONA ASSEMBLY CENTER – THE ASSEMBLY CENTER WAS BUILT ON THE DIRT PARKING LOT OF THE LA COUNTY FAIRGROUNDS IN POMONA – ROW AFTER ROW OF JERRY BUILT WOOD BARRACKS – CRACKS BETWEEN WOOD PLANKS OF WALLS & FLOOR LET IN DUST OF DUST STORMS THAT SWEPT ACROSS THE CAMP – OUR FAMILY OF 5 HAD A ROOM PERHAPS 12 x 12 – COTS WITH STRAW MATTRESSES – WELCOME TO CAMP USA – BEHIND BARBED WIRE WITH GUARD TOWERS & ARMED GUARDS – BUT IN SPITE OF THE OBVIOUS DOWNER SUFFERING SIDE OF THIS CATASTROPHIC SOCIAL EVENT FOR THE JA COMMUNITY & MY PARENTS & FAMILY I PERSONALLY AS A 15 OR 16 YR OLD KID WITH NEWLY MATURE BODY & BRAIN THOT IT A GRAND ADVENTURE – EVERY HAPPENING WAS FIRST TIME & NEW – RIGHT OFF TO BE RELEASED FROM PECULIAR MORES OF WHITE DOMINANT SOCIETY WITH ITS WEIRD SOCIAL NUANCES WAS ODDLY LIBERATING EVEN IF IT

WAS BEHIND BARBED WIRE FENCE – NOW ONLY BASIC HUMAN QUALITIES COUNTED – THERE WAS NO RACIAL CONSIDERATION BECAUSE EVERYONE WAS SLANT EYE – I COULD MOVE IN ANY DIRECTION SOCIALLY – FREEDOM & ADVENTURE EVEN IF IT WAS BEHIND BARBED WIRE – FREEDOM FOR ONE THING FROM FAMILY – THERE WAS NO LONGER A NEED FOR FAMILY – HAD A BED – EAT IN COMMUNAL MESS HALL – COMMUNAL BATH HOUSES – YOU SPENT YOUR DAYS WITH FRIENDS ROAMING IDLY THRU CAMP – GO HOME ONLY TO SLEEP – IT WAS FASCINATING TO SEE ONLY JAPANESE WITHOUT WHITES & MEXICANS – I HAD NEVER SEEN SO MANY JAPANESE TOGETHER IN ONE PLACE AT ONE TIME – BIGGER THAN A KENJINKAI PICNIC BY FAR OR NISEI WEEK IN LIL TOKYO LA – 1000'S – ALL THE HUMAN TYPES – ONE DAY I WAS ROAMING ALONG THE FENCE WHERE THE BACHELORS WERE HOUSED – GOING BY AN OPEN DOOR I LOOK IN & SEE A MAN PAINTING A PICTURE OF A WOMAN RISING LIKE A MOON ABOVE A LANDSCAPE OF OPEN ROLLING HILLS – HE TURNED & SMILED A GAP TOOTHED SMILE – HE HAD A MOUSTACHE LIKE THE MEXICAN ACTOR CANTINFLAS & A THIN LINE OF BEARD REACHED FROM HIS LOWER LIP TO HIS CHIN & HE HAD LONG HAIR TO BELOW HIS SHOULDERS – I HAD NEVER SEEN A JAPANESE HUMAN LIKE HIM BEFORE – HE REACHED UNDER HIS CHAIR & PULLED OUT A PAPER BAG FULL OF FRUIT – HAVE AN APPLE ORANGE BANANA HE SAID – DAYS PASSED SOMETHING NEW EVERY DAY – LEARNING EXPERIENCE IF HERE EVER WAS ONE – THEN ONE DAY WE TRUSTINGLY GOT ON TRAINS THAT WERE TO TAKE US TO A MORE PERMANENT CONCENTRATION CAMP FAR INLAND – WE HAD HEARD THEY WERE BUILDING CAMPS IN COLORADO WYOMING ARKANSAS ARIZONA UTAH IDAHO & A COUPLE IN CALIFORNIA – WE WERE TOLD WE WERE GOING TO A CAMP IN WYOMING – HEART MT RELOCATION CENTER IN THE NW CORNER OF THE STATE – THE TRAIN RIDE FROM POMONA TO WYOMING WAS A SUPER ADVENTURE – I HAD NEVER BEEN OUT OF CALIFORNIA TO THAT POINT IN MY LIFE – THESE RR CARS WERE OLD – PULLED BY OLD STEAM ENGINE LOCOMOTIVES MADE OF WOOD – YOU COULD OPEN THE WINDOWS & LEAN OUT – WE PASSED THRU TOWNS & DESERTS – THRU FORESTS OVER MTS & ALONG RUSHING RIVERS – THRU TUNNELS – OVER HIGH PLATEAU TILL WE REACHED THE MIDDLE OF NOWHERE – HEART MT RELOCATION CENTER WITH ITS OWN RR SIDING – BIG SKY – DISTANT MT RANGES – 1 MILE SQUARE SURROUNDED BY BARBED WIRE

WITH ENUFF BARRACKS TO HOLD 10,000 PEOPLE – SAME GUARD TOWERS & ARMED GUARDS LIKE POMONA – BASIC SET UP SAME AS POMONA – EXCEPT THE BARRACKS WERE TIGHTER FOR FRIGID WINTER WEATHER WITH HIGH WINDS – THE ROOMS WERE OF VARIOUS SIZES – ONE FAMILY PER ROOM – OUR ROOM WAS ABOUT THE SAME SIZE AS POMONA – EACH ROOM HAD A POTBELLY STOVE THAT BURNED COAL – COMMUNAL MESS HALLS & TOILETS – UNLIKE POMONA HEART MT HAD SCHOOL BUILDINGS – LIFE FELL INTO ROUTINE OF SCHOOL HANG OUT GO HOME SLEEP – FOR ADULTS THE MORE PERMANENT SET UP AT HEART MT WAS RELAXING AFTER HARD INITIATION INTO INCARCERATION EXPERIENCE IN ASSEMBLY CENTERS LIKE POMONA – VEGETABLE GARDENS & SMALL JAPANESE STYLE GARDENS IN FRONT OF FAMILY ROOMS APPEARED – A CLUB FOR EVERY IMAGINABLE INTEREST SPRANG UP – HAIKU CLUBS TANKA CLUBS GARDEN CLUBS HUNT FOR POLISHED DINOSAUR GULLET STONES CLUB SPORT CLUBS THE OLD KENJINKAI CLUBS – THERE WERE BUDDHIST & XTIAN CHURCHES ETC – A WORLD 1 SQ MILE BIG—MY FATHER STARTED A CAMP CHICKEN RANCH THAT EVENTUALLY MET THE NEEDS OF THE CAMP – MY MOTHER DID A LOT OF WRITING – SHE COULD WRITE WITHOUT INTERRUPTION – BUT LOST THOSE WRITINGS IN BIG POST CAMP MOVES CROSS COUNTRY – HEARTBREAKING – I RARELY SAW MY OLDER BROTHER BECUZ HE PRACTICALLY LIVED AT A RECREATION HALL GIVEN OVER TO ART CLASSES & A COMMUNAL PAINTERS STUDIO – MY BROTHER STUDIED PAINTING THERE WITH YOU GUESSED IT THE GUY WITH THE FUNNY MOUSTACHE & BEARD I SAW IN POMONA – BENJI OKUBO WAS HIS NAME – IN THE 30'S HE WAS HEAD OF THE ARTSTUDENTS LEAGUE OF LA – THERE WAS EVEN A ZEN MONK IN HEART MT – NYOGEN SENZAKI – I LATER STUDIED WITH THIS MAN IN LA – HEART MT WAS NOT A PLACE WHERE YOU COULD HAVE DIED FOR WANT OF SOMETHING TO DO – IN OTHER WORDS IT WAS A LIVELY PLACE – THE 1ST WINTER WAS A BLAST – TEMPERATURES 20 BELOW & LOWER – THEN ICE PONDS WERE DUG IN ALMOST EVERY BLOCK – AH TO GLIDE OVER FRESH ICE – EVERYONE SENT OFF FOR ICE SKATES THROUGH MONTGOMERY WARD & LL BEAN CATALOGS – NO HT MT WAS NOT ONE OF THEM NAZI CONCENTRATION CAMPS – I WAS EDITOR SCHOOL NEWSPAPER HT MT ECHO – I GRADUATED IN FIRST GRAD CLASS AT HT MT H S – I STARTED WRITING CALL EM VIGNETTES OF CAMP LIFE NOW FORTUNATELY DISAPPEARED – LOST – AROUND THIS TIME

THE GOVT DECIDED TO ALLOW PEOPLE TO LEAVE THE CAMP & GO TO ANY PLACE IN THE U S EXCEPT E & W COASTS – AFTER I GRADUATED H S THRU THE QUAKER FRIENDS SERVICE COMMITTEE I GOT A JOB AS BUS BOY IN U OF MICHIGAN FACULTY CAFETERIA – I THOT I'D TRY GETTING INTO U OF M EVENTUALLY BUT SOON AFTER MY 18TH BIRTHDAY IN ANN ARBOR MICH I WAS DRAFTED INTO THE U S ARMY – I SPENT OVER 3 YEARS IN ARMY AT CAMP SHELBY IN MISSISSIPPI & THEN IN ITALY WITH 442 – MY STORY IS TYPICAL – LOTS OF NISEI MY AGE LEFT CAMP ABOUT THIS TIME WITH ITS ODD SECURITY & WARMTH – WE LEFT CAMP & THE WORLD CRASHED IN ON US & OUR ADOLESCENCE RAN OUT & WE WERE CARRIED FAR FROM INNOCENCE OF HIGH PLATEAU SURROUNDED BY MTS – FAR FAR FROM PRE WW2 SAN GABRIEL VALLEY

MARIE –

CONTINUING ON – SOME OF MY VIEWS ON WRITING – AS AN ASIAN AMERICAN WRITER 3 IRONIES HAVE PRESENTED THEMSELVES ALWAYS ABOUT ENGLISH BEING MY NATIVE TONGUE & THE LANGUAGE I WRITE IN & THE LANGUAGE OF THAT MORE INTIMATE THAN INTIMATE VOICE ALWAYS AT MY EAR MY INNER VOICE – 1ST THE MENTOVISUAL PICTURE ENGLISH WORDS RUNNING THRU MONGOLIAN SKULL – SHOULD BE AN ALTAIC OR SINOTIBETAN LANGUAGE RUNNING THRU MY MONGOLIAN SKULL – OR MAYBE JUST BE FUTURISTIC & ACCEPT IT – SOME KIND OF BASIC IRONY HERE – 2ND THAT MY NATIVE TONGUE ENGLISH IS GENERALLY BY HISTORY UNFRIENDLY TO ME ANTI ASIAN & SPECIFICALLY ANTI JAP & A LANGUAGE THAT'S RACIST IN THE DIRECTION OF WHITE SUPREMACY TO BOOT – THINKING ABOUT THIS CAN TWIST YOUR HEAD AROUND – A DEEP DEEP IRONY HERE FOR ME – IF AS A CHILD I HAD INSIGHT INTO THIS ONE I SHOULD HAVE INVENTED MY OWN LANGUAGE – & 3RD THE KILLER IRONY TO LOVE THE LANGUAGE – LIKE I SAY IN MY "EARTH SLANGUAGE" & "IS LANGUAGE NECESSARY" (MARIE IF YOU HAVE ROOM IT MAY BE INTERESTING TO HH READER TO SEE THESE PRINTED IN ARTICLE) – WHEN I WAS A CHILD I WAS BILINGUAL BECUZ MY MOTHER SPOKE NO ENGLISH – I THINK BEING BILIGUAL GIVES LANGUAGE SENSITIVITY – NOW I HAVE LOST MOST OF MY JAPANESE THRU DISUSE THO ODDLY IT SEEMS TO BE COMING BACK AS I GROW OLDER – NOW I'M MAROONED ON ENGLISH & LIKE ANYONE WHO HAS ENGLISH AS THEIR MOTHER

TONGUE ENGLISH SPOKEN IN WHATEVER DIALECT OR CREOLE I'M A MENTAL HAOLE EVEN IF I'M A MONGOLIAN – TALK ABOUT IRONIES – I ACCEPT THIS NOW BUT I STILL FEEL LIKE I WANT TO USE THE LANGUAGE ON MY TERMS – I WANT TO CHANGE THE WAY ENGLISH LOOKS SPEAKS & MEANS – THAT'S WHY ALL CAPS & PUNCTUATION REDUCED TO DASH – I WANT TO TAILOR ENGLISH TO WHO I AM & TO MY SUBJECT – WHEN I READ WHAT I'VE WRITTEN I SEE THAT I'M A CRANK & THAT I HAVE JUST ONE BASIC RAP WHICH IS ABOUT HOW WE'VE FUCKED THIS ONE UP ROYALLY & WHAT CAN WE DO ABOUT IT – I HAVEN'T WRITTEN THE ASIAN AMERICAN EXPERIENCE BECUZ IT ISN'T MY SUBJECT – I'M BASICALLY AN IDEA PERSON – WRITING FOR ME IS EXPRESSING FEELINGS ABOUT IDEAS – I'M STILL TRYING TO FIND THE BEST WAY TO DO THIS

MY HAWAIIAN CONNECTION GOES BACK TO WW2 – MOST OF THE GUYS I SERVED WITH WERE FROM THE ISLANDS – FROM THE FIRST I LIKED EM – THEY LIKED TO PARTY & SING & I WAS A PARTY PERSON – THEY WERE DIFFERENT FROM KOTONKS WHO TEND TO BE QUIET & CONSERVATIVE – BUT IF I WAS TO HANG OUT WITH THE HAWAII GUYS THERE WAS THE LANGUAGE BARRIER – THEY SPOKE PIDGIN – I WOULD HAVE TO LEARN PIDGIN – THIS BECAME CLEAR TO ME ONE DAY WHEN WE WERE LEARNING HOW TO DISMATLE THE BROWNING AUTOMATIC RIFLE WHEN THE SERGEANT A GUY FROM HILO TURNED TO ME & ASKED FOR A TOOL FROM THE TABLE BESIDE ME – HAND ME DA KINE EH – I LOOKED AT THE TABLE – IT WAS COVERED WITH TOOLS – I LOOKED BACK AT THE SERGEANT – DA KINE DA KINE HE REPEATED – DA KINE I ASKED – HO DA DUMB BUGGAH DIS DON'T KNOW WHAT DA KINE IS O WAT – THEN HE EXPLAINED DA KINE HAMMA – & AFTER BEING ASKED WITH INCREASING HOSTILITY HOW COME YOU LIKE TALK LIKE ONE HAOLE I STARTED PICKING UP PIDGIN FAST – I STARTED GETTING AN IDEA OF THE POLITICS OF PLANTATION LIFE – THEY USED TO SAY AFTER THE WAR STAY COME HAWAII WE TAKE CARE OF YOU BUT AS IT HAPPENED ALMOST EVERY ONE OF MY HAWAII FRIENDS MOVED TO THE LA AREA AFTER THE WAR – THERE WAS QUITE A MOVEMENT OF HAWAII JA'S TO THE LA AREA RIGHT AFTER WW2 – I MADE IT OVER TO MAUI IN THE LATE 60'S & LIVED THERE A SHORT WHILE OUTSIDE HA'IKU – I LIKED IT –I LIKED THE RACIAL MIX – PACIFIC RIM PEOPLE & EUROWHITE PEOPLE IN NUMERICAL BALANCE – I LIKE THE FACT THAT JA'S ARE PART

OF THE POLITICAL PROCESS – AS A JA I'M PROUD OF THE FACT THAT JA'S WERE RESPONSIBLE IN LARGE PART FOR OPENING THE POLITICAL PROCESS TO EVERYONE HERE IN HAWAII – THAT MAKES ME FEEL GOOD – I LIKE THE LAND THE WATER THE AIR THE WEATHER THE SKY HERE – I LIKE WINDWARD SIDE RATHER THAN KONASIDE – MY WIFE & I LIVED MANY YEARS IN NORTHERN CAL – WE FOUND VOLCANO VILLAGE AT 4000' TO BE A LOT LIKE NORTHERN CAL – MISTY RAINY COOL – COOL ENUFF TO HAVE A WOOD FIRE – THE BIG ISLAND IS A MINI CONTINENT – A PLACE IN RAPID TRANSITION – WE LIKE THE SOCIAL AMBIANCE OF HILOSIDE – A PLEASANT LAID BACK PLACE FOR NOWADAYS

WELL MARIE I
REACHED MY LIMIT
FOR TALKIN ABOUT
MYSELF — HOPE
THIS INFO WILL BE
OF USE TO YOU
THANX FOR YOUR
EFFORTS IN MY
BEHALF
ALBERT

From: Laura Saijo
Subject: Albert passed on to the next
Date: June 3, 2011 9:00:19 PM HST

Dear all—some of you I have talked to already but I'm sending out to all of you who knew and loved Albert to say that he died here at home the way he wanted to with no tubes or drugs on a rainy night by a blazing fire on the hearth—I had the honor of helping him push through and got to be with him for the last breaths . . . I believe he is in Nirvana now—I believe he had the fierce Samurai heart and the compassionate intellect to see and merge with the clear light—as soon as he passed our two cats jumped on his bed and curled up purring at his sides and the dog came and licked his face—I now understand what it means to have a broken heart but I am also grateful for a beautiful death for him the way HE wanted it and that he is free of his suffering body and mind—we had an amazing 32 years of wonderful laughs and helping each other through hard times—he was the best husband imaginable—he was also at the beginning my guru-ji, my father, my passionate lover, my best friend, and, at the end, my child. I feel that every permutation of human relating we had together. He was the most intelligent and creative person I have known in my life, also the kindest, most generous, most compassionate, most accomplished and competent in every facet of human existence. I am truly blessed and I praise God for his presence in my life. We will be having a memorial service end of next week for the Volcano Village "neighbors" and if you would like to send a remembrance/reflection or "Albert story" I will collect them and share them at that time. Aloha and love from us from the Big Island . . . .

CANE HAUL ROAD, HAWAII
CANE HAUL ROAD, HAWAII
cane haul road, hawai'i
pua-kenikeni

Contributors

Ahimsa Timoteo Bodhrán, conceived in Niagara Falls, was born in 1974 on El Día de la Madre in the South Bronx to a multigenerational mixed-blood familia (Kanien'kehaka, Onodowaga, Puerto Rican, Irish, and German/Moroccan Jewish), and raised in Lenapehoking. He is the author of *Antes y después del Bronx: Lenapehoking* (New American Press) and editor of an international queer Indigenous issue of *Yellow Medicine Review: A Journal of Indigenous Literature, Art, and Thought.* An American Studies PhD candidate at Michigan State University, his prose and poetry appear in a hundred publications in Africa, the Américas, Asia, Australia, Europe, and the Pacific.

Sally-Jo Keala-o-Ānuenue Bowman's fiction and poetry have appeared in *'Ōiwi: A Native Hawaiian Journal, Hawai'i Review,* and the anthology *Honolulu Stories.* Her nonfiction books include *The Heart of Being Hawaiian,* a collection of her best profiles, essays, and articles. Her work has won several Pa'i Awards from the Hawai'i Publishers Association. She grew up in Kailua, O'ahu, graduated from Kamehameha Schools and holds BA and MS degrees in journalism. She taught writing at the University of Oregon for 20 years and now coaches developing writers. She lives in Springfield, Oregon, with her husband, David Walp.

Amalia B. Bueno's most recent poetry and short stories can be found in *Tinfish 20, Bamboo Ridge* Issue #98, and *Walang Hiya: Literature Taking Risks Toward Liberatory Practice* (Carayan Press). Her poetry chapbook, *On King You Go Left,* was published in 2010. When not eating, sleeping or writing, Amalia reinvents herself as a media relations consultant and poses as a graduate student at the University of Hawai'i at Mānoa pursuing an MA in English.

Donald Carreira Ching was born and raised in Kahalu'u. He received his BA in English from the University of Hawai'i at Mānoa and is pursuing his MA in Creative Writing. He recently completed his first novel, *Between Sky and Sea,* excerpted in *Hawai'i Review* and *Bamboo Ridge* (Issue #98).

Lee Cataluna is a journalist, playwright, teacher, and author of *Folks You Meet in Longs* and *Three Years on Doreen's Sofa* (Bamboo Ridge Press, 2005 and 2011).

Ghislaine D. Chock: I try to communicate thoughts and feelings into woven textiles most of the time, and on occasion, I let special moments become poems.

Lifelong storyteller and avid people watcher, **Doodie Cruz** has published a play, *Whose Nose Dat?,* and had several of her songs recorded: "Sittin' Around,"

"Every Child a Promise," "Where Are the Brothers?," "Natives," and "Sweet Child of Mine." After years of major writer's block, she will finally finish two plays and continue work on a collection of short stories about growing up in Pālolo Housing. Doodie credits her patient, supportive, and sometimes unsuspecting and reticent family and friends for providing a lifetime of stories on which she bases many of her works.

Myles De Coito: You know da joke about all a etnic group an dea weapon of choice? Somebody get knife, one oddah get can beer, and you-know-who get microphone. You know da one, ah? How come none a dem had pen? Mahalo to my parents, Glenn and Estrella De Coito, and my siblings, Dawn and Scott De Coito. My home nurtured me with the greatest weapon of all: storytelling. To my wife, Elsa, and son, Sam, thank you for allowing me to swing da sucka all ovah da place! As not blood, as jess ink.

Jesse S. Fourmy: I spent a decade living, surfing and working on the Big Island of Hawai'i. I was recently reassigned back to Southern California with the government. I can't wait to return to the place where "I grew up." Mahalo.

J. Freen lives on in Kalihi.

Norma W. Gorst writes poetry and short fiction. Her poetry chapbook, *At the Edge of Speech*, was published in 2005 and in 2006, she collaborated with Carol Catanzariti on the chapbook *Seeking an Answer*, a book of linked poems (both published by Finishing Line Press). Her poetry has appeared in *Chelsea*, *Chaminade Literary Review*, *Cottonwood*, *Hawai'i Review*, *Hawai'i Pacific Review*, and *Kaimana*, among others. "Rowan," a short story, appeared in *Bamboo Ridge* (Issue #75) in 1999. She holds a John Unterecker Prize for Poetry from Chaminade University.

Marie M. Hara: In the era of Territorial Hawai'i, I was a young child living on an isolated plantation. My grandparents, who were close to the end of life, tried to get me ready for the future. Loving them as I did, I wrote about them as soon as I knew how. Writing and books remain my great pleasure. In the late 1990s I found it difficult to give up the typewriter for the computer, even for emailing. I resisted the cell phone. But now I'm trying out the Kindle, blogs, cell phone photos/videos, and text messaging. Ojiji, Obaban, surprise! BRB (be right back)

Gail N. Harada is a graduate of Stanford University and the University of Iowa Writers' Workshop. She lives and works in Honolulu.

Jim Harstad: What an honor to have my story in this landmark edition! Thank you Darrell and Eric and everybody in the family of angels that produces *Bamboo Ridge*. The next 100 editions will be even better, I'm sure, as the tradition grows stronger. (I'll only be 96 by then, so I should be able to crank out another story for your consideration.) Again, thank you.

Cathy Kanoelani Ikeda lives in Hilo, Hawai'i, but deep down she's a Lahaina girl with the red-dirt-stained slippers to prove it. She has begun telling the story of her grandpa Peanut's life. In January 2011, he turned 95.

Ann Inoshita was born and raised on O'ahu. She co-authored *No Choice but to Follow,* a book and CD of linked poems, with three other poets, published by Bamboo Ridge Press. Kahuaomānoa Press published her book of poems, *Mānoa Stream.* Her short play, *Wea I Stay: A Play in Hawai'i,* was included in *The Statehood Project* performed by Kumu Kahua Theatre and published by Fat Ulu Productions. Mahalo Bamboo Ridge Press for publishing these fictional poems and for accomplishing so much for writers, readers, and literature.

David James' second book, *She Dances Like Mussolini,* won the 2010 Next Generation Indie Book Award for poetry. His one-act plays have been produced from New York to California. He teaches at Oakland Community College in Michigan.

Darlene M. Javar's poems have been published in *Bamboo Ridge, Kaimana, Chaminade Literary Review, Tinfish, Hawai'i Pacific Review, Earth's Daughters, Storyboard 8, Into the Teeth of the Wind, The Distillery,* and *The East Hawaii Observer.* Her poetry has been recorded by "Rural Voices Radio II," National Writing Project, and *Aloha Shorts,* a co-production with Hawaii Public Radio and Bamboo Ridge Press. "Thank you, Bamboo Ridge, for your years of dedication to the voices of Hawai'i. I am honored to be included in this 100th edition."

Frances H. Kakugawa was recognized in *Living Legacy: Outstanding Women of the 20th Century in Hawai'i.* Her books include *Breaking the Silence: A Caregiver's Voice*; *Sand Grains*; *White Ginger Blossom*; *Golden Spike*; *The Path of Butterflies*; *Mosaic Moon: Caregiving Through Poetry*; *Teacher, You Look Like A Horse!* and award-winning children's books, *Wordsworth the Poet* and *Wordsworth Dances the Waltz.* A leading advocate of the power of poetry in easing the burden of long-term family care, she resides in Sacramento and gives lectures and writing workshops throughout the U.S. Her two previous appearances in *Bamboo Ridge* were in Issues #9 and #98. Work in this issue is excerpted from the newly released *Kapoho: Memoir of a Modern Pompeii.*

Lisa Linn Kanae is the author of *Islands Linked by Ocean* and *Sista Tongue.* She is also the recipient of the 2009 Elliot Cades Emerging Writer Award.

Now retired from the DOE, **Milton Kimura** is contemplating a move to a large city on the mainland where he can better feed the addiction that Miss Halstead started nearly 50 years ago. While there is little chance that he'll find another Price, he relishes the hunt.

Christine Kirk-Kuwaye has lived for most of her life on O'ahu and for more than 20 years in Ka'a'awa. She continues to have a love-hate relationship with writing, especially her own. On a more positive note: as a result of years working with students at the University of Hawai'i at Mānoa, she—along with colleagues and friends—shares lessons learned at collegewisdom.com, a site for parents and others who are interested in college students. She also continues to research the early territorial period of Hawai'i, including eugenics, the Girl's Industrial School, and the University of Hawai'i.

Juliet S. Kono is the author of *Anshū: Dark Sorrow,* a novel published by Bamboo Ridge Press in 2010. She teaches at Leeward Community College and lives with her husband in Honolulu.

Brenda Kwon is a writer, language arts instructor, musician, and yoga teacher. She thanks her mother for allowing her to be all these things.

M. Jane Lambert graduated with a BA from the University of Hawai'i at Mānoa. Currently, she lives in Mililani, writing poetry and short fiction.

Mel Lau was born and raised in Kalihi. She is married to a great guy who completes her. They have two daughters who make them proud. Mel writes for fun, but secretly wishes, one day, that it will replace her day job.

Lanning C. Lee was born and raised in Honolulu. He attended the University Laboratory School beginning at age 3. Except for a few years attending the University of Wisconsin – Madison for his MA in English and working in the private sector, he has spent most of his life on the UH Mānoa Campus, where he earned his BA and PhD in English. He currently works as a counselor for the UH Mānoa KOKUA Program. "One Devil in Baggy Pants" is dedicated to his father, Staff Sergeant Henry C. Lee of the 82nd Airborne Division, 504th Parachute Infantry Regiment (aka The Devils in Baggy Pants). "A New Lease" is written for Haruki Murakami.

Jeffrey Thomas Leong's poems have appeared in *Cimarron Review, Crab Orchard Review, Flyway: A Literary Review, Asian Pacific American Journal, Cha: An Asian Literary Journal, nycBigCityLit,* and other publications. He and his wife are parents of a precocious nine-year-old girl adopted from Jiangsu, China. Jeffrey has worked many years as a public health administrator and has degrees in Asian American Studies and law from UC Berkeley. In his poetry, Jeffrey seeks to explore the mysteries of gender, race, and family in a global, multicultural world, and within his Chinese-American ancestry. He lives in the San Francisco Bay Area.

R. Zamora Linmark has authored two poetry collections, *Prime Time Apparitions* and *The Evolution of a Sigh,* both from Hanging Loose Press, and two novels, the best-selling *Rolling The R's,* which he's adapted for the stage, and the just-published *Leche.* He resides in Honolulu and Manila, and is at work on a novel and a play, *But, Beautiful.*

The perils of Walter Yamada continue. First seen dangling from the roof of his Kaimukī home on a stormy night ("Walter! Walter!"), then caught dreamcheating with Nicole Kidman and Winona Ryder in a Waikīkī hotel room ("Walter and the Dream Girls"), and now this, wrestling with the annual angst of Valentine's Day ("Walter Gets Romantic"). **Michael Little** is the author of *Queen of the Rodeo* (2001) and *Chasing Cowboys* (2009). His novel about Barbie's escape from the dream house is aging quite nicely in a desk drawer. He has never been busted for dreamcheating with Winona Ryder.

Mary Lombard Mulder lives in lovely Kailua and, when not writing short stories, is volunteering at the best used bookstore in Honolulu—the Friends of Kailua Library Bookstore—or living it up with her canasta buddies. She is especially honored to be among the fine writers in this 100th edition of *Bamboo Ridge.*

Christina Low graduated with her MA in Creative Writing from the University of Hawai'i at Mānoa, where she teaches English. She also teaches at Kapi'olani Community College. She has been published in *Make/Shift Magazine, RipRap Journal, Muscle and Blood Magazine, ViceVersa Journal,* and *Hawai'i Review.*

Darrell Lum has served as co-editor of *BR* and general pain-in-the-ass since 1978.

Wing Tek Lum's work in this issue is from his next collection of poetry, *The Nanjing Massacre: Poems,* scheduled to be released as *Bamboo Ridge* Issue #102 in 2012. Bamboo Ridge Press also published his first collection, *Expounding the Doubtful Points,* in 1987.

Christina Minami grew up in Honolulu and now lives in Chicago, IL.

Terri Nakamura, aka Aria Soyama / A. Soyama, like fo say tanks to her ohana, frenz and teachas fo she nothing witout dem. Props out to Bamboo Ridge fo da choke support and to da Albino Gorilla, fo his ginormous heart and mean cleaning skills.

Angela Nishimoto grew up on the windward side of O'ahu. She teaches botany and biology at Leeward Community College. Angela lives in Honolulu with her husband, Andrew McCullough.

Carrie M. O'Connor is a fourth-generation native of Hawai'i. After earning a Master of Arts degree at Marquette University, she made her home in Milwaukee, where she works as a writer and proofreader. Her recent work includes a *Milwaukee Journal Sentinel* opinion piece and an essay that aired on Milwaukee Public Radio. Her fiction has been published in *Bamboo Ridge: Journal of Hawai'i Literature and Arts, Auscult, Wild Violet,* and *Bartleby Snopes Literary Magazine.*

In 1951, **Shelley Ayame Nishimura Ota** published *Upon Their Shoulders,* the first historical novel by a Japanese American. Her novel is recognized in the *Encyclopedia of Japanese American History,* by the National Endowment for the Arts, and the anthology *Honolulu Stories.* She was born in Waiākea in 1911, graduated from the University of Hawai'i, and died in Hilo in 1987. Her second novel, *Hawaiian Kaleidoscope,* was never published because she lost her vision. After fifty years, her son, William T. Ota, a retired publisher and Harvard MBA, resurrected this historically significant manuscript. *Bamboo Ridge* is first to publish an excerpt.

Christy Passion: Following up on her first collaborative book of *renshi* (linked poetry), *No Choice but to Follow,* Christy is currently embarking on a focused *renshi* of the infamous Massie Trial. Her poetry has won both local and national awards and has most recently been published in *Mauri Ola, ʻōiwi,* and *Bamboo Ridge*. She currently works at the Queen's Medical Center as an RN in the surgical ICU while finishing up her Master's degree to become a Clinical Nurse Specialist. Lifelong projects include not taking herself too seriously and meditating for longer than five minutes at a time.

Elmer Omar Pizo: Borrowing a line from the Bee Gees, "words are all I have..." and my most heartfelt thanks to Bamboo Ridge Press. Through the years you have produced/published anthologies that are succulent, delicious, and a good source of knowledge.

Mayumi Shimose Poe is the Managing Editor of *American Anthropologist*. Her fiction, essays, and poetry have appeared or are forthcoming in *American Anthropologist, Bamboo Ridge, Dark Phrases, Drunken Boat, Eternal Portraits, Frontier Psychiatrist, Hawaii Women's Journal, The Honolulu Advertiser, Hunger Mountain, Hybolics, Japan Subculture Research Center,* the *Phoenix,* and *Stepping Stones*. She lives in Los Angeles. www.mayumishimosepoe.com

Darlene Rodrigues descends from a long line of rice farmers, chance takers, and pineapple pickers. She heeds the words of her uncle and looks into the eyes of her cats everyday. Her poetry and essays have appeared in *Amerasia, disOrient, Katipunan,* and in the anthologies, *Babaylan: Writings by Filipina and Filipina American Writers* and *Words Matter: Conversations with Asian American Writers*.

Brian Rugen teaches in the Department of Languages and Applied Linguistics at Hawai'i Pacific University. He grew up in Colorado and has spent the last ten years bouncing back and forth between Japan and Hawai'i. According to his wife and daughter, he is now settled in Hawai'i.

Laura Saijo has for thirty years been a teacher of music and high school and adult ed math and English. Her Ka'u High music students this past year won first place in two statewide contests: one as the only neighbor island participant against twenty O'ahu schools in a live competition, and the other for best music video of a student-written and arranged original song. Laura is a published writer and songwriter who also loves to garden, cook, and bake. She was married for thirty-three years to the poet Albert Saijo, who died this past June. She lives in Volcano Village in the last of four houses Albert designed and built for them in California and in Hawai'i.

Jhoanna Calma Salazar was born in the Philippines, raised in Chicago, has lived on Maui, O'ahu, and in Italy. Her poem "after the doctors tell her . . ." is based on some true events and is part of the difficult process of sorting out faded memories, unanswered questions, and unyielding regrets that sometimes remain long after loss.

Salt is the name **Nancy S. Young** chose for her creative work. She is traveling with her husband for a few years while he does interim ministries for Unitarian Universalist Churches. They intend to return to their home up Kalihi Valley in another year or so. Her thoughts are often up Kalihi, especially at night when her poems come out in images from her dreams.

Normie Salvador received his BA in English with Highest Honors and MA in Creative Writing from the UH-Mānoa. His work has appeared in literary journals, magazines, newspapers, on the *Aloha Shorts* radio program, and online. He has read at the university, community colleges, conferences, and coffee shops. Tinfish Press published *Philter,* his poetry chapbook, in 2003. Currently, he is a lecturer at Kapiʻolani Community College teaching English Composition and Creative Writing. During summer and winter breaks, he is a freelance editor for individual authors, presses, and publishers here, elsewhere, and online.

Misty Sanico is a writer and editor for Hawaiʻi Book Blog, a local literary website devoted to Hawaiʻi books and authors. As a resident of Honolulu, she is often found at author readings, trolling book sales, or hidden in the library. With a passion for books, reading, and writing, there is always a project to work on, a lesson to learn, or an adventure to be had. She also loves laulau.

Susan M. Schultz is editor of Tinfish Press, out of her Kāneʻohe home and her UHM office. She is author of several books of poetry & prose, including *And Then Something Happened* (Salt), *Dementia Blog* (Singing Horse, 2008), and *Memory Cards: 2010-2011 Series* (Singing Horse, 2011). She blogs at http://tinfisheditor.blogspot.com.

Eric Paul Shaffer is author of five books of poetry, including *Lāhaina Noon* and *Portable Planet.* His poetry appears in *Ploughshares, Slate, North American Review,* and *The Sun Magazine*; Australia's *Island* and *Quadrant*; Canada's *CV2, Dalhousie Review, Event,* and *Fiddlehead*; Éire's *Poetry Ireland Review* and *Southword Journal*; England's *Stand* and *Magma*; and New Zealand's *Poetry NZ* and *Takahe.* Shaffer received the 2002 Elliot Cades Award, a 2006 Ka Palapala Poʻokela Book Award for *Lāhaina Noon,* and the 2009 James M. Vaughan Award for Poetry. After ten years on Maui, he now lives on Oʻahu and teaches at Honolulu Community College.

John E. Simonds, a resident of Hawaiʻi since the 1970s, is a retired Honolulu newspaper editor and author of *Waves from a Time-Zoned Brain,* a book of poems, published in 2009.

Sally Sorenson: I love writing fiction. After years of business publications, newsletters, and press releases, fiction allows me to stretch the truth in creative ways. "Mango Wars" might have been inspired by real people, but no interviews were conducted or fact-finding missions undertaken. I've been a member of the Aloha Chapter of Romance Writers of America for more than a decade. My short stories have appeared in several anthologies; non-fiction articles in the Honolulu newspaper(s).

Joseph Stanton's books of poems are *A Field Guide to the Wildlife of Suburban Oʻahu, Cardinal Points: Poems on St. Louis Cardinal Baseball, Imaginary*

Museum: Poems on Art, and *What the Kite Thinks*. He has published poems in *Bamboo Ridge, Poetry, Harvard Review, Poetry East, New York Quarterly*, and many other journals. His other sorts of books include *Looking for Edward Gorey, A Hawai'i Anthology, The Important Books: Children's Picture Books as Art and Literature*, and *Stan Musial: A Biography*. He is a Professor of Art History and American Studies at the University of Hawai'i at Mānoa.

Carrie Y. Takahata has a BSW in Social Work and an MA in English with an emphasis in Creative Writing from the University of Hawai'i at Mānoa. She's currently employed as a legal secretary in San Francisco.

Moriso Teraoka: I am a student at Kapi'olani Community College. I have come to realize that poetry writing is tasking but enjoyable. I have tossed ideas in my head for many hours of the day and was never able to put those ideas in writing. And yet, there are moments when ideas jell into words and before I know it, a poem is written. My recollection of my kid days resulted in "We Go Catch Frog." "The Accordion" was memorable as I will never forget my relationship with the POW after World War II ended in Italy in 1945.

Bill Teter teaches high school English at the University Laboratory School in Honolulu.

Mark Thiel's work has been published in *The Mid-American Review, Hawai'i Pacific Review, Bamboo Ridge* (Issue #98), and *Hawai'i Review*, where he was awarded the 2011 Ian MacMillan Poetry Prize. He lives with his wife in Honolulu.

Delaina Thomas is a member of the Maui Ryukyu Culture Group.

Ken Tokuno has been writing and publishing poetry since 1986. He has published in *Bamboo Ridge, Seattle Review, Hawai'i Review, The Bellowing Ark*, and several other magazines. *Orchard*, a collection of his poems, was published by the Bellowing Ark Press in 2007. He works at the University of Hawai'i at Mānoa and lives in Kāne'ohe with his wife, artist Diane Nushida Tokuno.

"Da Pidgin Guerrilla" **Lee A. Tonouchi** is da writer of da award-winning book of Pidgin short stories *Da Word* (Bamboo Ridge, 2001); author of da Pidgin essay collection *Living Pidgin: Contemplations on Pidgin Culture* (Tinfish, 2002), compiler of *Da Kine Dictionary: Da Hawai'i Community Pidgin Dictionary Projeck* (Bess, 2005), and editor of *Buss Laugh: Stand Up Poetry from Hawai'i* (Bess, 2009). His latest book is *Significant Moments in da Life of Oriental Faddah and Son: One Hawai'i Okinawa Journal* (Bess, 2011).

Jean Yamasaki Toyama is a poet, scholar, translator, and writer of fiction. Her latest publications include *No Choice but to Follow, Kelli's Hanauma Friends*, and a selection of poems in *Wavelengths: 2011 Savant Anthology of Poetry*. "The Ant Massacre" comes from her yet-to-be-published collection, *The Piano Tuner's Wife*. She lives in Hawai'i where she was born and raised.

Joe Tsujimoto has published two teacher texts: *Teaching Poetry Writing To Adolescents* (NCTE/ERIC) and *Lighting Fires: How the Passionate Teacher Engages Adolescent Writers* (Heinemann). He has also published a collection of short fiction, *Morningside Heights: New York Stories* (Bamboo Ridge), which was a finalist for the 2010 William Saroyan International Prize for Writing. Winner of the 2008 Elliot Cades Award for Literature, Tsujimoto teaches 8th graders English at Punahou School.

Amy Uyematsu is so pleased to be included in this 100th issue of *Bamboo Ridge*. She is grateful for *Bamboo Ridge*'s support, going back to 1986, when the journal published "Sansei Line Dance." Amy is a recent high school math teacher retiree and twice-lucky grandma (known as Gum Gum Amy).

Sylvia Watanabe, a third generation Asian settler, will never know any other home but Hawai'i. For 25 years, she has been on temporary assignment in the American Mid-West—the last 15 as co-director of the creative writing program at Oberlin College. The excerpts in the current issue of *Bamboo Ridge* are taken from an ongoing project called *Atomic Histories*, a collection of lyric prose pieces about America's legacy of nuclear colonialism in Asia and the Pacific.

Lois-Ann Yamanaka is the author of *Behold the Many, Father of the Four Passages, Heads by Harry, Blu's Hanging, Wild Meat and the Bully Burgers, Saturday Night at the Pahala Theatre, Name Me Nobody,* and *The Heart's Language*. She is currently at work on a young adult novel *Bully Bastard* and a novel *The Mother Mary Stories*. She is co-director of Na'au: A Place for Learning, in Honolulu.

Kristel Yoneda was in high school when she started telling people she was a writer. Of course, she wasn't really a writer back then. She was a socially awkward teenager who really loved daily journal writing in English and often scribbled lines of poetry in the margins of her Calculus homework (which did not give her extra credit). She believed, however, if she repeated it enough, some day it might feel true. A contributing writer for the *Hawaii Women's Journal*, she was recently featured in the book *It Gets Better*, based on the YouTube sensation of the same name. She continues to tell people she's a writer, in hopes of it one day being true.

Beryl Allene Young graduated from Saint Andrew's Priory in Honolulu in 1962 and studied English at the University of Hawai'i at Mānoa, where she obtained her BA in 1966. She was awarded an MA in English in 1970 and earned an MLS in Library Studies in 1973. After teaching English composition at Kapi'olani Community College in 1992, she nursed her mother through her final illness until 2008. Now, she writes poems in her spare time.

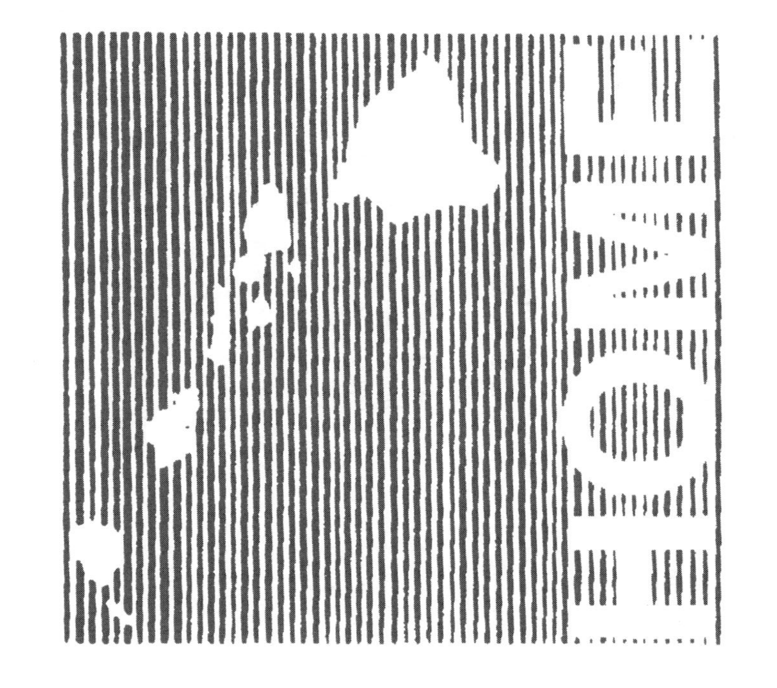
HOME